Growing Roses
Organically

Growing Roses
Organically

Your Guide to Creating an Easy-Care Garden
Full of Fragrance and Beauty

Barbara Wilde

RODALE

Pour Denis Gardeur

**WE INSPIRE AND ENABLE PEOPLE TO IMPROVE
THEIR LIVES AND THE WORLD AROUND THEM**

We're always happy to hear from you. For questions
or comments concerning the editorial content of this
book, please write to:

Rodale Book Readers' Service
33 East Minor Street
Emmaus, PA 18098

Look for other Rodale books wherever books are
sold. Or call us at (800) 848-4735.

For more information about Rodale Organic Living
magazines and books, visit us at

www.organicgardening.com

Editor: Vicki Mattern
Project Manager: Christine Bucks
Cover and Interior Book Designer: Gavin Robinson
Interior Illustrators: Michael Gellatly
    and Adam McCauley (garden design)
Cover Photographer: Howard Sooley
Photography Editor: Lyn Horst
Photography Assistant: Jackie L. Ney
Layout Designer: Donna G. Bellis
Digital Output Specialist: Dale Mack
Researchers: Sarah Wolfgang Heffner
    and Pamela R. Ruch
Copy Editor: Erana Bumbardatore
Product Specialist: Jodi Schaffer
Indexer: Lina Burton

RODALE ORGANIC LIVING BOOKS
Executive Creative Director: Christin Gangi
Art Director: Patricia Field
Content Assembly Manager: Robert V. Anderson Jr.
Copy Manager: Nancy N. Bailey

On the cover: Roses can add romance to any garden, including yours. And getting roses to flourish isn't that difficult—you just need to begin by choosing healthy,
hardy varieties.

**Library of Congress Cataloging-in-Publication
Data**
Wilde, Barbara.
    Growing roses organically : your guide to creating an
easy-care garden full of fragrance and beauty / Barbara
Wilde.
        p.   cm.
    Includes bibliographical references (p.   ) and index.
    ISBN 0–87596–880–5 (hardcover : alk. paper)
    1. Rose culture. 2. Roses. 3. Organic gardening.
I. Title.
SB411 .W54 2002
635.9'33734—dc21
                                                    2002001042

Distributed in the book trade by St. Martin's Press

2 4 6 8 10 9 7 5 3 1   hardcover

RODALE
Organic Gardening Starts Here!

Here at Rodale, we've been gardening organically for more than 60 years—ever since my grandfather J. I. Rodale learned about composting and decided that healthy living starts with healthy soil. In 1940, J. I. started the Rodale Organic Farm to test his theories, and today the nonprofit Rodale Institute Experimental Farm is still at the forefront of organic gardening and farming research. In 1942, J. I. founded *Organic Gardening* magazine to share his discoveries with gardeners everywhere. His son, my father, Robert Rodale, headed *Organic Gardening* until 1990, and today a third generation of Rodales is growing up with the new *OG* magazine. Over the years we've shown millions of readers how to grow bountiful crops and beautiful flowers using nature's own techniques.

In this book, you'll find the latest organic methods and the best gardening advice. We know—because all our authors and editors are passionate about gardening! We feel strongly that our gardens should be safe for our children, pets, and the birds and butterflies that add beauty and delight to our lives and landscapes. Our gardens should provide us with fresh, flavorful vegetables, delightful herbs, and gorgeous flowers. And they should be a pleasure to work in as well as to view.

Sharing the secrets of safe, successful gardening is why we publish books. So come visit us at www.organicgardening.com, where you can tour the world of organic gardening all day, every day. And use this book to create your best garden ever.

Happy gardening!

Maria Rodale

Maria Rodale
Rodale Organic Gardening Books

Contents

Acknowledgments

I am indebted to the help, support, and inspiration of many people for the writing of this book. First and foremost to my companion, Denis Gardeur, whose quotidian enthusiasm, interest, and synergies made this book possible. To my children, Gabrielle and Jesse, whose very existence affirms my own. To Harrison Flint, the sort of teacher we are lucky to encounter once in a lifetime, who launched me into both professional horticulture and writing. To my nursery and landscape clients over the years, whose warmth, enthusiasm, and insights continue to inspire me, and especially among those to Dave and Katrina Seitz, John and Linda Zimmerman, and Herb Kirst and Peggy Hillman. To Thomas Proll of W. Kordes Söhne, who shared so much information so generously and taught me that breeding healthy roses doesn't happen overnight. And finally to my editor, Vicki Mattern, and project manager, Christine Bucks, who always read their e-mail and so afforded me the luxury of writing this book from my home in Paris.

Beautiful Roses the Organic Way

In completing this book, I take my humble place in a long line of gardener-writers who have made personal efforts to share what they know about roses, whether from a standpoint of classification and description, practical cultural information, or both. For centuries, writers have been describing the theories in vogue on how to make these beautiful plants prosper, drawing on their own experiences and that of others. I'm no different, except that I've brought to the table of growing this sometimes temperamental plant the additional requirement that the methods I recommend use no toxic chemicals or synthetic fertilizers. That's right—I grow my roses organically.

Because rose growing for the last 100 years has relied ever more heavily on using chemical fungicides to control rose diseases, many rose gardeners scoff at the idea of even *thinking* about growing roses organically. The breeding of modern roses—with its heavy interest in hybrid tea roses of increasingly bright colors—unfortunately evolved right along with the idea of using readily available horticultural chemicals as a sort of magic bullet to enable gardeners to grow even the weakest, most disease-prone roses without problems. Breeders threw concern for rose health to the wind in their genetic selection of roses with ever-bigger blossoms in previously unknown combinations of crimson, coral, orange, and yellow—genetically speaking, the most disease-prone colors.

But after reaching its heyday in the 1950s and '60s, gardeners' innocent faith in better living through chemicals began—almost imperceptibly, at first—to wane. Beginning with the publication in 1966 of Rachel Carson's prescient book, *Silent Spring,* which detailed the horrific effects of DDT on the environment, some gardeners began to realize that their beloved magic bullets were ripping huge wounds in the fabric of life around them.

A grassroots movement to find gentler, environmentally sustainable methods of gardening began, and it has often meant going back to more old-fashioned ways of doing things. Gardeners began once more to make compost and look for less-harmful means of controlling disease and insect damage in their gardens. And, responding to a groundswell of interest in organic gardening, many modern research facilities began to investigate new methods and products to modernize organic gardening. Marketing jumped in to fill the gap between many gardeners' disillusionment with the old chemical methods and the need for commercially available organic gardening products and supplies.

However, because of the terrible disease susceptibility of so many modern roses, growing roses organically didn't become popular with rose gardeners. Trying to grow these plants without systemic chemical fungicides was just too frustrating. But in the 1980s, a resurgence of interest in the old rose varieties—with their superior health and hardiness—grew out of gardeners' frustration with modern roses and a nostalgia for the "good garden plant" characteristics of the old shrub roses. Many gardeners simply no longer had the time to fuss over their hybrid teas, dousing them in sprays and feeding them a virtual IV line of soluble chemical fertilizers. And many rose breeders—to their credit—responded with a new emphasis on health and hardiness in their selections, releasing scores of healthy, hardy new cultivars. Today, you can choose from an unsurpassed selection of both old and new rose varieties that you can grow successfully using organic methods.

Of course, keep in mind that growing roses organically requires a holistic approach, rather than a linear one. By sharing my knowledge about choosing healthy varieties, preparing the soil carefully, and gently intervening when it comes to pest and disease problems, it's my fondest hope that my own experiences growing these wonderful plants will enrich your own.

Barbara Wilde

Barbara Wilde
Paris, June 13, 2001

PART I

starting out

Growing roses organically for the first time can be like trying to negotiate someone else's house in the dark: You keep bumping up against things you didn't know were there. But that's where the first part of this book comes in. In the following pages, I'll shine a bright light on those unknowns, so that your roses start off on the right track.

To begin, I'll give you the information you need—including a brief look at the history and classes of roses—to choose the right varieties for your organic garden. I'll also teach you how to prepare a rich, nourishing soil that's tailored to your roses' needs; it's your best insurance for success. Finally, I'll cover planting, including specifics for roses that are grafted, as well as roses that have their own roots.

These pages will teach you all you need to know to start your rose garden right and reap years of pleasure from it.

1

By making wise choices from both old and new varieties, the voluptuous beauty of roses is well within the reach of today's organic gardener.

roses: perennial favorites

Who can resist the rose's

breathtakingly beautiful blossoms and heavenly fragrance? People have admired these special plants for thousands of years, making them the subjects of legends and the focal points of gardens.

And for all but a tiny fraction of that time, roses flourished under the care of gardeners who used only naturally available materials. Yet over the last several decades we've become convinced that roses cannot prosper without harmful, synthetic chemicals. We've come to think of the rose as a delicate plant, prone to disease and likely to die out during harsh winters. For many of us, the ubiquitous hybrid tea rose is little more than a very expensive annual—and it's much less rewarding!

The good news is that gardeners can choose from among hundreds of cold-hardy, disease-resistant roses. Some of these tough roses are "old" or heirloom types that have been in cultivation since antiquity, while others were bred more recently, just 100 to 300 years ago. Still others really *are* new and improved. Innovative breeding programs have focused on producing roses that are extremely cold-hardy, resistant to disease, and suitable for a host of landscape situations.

With so many rugged but beautiful old and new roses to choose from, you'll find that gorgeous, chemical-free roses are well within your reach.

Antique Roses for Today's Gardens

Almost any gardener interested in growing roses has heard of "heirloom" or "old" roses. And if you've delved a little deeper into the topic of old roses, you've probably also encountered terms such as "Bourbon," "hybrid musk," "hybrid perpetual," "hybrid rugosa," "Noisette," and "polyantha."

If you find these terms bewildering, that's because they are! The history of roses and their breeding is anything but clear. In fact, it's about as muddled and complicated as the story of any human undertaking can be. But having a basic understanding of the above terms can help you make smart decisions when selecting roses for your organic garden. Let's start, then, by putting the many rose classes into historical perspective.

The Ancient Roses

Roses have been a part of human history for thousands of years. In the Western world, roses were cultivated first in Europe and the Middle East—areas endowed with beautiful species of wild roses. Unlike our native American roses, many of these roses bear double flowers that are intensely perfumed. As wildflowers go, they are beautiful and spectacular plants, so it was only natural that people planted them in the very earliest gardens.

The three primordial rose types were *Rosa alba, R. damascena,* and *R. gallica.* Together with the centifolias (a hybrid group of unknown parentage), they are commonly known as the "old" roses. To distinguish them from some of the early repeat-blooming hybrids, we'll call them the "ancient" roses. Almost all of the ancient roses bloom just once per growing season, with one long, sumptuous flowering in early summer. But, partly due to this once-blooming quality, all of these ancient roses also offer superior hardiness and disease resistance. (See "The 4 Classes of Ancient Roses" on the opposite page for a summary of their characteristics.)

Ancient roses are such remarkable plants that garden writers were already obsessing about them before the time of Christ. Sometime in the third or fourth century B.C., the Greek philosopher and botanist Theophrastus described various rose species of Egypt and gave recommendations for growing them. He also noted famous gardens of the time that were replete with rose bushes planted in giant silver pots. Wreaths of damask roses (*R. damascena*) have even been found in some ancient Egyptian tombs.

Over time, roses began to flourish in symbolism and myth—first in Greek and Roman mythology, and later in Christian symbolism and secular folktales. Many of these mythical roses were probably *R. alba,* which continued to be depicted by artists as varied as Botticelli and Crivelli.

The ancient Romans featured roses prominently in their rites and festivals. In fact, the Romans were so fanatical about roses that they developed hothouses for forcing the plants into bloom. When that didn't

Old roses have been thriving for centuries in historic church gardens in France. Monks and nuns used the flowers to grace the altar and for medicine. The gardens are still tended organically today.

The 4 Classes of Ancient Roses

Here's a quick glance at the ancient roses, along with the characteristics that differentiate them from one another.

Rose	Origin	Habit	Bloom	Fragrance	Cultural Notes	History
Rosa × alba (alba or white rose)	Europe; thought to be a natural hybrid of *R. canina* with *R. damascena* or *R. gallica*.	Tall, wide shrub of 4' to 6' or more with gray to blue-green matte foliage. Very thorny, with a full, arching form, it makes a superb shrub.	Loosely double to very double rosette forms; petals sometimes form cupped, flat blossoms; colors range from pure white through many delicate shades of pale and shell pinks.	Superb, complex fragrances, often with citrus overtones.	The healthiest of all the ancient roses, it tolerates partial shade and is very long-lived and easy to grow.	Mentioned in Pliny's *Natural History* in 79 A.D., this rose was grown by the Romans and often depicted in paintings.
Rosa centifolia (cabbage rose; provence rose)	Hybrids of unknown origin, probably involving complex crosses of *R. canina, R. damascena, R. gallica, R. moschata,* and *R. phoenicia.*	Somewhat lax-growing shrub (it has thin stems, so they may arch heavily under the weight of the flowers), 3' to 5' tall, with matte foliage.	Sumptuous, rounded blossoms are tightly packed with petals; colors range from white through delicate pinks. Single, profuse flowering in June, though some moss roses (a deviation of this group) repeat lightly.	Intoxicating, rich, heady perfume.	Slightly prone to mildew diseases. Plants may need support under the weight of the heavy blossoms, and flowers are sometimes spoiled by wet weather.	Often featured in paintings by the Dutch masters.

(continued)

Rose	Origin	Habit	Bloom	Fragrance	Cultural Notes	History
Rosa damascena (damask rose)	Asia Minor; a complex of garden hybrids derived from crossings of *R. gallica* with *R. moschata* and *R. fedtschenkoana*.	Tall, arching, 4' to 6' shrub with downy, gray-green foliage and thorny shoots. The repeat-flowering subgroup Portland damasks are small, bushy, 3' to 4' shrubs.	Delicate semi-double to heavily doubled, swirled flowers in colors ranging from white to delicate pink, warm pink, or rich cerise. Profuse bloom in June; Portland damasks bloom repeatedly, while autumn damasks bloom heavily in June and again, lightly, in fall.	Grown for essential oil (attar of rose), used to make perfume. It has the quintessential rose fragrance, complex, fruity, and rich.	Tough; easy to grow, even in gravelly soils.	Associated with the ancient city of Damascus, brought to Europe by the crusaders, and grown for perfume in North Africa and the Middle East. Striped 'York and Lancaster' symbolized the end of the War of the Roses.
Rosa gallica (provins rose)	Europe and southwest Asia.	2½' to 4' shrub, occasionally taller, with matte, dark green to gray-green foliage and sparse thorns. It has a mildly suckering habit and an upright to arching form.	Single; semi-double; or heavily double, swirled, and quartered blossoms. Colors range from deep violet cerise through clear, warm pinks to nearly white, though it blooms mostly in deep, rich tones. Some swirled and striped colors. June-blooming, with attractive hips.	Heavily perfumed with a rich, permeating, sometimes spicy scent.	Easy to grow and tolerates relatively poor soil.	The most ancient of roses, used medicinally for centuries. 'Apothecary's Rose' (*R. gallica officinalis*) and *R. alba* were adopted as symbols of opposing sides in the War of the Roses.

produce enough blooms, they imported additional roses from Egypt. For one especially extravagant banquet, Emperor Nero blanketed a beach near Naples with rose petals for the delight of his guests.

By the Middle Ages, roses were an integral part of the culture of Christianity. Church and cloister gardens grew them for both symbolic and medicinal purposes. *R. gallica officinalis*, the oldest rose of all, continues to be known as the 'Apothecary's Rose'. Remarkably, ancient gallica, damask, and alba shrubs still grow in France's historic church gardens, known as *jardins de curé*, which are tended organically—a living testimony to the ruggedness and beauty of these old roses!

Despite the importance of roses, fewer than 30 different varieties existed during the Middle Ages. These early varieties usually were propagated by divisions of suckers and by rooting cuttings. All of that changed by the mid-1700s, though, when the Dutch emerged as consummate horticulturists and merchants. Besides trading flower bulbs, the Dutch were the first Europeans to actually breed roses and grow new varieties from seed. By 1810, about 200 different roses were available, including the cabbage roses (*R. centifolia*) depicted in so many paintings by the

The centifolia roses bred by the Dutch in the 17th and 18th centuries still charm gardeners today. Disease resistance, hardiness, and ease of culture make centifolias, or cabbage roses, and their deviations, moss roses, well suited to organic techniques.

Dutch masters. The breeding origins of these sumptuous, double roses remain a mystery, however, as the centifolias themselves are sterile.

Around 1800, the French became active in rose development. Empress Josephine, consoling herself over her divorce from Napoleon, began collecting roses for the first all-rose garden, or *roseraie,* in France, at her personal palace of Malmaison. (Before that time, roses in France had always been planted in mixed borders.) Before long, Josephine had hired several rose breeders to fuel her passion. Under her patronage, several hundred new cultivars of the ancient species (albas, centifolias, damasks, and gallicas) were created.

Repeat-Blooming Old Roses

As Josephine's rose breeders worked to supply her with new roses, the introduction of an entirely different kind of rose from the Orient was revolutionizing rose breeding throughout the rest of Europe. Unlike most European rose species, these "new" China and tea roses flowered almost continuously, a trait that rose breeders couldn't wait to pass along. Unfortunately, the new roses also carried some undesirable traits: From this point on, the roses that breeders developed would vary greatly in their hardiness and disease resistance.

Hybrid perpetuals. The prospect of breeding roses that would flower throughout the growing season caused a fury of excitement. French breeders crossed the new roses with autumn damasks and Portland damasks to produce what became known in the 1840s as the "hybrid perpetuals." Of the several hundred hybrid perpetuals developed, fewer than 100 still exist. Although we usually bemoan the loss of heirloom cultivars, in this case it was probably for the best. Breeding had been so fast and furious that just about every new cross was released and sold, whether or not it had any merit. Today, the surviving hybrid perpetuals are at best a mixed bag for organic gardeners. Some are very beautiful, but others are very weak growers, especially as grafted plants.

Bourbons. Around the time that hybrid perpetuals were being developed, a seedling of a cross

(continued on page 10)

The 6 Groups of Repeat-Blooming Old Roses

With sizes ranging from 2 to 10 feet, climbing, arching, and upright habits, and a palette of beautiful colors, repeat-blooming old roses offer something for every gardener.

Rose	Origin	Habit	Bloom	Fragrance	Cultural Notes
Bourbon	Isle of Bourbon (now Réunion); natural cross between a repeating damask and a China rose. Cultivars developed in France in the early to mid-1800s.	Shrubs from 3' to 6' or more; some are climbers, and their form varies from short and bushy to tall and arching.	Elegant, very double, often cupped blossoms of white, translucent shell pink, warm pink, raspberry pink, or carmine; one striped. Strongly repeat flowering.	Rich, heady scent.	Vary in vigor; some tolerate partial shade. Disease tolerant and hardy to Zone 5.
Hybrid Musk	England; hybrid of Noisette and multiflora stocks. Developed as early as the early 1900s.	Variably bushy and upright to arching and even climbing. 2' to 8', depending on climate.	Clusters of small, semidouble flowers in white, pale yellow, pink, and apricot shades, with visible stamens. Nearly nonstop flowering and attractive hips.	Musky scent.	Vigorous and easy to grow. Disease tolerant to resistant, and hardy to Zone 5.
Hybrid Perpetual	France; complex hybrids of China and tea roses and autumn and Portland damasks, developed from the mid 1830s to 1900.	Shrubs from 3' to 5', varying from rigidly upright to lax and arching.	Highly variable, but usually very double; colors from white through all shades of pink and red, and some stripes. Slight to medium repeat flowering.	Varies from no fragrance to rich, "old-rose" scent.	Many produce weak plants that are prone to disease but cold-hardy.

Rose	Origin	Habit	Bloom	Fragrance	Cultural Notes
Hybrid Rugosa	Species from Japan; hybridized in France, Germany, and the United States, mostly in the late 1800s and beyond.	Shrubs from less than 2' to more than 6', often wider than tall, with an upright habit. Dense and thorny, with thick, crinkled leaves.	Single to fully double, loosely formed flowers with scrolled buds in small clusters. Colors range from pure white to warm pinks, deep mauves, and magentas. Most repeat strongly from spring through fall and have huge, decorative hips.	Rich, spicy scent permeates the air around these roses.	The easiest, most vigorous roses to grow. Tolerant of drought and salt. Hardy to Zone 3; many are nearly immune to disease.
Noisette	America and France; hybrid of China rose and musk rose, developed in the early to mid-1800s.	Vigorous arching shrubs to 10' or more; some are climbers.	Clusters of medium-size, double flowers in white, pale pink, peach, and soft yellow. Nearly constant bloom.	Lightly fragrant.	A few cultivars are hardy to Zone 5, but they're best in Zone 7 and southward. Vigorous and disease tolerant.
Polyantha	France; hybrid of multiflora and tea stock in the late 1800s.	Dwarf bushes to 3'. Thorny, with small, glossy leaves.	Clusters of small, double blossoms in pink, white, or cerise. Nearly non-stop flowering.	Little to no scent.	Very easy to grow, even in difficult conditions; good disease resistance. Most cultivars are hardy to Zone 4 or 5.

Hybrid musk 'Buff Beauty' is one of the best-loved examples of this somewhat modern group of repeat-flowering old roses. In Zones 7 through 9, gardeners can grow 'Buff Beauty' and several others of its tribe as small climbers. In Zones 5 and 6, however, most hybrid musks are more like medium shrubs in size.

between a China rose and an autumn damask from the Isle of Bourbon in the Indian Ocean was sent to the breeders of Malmaison. Dubbed *R. borboniana* or 'Bourbon Jacques', this hybrid became the first of the Bourbon roses, a small tribe of repeat bloomers. Although the Bourbons are more hardy and disease-resistant than most modern roses, they are less iron-clad than the four ancient classes of roses. In general, the toughest Bourbons more closely resemble their damask (rather than their China) parent; examples include 'Louise Odier' and 'Zéphirine Drouhin'.

Noisettes. The hybridizing frenzy that occurred during the first three decades of the 19th century also produced the Noisettes, another major group of repeat-flowering old roses. That story begins in America, but it still has a French connection. Working just after 1800, John Champneys of Charleston, South Carolina, crossed the musk rose (*R. moschata*) with a China rose. The result was 'Champneys' Pink Cluster', a vigorous but fairly tender plant with long canes and clusters of very fragrant pale pink flowers.

Champneys' neighbor, a transplanted Frenchman named Philippe Noisette, planted seeds from this plant and selected 'Blush Noisette' from the progeny. Still in trade today, 'Blush Noisette' is more compact and hardier than its parent and has larger, more fully double flowers.

Noisette sent stock plants to his brother, a nurseryman outside of Paris, who finally introduced the American beauty into commerce. In the hands of the French, one Noisette quickly became many; within a decade, hundreds of Noisette hybrids were available on the market.

Hybrid musks. The charming repeat-blooming roses known as hybrid musks were first bred in the early 20th century by a British clergyman named Joseph Pemberton. By crossing a musk rose with a hybrid tea, Pemberton developed a group of rugged, disease-resistant shrubs that bear fragrant clusters of small, semidouble flowers. In warm regions, gardeners can grow them as climbers. As a group, hybrid musks are fairly tolerant of partial shade and lean soil.

Hybrid rugosas. For organic gardeners, the introduction of the rugosa rose (*R. rugosa*) from Japan represents one of the most important chapters in the history of roses. This rose embodies all that is good in roses: excellent hardiness; virtual immunity to disease; strong repeat bloom; powerful fragrance; huge, showy hips; colorful autumn foliage; and even salt- and drought-tolerance. Rugosas are distinguished by their thick, semiglossy, deeply crinkled leaves. This rough leaf surface, described as "rugose" in botanical terms,

seems to render them more resistant to foliar diseases than any other group of roses.

Although some rugosa selections and crosses showed up in the late 18th and early 19th century, interest in this group of roses really heated up around the turn of the 20th century, when the French breeder Gravereaux bred many outstanding rugosa hybrids. His garden, *La Roseraie de l'Hay du Val de Marne,* is still maintained as one of the finest public rose gardens and centers of rose research today.

Dwarf polyanthas. One other group of old roses, the hybrid polyanthas, is worth noting. These roses are small in every way, from the size of their flowers to the stature of the plants themselves. The first real polyantha was derived from *R. multiflora* stock by the French breeder Guillot around 1875. 'The Fairy', the best-known and most-beloved polyantha, was bred in the 1930s by J. A. Bentall, Pemberton's apprentice. This hardy rose will bloom nonstop almost anywhere.

No other rose species has contributed as many positive qualities to rose breeding as *Rosa rugosa*. Organic gardeners will find the most easy-care roses among rugosa hybrids old and new.

'The Fairy's' hardiness, prolific bloom, and disease resistance make up for its lack of fragrance in every way.

Modern Rose Breeding

Before the hybrid perpetuals were developed, all roses were great candidates for organic gardens in America and Europe. But by the mid-19th century, though, the influx of genes from the China and tea roses had diminished hardiness and increased disease susceptibility among the newest roses. As rose breeding continued throughout the 19th and 20th centuries, the high-centered, pointed buds of the tea rose became the vogue, while the round, voluptuous shape of the old roses fell from favor. To achieve the new look, breeders crossed mostly tea and China roses, producing roses that were increasingly tender and prone to disease.

Breeders in the first half of the 20th century focused their efforts on creating roses suitable for use as cut flowers, and the qualities of the plant itself became less important. For gardeners—especially those who didn't want to douse their plants with chemical fungicides every week—growing hybrid teas in the garden became more frustrating and less rewarding.

Organic rose growers suffered yet another blow with the introduction into breeding of *Rosa foetida bicolor*, or 'Austrian Copper', valued for its brilliant yellow and orange colors. Although this rose is very hardy, it is enormously susceptible to black spot. That's why most modern yellow and orange roses also suffer from this debilitating disease—they inherited the flaw from their ancestor.

Fortunately, trends change. During the final decades of the 20th century, rose breeders shifted their attention toward developing roses that were healthy, repeat-flowering, and functional. Many of these roses are nearly perfect for the organic garden. And with today's demand for colorful, low-maintenance plants, this positive direction in rose breeding is bound to continue. (For a summary of the best modern rose-breeding programs, see "Best Rose Breeders for Organic Landscapes" on the opposite page.)

Unfortunately, 'Austrian Copper' [species rose] contributed not only its brilliant colors to modern rose breeding but also its extreme susceptibility to black spot.

Best Rose Breeders for Organic Landscapes

When selecting roses for your organic landscape, look for introductions from the following breeders. Roses from these programs are sure to be not only beautiful but also disease-resistant and cold-hardy. (Most rose catalogs state the breeder's name in parentheses after the name of the rose.)

Baum (Pavement series). The German breeder Baum began introducing the superlative Pavement series of roses beginning in the late 1980s. Regardless of the clumsy moniker (an unfortunate translation of the German word for "groundcover"), to know these roses is to love them. All are low, spreading rugosa hybrids with enough rugosa genes to make them wonderfully cold-hardy and essentially immune to disease. They're as beautiful as they are rugged, blooming with large semi-double to fully double, very fragrant flowers from late spring through fall. Most bear a bountiful crop of showy red rosehips, as well. And because they root so easily, they're often offered as own-root stock—another boon to organic gardeners.

Kordes. Wilhelm Kordes began breeding roses in the 1930s. As part of his commission to develop roses for German parklands, Kordes bred landscape-size roses that were vigorous, cold-hardy, and completely carefree. Under the guidance of the fourth generation of the family, the family business has stepped up its focus on breeding healthy roses. Over the last 5 years, the company has released many healthy new varieties of floribundas, shrubs, climbers, and groundcovers.

Poulsen (Towne & Country series). The Poulsen family has been breeding hardy roses for their cold Danish climate since the 1920s, when brothers Dines and Svend began their work. Originators of what was later termed the floribunda rose, Poulsen today is known for the disease-resistant and hardy Towne & Country series of shrub roses.

Svejda (Explorer series). Dr. Felicitas Svejda of the Morden Station of the Canadian Department of Agriculture developed the outstanding Explorer series of healthy, hardy roses. The group includes 'William Baffin' (the hardiest climbing rose in existence), 'Jens Munk', and a host of other excellent shrubs named after Canadian explorers.

Outstanding breeders, such as those working at the Canadian Department of Agriculture, continue to turn out brand new, healthy, hardy shrub roses, such as 'De Montarville'.

Selecting naturally healthy
roses is the key to growing roses
successfully in your landscape.

choosing healthy roses

The most important step

you can take toward successful organic rose growing is to start with healthy roses. Roses vary enormously in their ability to resist or tolerate fungal diseases, and combating these diseases is the most frustrating problem that organic gardeners face. But if you choose your roses wisely, your plants will be able to resist or survive these diseases—with minimal help from you. So before you buy, make sure you know the health heritage of the roses you're interested in, as well as which rose groups are the most susceptible to disease.

When you go to your garden center or sit down with your favorite rose catalogs, keep a short list of the major classes of roses suitable for organic gardens close at hand. Better yet, make your own most-wanted list from the varieties in this book—and stick to it. Choosing healthy roses is the best way that you can ensure success in your organic garden.

Choose Roses You Can Live With

When choosing roses for your landscape, first ask yourself, "What kind of gardener am I?"

Are you mainly interested in having a carefree landscape—one in which plants flourish with no help other than proper soil preparation, planting, and occasional feeding and watering? If so, you'd better stick to extremely healthy roses, such as the rugosa hybrids and a few others.

Are you impassioned by the many forms, colors, and fragrances of roses? Maybe you don't mind tending your roses—even if that means spraying with nontoxic products a few times a year and cleaning up carefully at the end of the growing season. From your perspective, these may be satisfying activities that allow you to enjoy a wider array of blooms for cutting and all-season color.

Organic gardeners who've been bitten by the rose bug will still enjoy growing old roses, such as the hybrid perpetuals 'Mrs. John Laing' and 'Reine des Violettes' *(above)*, for their beautiful flowers and intense perfumes. These roses are quite hardy but more disease-prone than the rugosas. They respond well to a good program of disease prevention.

In that case, you may want to explore the many roses that are slightly more susceptible to diseases but still relatively healthy. For instance, you may not mind fussing a bit with 'Mrs. John Laing', a hybrid perpetual with repeat-blooming flowers but a tendency to contract black spot more readily than, say, an alba rose, which flowers only in early summer.

Also, consider your expectations for your roses over the course of the season. If you're a perfectionist, a couple of mildewed leaves—even for a brief period—may be more than you can stand. On the other hand, you may be more easygoing and willing to endure a bit of black spot, as long as you know it's not endangering the long-term health and survival of your rose.

Your expectations and the amount of time you plan to spend in your garden will help you decide which roses you'll enjoy most.

Know the Health Heritage of Your Rose

Besides your own expectations, the other key consideration when selecting roses is their background. The genetic heritage of a rose plays an enormous role in its resistance—or susceptibility—to disease, as well as in its hardiness. Knowing what group a rose belongs to will give you a pretty good idea of what to expect in terms of its disease resistance and hardiness.

Roses range from extremely healthy (such as the rugosas and their hybrids, which are virtually immune to disease) to quite weak (such as many modern hybrid teas and floribundas). Between these two extremes are roses with every conceivable level of inherent, genetic resistance to disease. Although some of these in-between roses are very beautiful, they may get black spot on, say, 30 percent of their foliage in very humid climates. If left untreated, these roses may grow and flourish from year to year, but they won't look their best for much of the season.

Let's take a closer look at the inherent health of the roses introduced in Chapter 1.

Rugged Ancient Roses

The four ancient groups of roses—albas, centifolias, damasks, and hybrid gallicas—are all excellent candidates for organic gardens. Most of these roses bloom just once per season (for several weeks, peaking in June in most parts of the country), but their bloom is something to anticipate and revel in when it arrives. These old garden roses put on the sort of sumptuous show depicted in coffee-table garden books. The sheer abundance of their flowers saturates the air with perfume and causes their branches to arch beneath their weight.

What's more, this single, annual bloom is a boon to organic gardeners because it renders the plants hardier and more disease-resistant than repeat-blooming roses. Once-blooming roses put out a big burst of growth in spring prior to flowering. Flower buds on the previous year's growth develop into blossoms, the new shoots that grew the previous year develop flower buds, and vegetative buds elongate into new shoots. This spurt of activity pretty much ceases by July (although exactly when depends on your hardiness zone).

For the remainder of the season, the existing growth goes through the process of hardening off: Foliage becomes more leathery and develops a thicker, waxy cuticle. Shoots become harder and woodier, with a tougher bark. This hardening-off process both prepares the rose to face freezing winter temperatures and helps protect the plant from the airborne spores of fungal diseases.

Repeat-blooming roses, on the other hand, constantly produce new, tender growth. The new growth is not only prone to winter-kill but also is more susceptible to invasion by disease spores. In general, the more a rose flowers over the course of a season, the more difficult it is for the rose to resist disease. So, for your organic garden, a once-blooming rose usually is a better bet than a repeat-blooming rose.

None of the ancient, once-blooming roses becomes diseased seriously enough to threaten the survival of the plant. Still, some of these tough ancient groups are more prone to disease than others.

Albas. Of the four groups, albas are the healthiest. Although they are not immune to disease, alba roses rarely suffer from mildew or black spot when planted in the proper site.

Disease Susceptibility

The major rose groups are listed below from least susceptible to most susceptible. Although many floribundas and hybrid teas aren't suited to organic gardens, I've included them here for comparison. Also, keep in mind that a host of other factors, including weather conditions and plant selection, will influence the actual incidence of disease in your own garden.

Rugosa roses

Alba roses

Hybrid gallica roses

Damask roses

Centifolia roses

Polyantha roses

Hybrid musk roses

Bourbon roses

Noisette roses

Hybrid perpetual roses

Floribunda roses

Hybrid tea roses

Hybrid gallicas. Hybrid gallica roses seem to be a bit more susceptible to disease. But, in my experience, the problem usually isn't serious enough to require treatment.

Damasks. Damask roses suffer from black spot to varying degrees. But, again, the problem usually isn't serious enough to require intervention. Unfortunately, fragrance seems to be associated with a susceptibility to black spot, especially among repeat-flowering roses. Maybe that explains why damasks (particularly the repeat-blooming Portland roses and autumn damasks) suffer from black spot a little more than other ancient roses. Even so, damask roses are tough enough to merit a spot in any organic landscape. And, as the coming chapters will explain, a simple prevention program can make this slight problem almost nonexistent.

Centifolias. Centifolia roses vary in their disease susceptibility because of their complex hybrid origins. But none of them is so vulnerable that the viability of the plant is endangered by disease, even if you take no special measures to prevent or control it. As a group, centifolias are less prone to fungal diseases than any of the repeat-blooming varieties, with the exception of the rugosas.

Disease-Resistant Repeaters

As mentioned earlier, repeat-blooming roses generally are more prone to disease. There are several notable exceptions, however.

Polyanthas. These diminutive shrubs generally show good vigor against disease, thanks to the

influence of multiflora roses in their heritage. 'The Fairy', a very popular polyantha cultivar, is a great example of the tough nature and hardiness of this group. One drawback of the polyanthas is their tendency to drop their leaves in late summer, especially if exposed to overhead irrigation. Don't let this discourage you from including some of these long-blooming little roses in your garden, though. Just consider it a perfect example of how good cultural practices can mitigate genetic destiny.

Hybrid musks. Joseph Pemberton really was ahead of his time when he bred his tough tribe of hybrid musk roses in the early 1900s. Unlike many other breeders, Pemberton incorporated genes for health along with those for rebloom in his creations. The glossy foliage of the hybrid musks resists disease remarkably well, especially when supported by a good program of preventive maintenance. Considering that hybrid musks are in nonstop bloom from late spring through late fall, their disease resistance is extraordinary.

Polyantha roses such as 'The Fairy' are tough, tidy little shrub roses that provide almost nonstop color—and are quite disease-resistant.

'Ferdinand Pichard' is the healthiest of the hybrid perpetuals and also one of the most beautiful. With relatively disease-resistant, gray-green foliage; sumptuous ivory blossoms striped with raspberry; and a rich, fruity fragrance, this rose merits the attention of any organic rose lover.

Disease-Fighting Foliage

Rose varieties that have highly glossy foliage are not only attractive, they're also often more resistant to fungal leaf diseases. That's because the gloss is a thick waxy coating, or cuticle, on the surface of the leaves. This coating helps prevent germinating fungal spores from penetrating the leaf surface with their mycelia.

Bourbons. Bourbon roses are a bit more susceptible to disease than the repeat-flowering damasks are. Without a little extra care, they may succumb to black spot enough to become unattractive by late summer. Again, a good program of prevention can help keep these lovely roses looking their best.

Hybrid perpetuals. In terms of disease susceptibility, this diverse clan includes some pretty difficult characters. As mentioned in Chapter 1, these roses were the result of rather hurried and haphazard breeding. While the hybrid perpetuals are relatively hardy (most to Zone 5 and some to Zone 4), almost all require both preventive maintenance and remedial measures during wet weather to keep black spot in check. Still, if you love delicious fragrance and unusual bloom colors, you may find the hybrid perpetuals well worth the fuss.

Rugosa Roses: The Organic Gardener's Dream

Rugosa roses blithely break nearly all of the rules that apply to the other groups of roses. These roses bloom repeatedly from late spring through frost, yet they're virtually immune to disease. This unique health is due to the rough, crinkled leaf surface—described as "rugose"—that characterizes the group. Something about the surface structure of these leaves makes them nearly impossible for germinating fungal spores to penetrate.

In rugosa hybrids, disease resistance of a given variety correlates directly with the degree of roughness of the leaf surface. Hybrids that have smoother leaves, such as 'Conrad Ferdinand Meyer', are less disease-resistant.

Another bonus with rugosas is that even insects find rugosa leaves less appetizing. The downside is that roses with rugose leaves do not seem to tolerate sprays of any kind—even foliar feedings. In my experience, rough-leafed rugosas burn easily when sprayed with even the mildest foliar fertilizer solution. Perhaps the rough leaf surface traps and holds more spray than a smooth surface would, resulting in burning. But despite this minor flaw, rugosas remain the consummate roses for organic gardeners. No other rose offers the same combination of superior disease and pest resistance, along with drought and salt tolerance.

Healthy Modern Roses

Finally, don't forget the roses hybridized by intrepid breeders (see "Best Rose Breeders for Organic Landscapes" on page 13). These hybridizers have made rose health a top priority. Breeders such as Kordes of Germany and those at the Canadian Department of Agriculture continue to enrich the palettes of organic gardeners everywhere with healthy roses. Learn to recognize these breeders' names so you can spot their new introductions in catalogs.

The Color Conundrum

Although every rule has exceptions, keep in mind that red and yellow roses, together with the orange shades that lie between, tend to be more susceptible to black spot than other colors are.

As we saw in Chapter 1, the genetic link between some yellow and orange blossom colors and black spot stems from the use of *Rosa foetida* and *R. foetida bicolor* in the breeding of modern roses. These two roses—while quite hardy—seem to pass on to their progeny their extreme black spot susceptibility. The link between crimson and scarlet shades and the disease may be due to some of the red *R. chinensis* varieties used in the hybridization of modern teas and floribundas.

Fortunately for those of us who appreciate bright colors, some healthy red and yellow roses do exist.

Purchasing Healthy Roses

Once you've made a list of the healthy roses you want to acquire for your garden, the next decision is where you are going to purchase them. Your best bet when selecting a rose merchant is to buy from a grower who is as impassioned about roses as you are—or even more so!

For the greatest selection of disease-resistant heritage and modern roses, you'll probably need to rely on a mail-order supplier. A good rose nursery will have a catalog or Web site packed with useful, first-hand information. The nursery should be willing to respond to your inquiries and offer helpful guidance—especially if you contact them before their peak season.

If possible, find a supplier that's willing to give honest appraisals of the roses in their catalogs, listing their weaknesses as well as their strengths. Some catalogs ooze with hyperbole, making their roses sound as though they can do everything but plant themselves and bloom in the snow. Unfortunately, these suppliers may be setting you up for disappointment—too often, their roses fail to live up to their lofty descriptions.

Also find out whether the nursery offers roses grown on their own roots, as opposed to strictly grafted stock. Growers that offer at least some own-root roses usually are very dedicated to promoting rose health. If you have a choice, always choose own-root roses. Any given variety grown on its own roots will be more vigorous and less prone to disease than a grafted variety. Although grafting or budding is an economical way to reproduce rose varieties true to name, this method of propagation can transmit viral diseases that could compromise the vigor of your plant. If you're considering a grafted rose, be sure the rootstock is certified virus-free.

Healthy Red and Yellow Roses

Looking for healthy, hardy red or yellow roses? Consider these varieties:

Red Roses

'Dart's Dash' [hybrid rugosa]

'Dortmund' [hybrid kordesii]

'Elmshorn' [shrub]

'Geranium' [hybrid moyesii]

'Hunter' [hybrid rugosa]

'Linda Campbell' [hybrid rugosa]

'Robusta' [shrub]

Yellow Roses

'Father Hugo's rose'* [species]

'Frühlingsgold'* [hybrid spinosissima]

'Gloire de Dijon' [climbing tea] (Zones 6
   to 7 and southward)

'Goldbusch' [shrub]

'Harison's Yellow'* [hybrid foetida]

Incense rose [species]*

'J. P. Connell' [shrub]

'Leverkusen' [hybrid kordesii]

'Topaz Jewel' [hybrid rugosa]

*These roses bloom very early, beginning in the second week of May in Zone 5.

Buy the Best Bareroot Plants

Almost all mail-order nurseries ship bareroot roses. This is standard practice and an excellent way of shipping.

Bareroot roses are graded according to the size and number of their canes. Make sure to determine the grade of plants the nursery sells, and whenever possible, order No. 1 grade. The increased vigor of a husky plant is more than worth the difference in price between a No. 1 and a No. 1½ or No. 2 plant.

Choosing Container-Grown Roses

If you're shopping at a local nursery that offers the varieties you want in containers, apply the same rules to buying pot-grown roses that you would to any other containerized plant. Look for roses that are disease-free and well rooted but not rootbound.

To find out whether a prospective rose is well rooted, ask a nursery employee to lift the plant out of the container for you. If he or she isn't willing to do that, don't buy the rose; the rose was most likely potted up recently and hasn't rooted adequately yet. Nothing will kill a container-grown rose more quickly than dumping it out of its pot before it has enough roots to hold the potting medium firmly in place. When this is the case, the potting mix will fall away, breaking off the newly formed feeder roots and shocking the rose so much that it won't be able to recover. And that's just what will happen if you take home that insufficiently rooted rose and try to plant it in your garden.

A rootbound rose, on the other hand, may not be the best plant to buy, but you can plant it and expect it to take hold in your garden. A rootbound plant's roots usually grow in a circular pattern and may even emerge from the bottom of the pot because they've run out of growing space. If the rose you've decided on is available only as a rootbound plant, you can go ahead and purchase it. Just be sure to read Chapter 4, "Planting New Roses," and plant the rose according to the special instructions for rootbound roses given there.

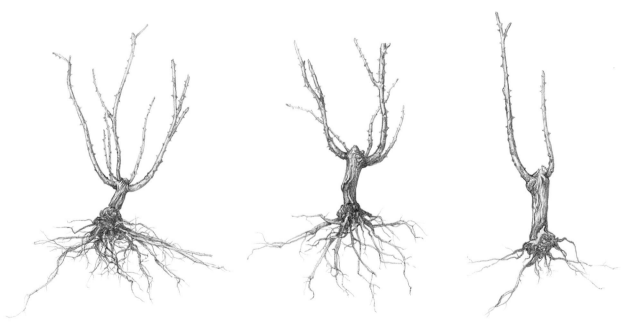

Always buy No. 1 grade plants. A No. 1 plant *(left)* has at least three large (⁵⁄₁₆-inch-diameter) canes branched not more than 3 inches above the graft union. A No. 1½ plant *(middle)* has two large canes branched not more than 3 inches above the graft. A No. 2 plant *(right)* has at least two canes, one of which is at least ¼ inch in diameter.

Prepare your soil generously and thoroughly, and your roses will reward you with years of lavish, low-maintenance bloom.

chapter 3

laying the groundwork

In addition to choosing healthy rose varieties that are hardy in your area, preparing your soil thoroughly is one key to success when growing roses organically. Building good soil for your roses takes some effort, but think of it as an investment: If you prepare your soil properly now, both you and your roses will have fewer problems later. You won't need to spend as much time watering and fertilizing, and your roses will be less likely to suffer from diseases, insect pests, and winter dieback. Best of all, your new plants will root quickly and establish themselves vigorously the very first season. In short, good, organic soil preparation pays off by making growing roses that much more rewarding.

Preparing your soil properly isn't as daunting as it sounds, either. You just need to ensure that your soil has good drainage and that it will provide the nutrients essential to your roses. With those fundamentals in place, your roses will be off to a great start.

What Roses Need

To produce the profusion of flowers that we gardeners enjoy, roses require "fuel" in the form of nutrients and water. Their soil must act as a reservoir of these two necessities. What is "adequate water" for roses? The soil should retain enough moisture so that the plants don't experience extreme dryness when rainfall is scarce, yet the soil doesn't become waterlogged. Roses need soil that contains plenty of tiny air spaces so that their roots have access to the oxygen they need for growth.

The ideal soil for roses is a well-drained, fertile clay loam with a pH around 6.5. If you don't already have that sort of soil, adding plenty of organic matter in the form of compost will go a long way toward fulfilling all of a rose's requirements. Compost slowly releases nutrients to your roses, including the micronutrients essential to rose health. And while it may seem paradoxical, organic matter both helps keep the soil porous and increases the soil's ability to retain water.

Finally, remember that roses love full sun, especially in Zone 7 and colder. In Zone 8 and warmer, they can take a few hours of shade in the heat of the afternoon, but they don't require it. In cooler zones, even the most shade-tolerant roses need a minimum of 5 to 6 hours of direct, unfiltered sunlight per day—any rose that receives less than that will produce far fewer blooms and be more likely to become diseased.

Plant roses where you can admire them often, such as flanking an entry, along a path, or as part of your favorite perennial border.

will rarely see them. After all, the reason we plant roses is to enjoy the sensual pleasures they bring to the garden: the colors of their blossoms, their fragrances, the forms of the plants themselves, the foliage textures, and even the ornamentation of red and orange hips through fall and winter.

Selecting a Site

When deciding where to plant your roses, try to balance the rose's needs with your own. Choosing a site that allows you to really enjoy your roses is just as important as finding a site that provides what roses need.

Plant Roses Where You Can Enjoy Them

Plant your roses in a place you pass by frequently or a location that's easily viewed from inside your home. There's little point to planting your roses where you

Look on the Sunny Side

When it comes to choosing a site that will meet the needs of your roses, make sunlight a top priority. If sunlight does not reach your roses, they will not thrive. And nothing you do—short of removing the obstruction to the sun—will change that.

If you must plant roses in partial shade, try to find a spot that receives at least several hours of direct morning sun. That way, the foliage of your roses will dry quickly and be less prone to disease. If shade from trees blocks the sunlight, consider removing some of the limbs to open up the canopy over your roses. And choose the most shade-tolerant, disease-resistant roses you can find. Remember that even these varieties need at least 5 to 6 hours of *unfiltered* sunlight per day.

You can grow roses successfully next to your home if you observe these guidelines:

■ If you are deciding between a sunny, east-facing wall and a west-facing wall, choose the east wall. The morning sunlight will help dry rose foliage promptly, minimizing the chances of disease.

■ If you plant roses on the west side of your house, use extremely disease-resistant varieties, such as rugosas. With a western exposure, rose foliage remains moist for most of the morning, making it more susceptible to disease.

■ Don't plant roses on the east or west side of your home if the area is shaded by trees or other obstructions. This creates full shade, which roses can't tolerate.

■ If you want to plant along a south-facing wall, keep in mind that the site will become extremely hot in summer. You'll need to water often, and your roses will be more prone to insect attacks.

■ Avoid the north side of your home altogether; it's too shady.

Find a Gentle Breeze

If possible, plant your roses where they'll receive gentle breezes. Good air circulation reduces moisture on rose foliage and, in turn, minimizes fungal disease problems.

Avoid extremely windy areas, though. Windy spots are effectively colder, and they're more drying. In very windy sites, rose canes are more susceptible to winter dieback and buds are more likely to suffer frost damage in early spring. Strong winds also can be very damaging to the flowers themselves. Rose blossoms transpire enormous amounts of water, so drying winds cause them to wilt and tatter easily.

Savoir Faire…

For extremely windy locations, choose drought- and wind-tolerant rugosa roses or varieties with thick, glossy foliage. This leathery foliage allows roses to withstand drying winds.

Choose a Spot with Good Drainage

Roses don't like wet feet, so try to select a spot that has good drainage. Your roses should do fine if there is any apparent slope—however slight—away from the spot where you want to plant. Even entirely flat locations are okay, as long as the area is not *lower* than the surrounding terrain. Locations where water stands during periods of heavy rainfall are obviously low and poorly drained. These spots are better suited to moisture-loving plants, such as astilbe and queen of the prairie, than to roses. If you must grow your roses on such a site, you'll need to install perforated drain tile (as explained on page 27) so that your roses can thrive there.

Evaluating Your Soil

Once you've selected the site for your roses, determine what sort of soil you have in that location. Although there are three major soil types (sand, loam, and clay), most soils are somewhere in between the major categories. Nevertheless, you'll find that your soil will be identifiably closer to one of these types than to the other two.

Remember that your soil will contain particles of all three types—sand, loam, and clay. It's the *predominant* particle size that determines how your soil behaves and that constitutes its type. Knowing your soil type will give you a good indication of how easily your soil drains and how well it retains nutrients and water.

Determining your soil type is as easy as making a mud pie—or even easier. First, scoop up a small handful of soil. If it's dry, add enough water to make a stiff paste. Then, take your finger and rub the soil mixture in your palm. Sandy soils feel abrasive, clay soils feel slippery, and loam feels both gritty and smooth.

In addition to examining the soil itself, take a close look at what's growing in that soil. Indigenous plants (those you haven't planted yourself) sometimes provide additional clues about the soil conditions. While not foolproof, a casual inventory of existing weeds can give you a pretty good idea of what your soil is like.

Correcting Less-Than-Perfect Soil

Roses *want* a well-drained, fertile, clay-loam soil with a pH of 6.5. But few gardens are naturally blessed with such ideal soil. By now you've probably figured out what type of soil you have, and you can begin adjusting it to meet the needs of your roses.

Improving Drainage

Of all the possible shortcomings your soil can have, poor drainage may be the most deadly. Roses planted in poorly drained, perennially wet areas fail to thrive and are prone to a host of fungal and bacterial diseases.

If your site is poorly drained, take the following steps, ranging from least to most drastic, before planting your roses. This will ensure that excess water flows away from their roots.

Add coarse sand to the soil. Improve heavy clay soil by incorporating at least a couple of inches of coarse sand. If drainage is noticeably poor, you can carry this one step further by not only mixing sand into the topsoil but also digging an extra-deep hole at planting time and lining the bottom of it with sand or pea gravel.

Plant in a raised bed. Raising the level of the planting bed several inches above the surrounding soil is a good way to correct a mild drainage problem. It isn't difficult to do. In fact, you may find that simply adding amendments to the soil produces the desired effect. If you build a raised bed, be careful that it isn't in the

What Weeds Say about Your Soil

These "indicator weeds" tend to grow in the following soil conditions.

Weed	Preferred Soil Condition
Black medic (*Medicago lupulina*)	Dry, sandy soil
Chickweed (*Stellaria media*)	Clay soil; compacted soil
Common violet (*Viola papilionacea*)	Moist to wet soils
Common yarrow (*Achillea millefolium*)	Dry, infertile soil
Curly dock (*Rumex crispus*)	Wet clay soil
Dandelion (*Taraxacum officinale*)	Clay soil
Ground ivy (*Glechoma heracea*)	Poorly drained soil
Henbit (*Lamium amplexicaule*)	Rich, loamy soil
Plantain, wide leaf (*Plantago major*)	Clay soil
Prostrate knotweed (*Polygonum aviculare*)	Compacted clay soil
Prostrate spurge (*Euphorbia humistrata*)	Dry clay or sandy soils
Stinging nettle (*Urtica dioica*)	Moist, rich loam soil
White clover (*Trifolium repens*)	Compacted clay soil
Yellow nutsedge (*Cyperus esculentus*)	Moist to wet clay soils

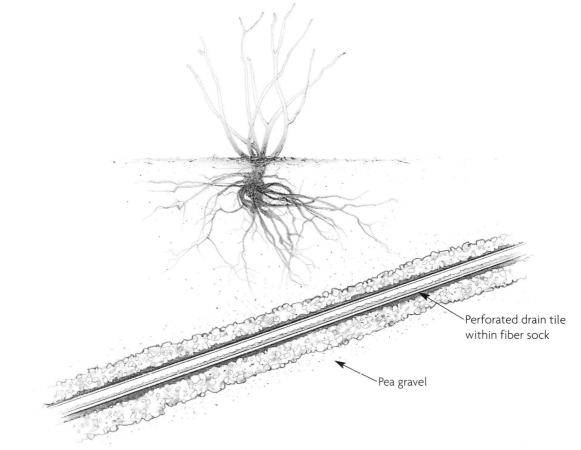

Perforated drain tile within fiber sock

Pea gravel

Correctly installed drain tile is the ultimate solution to the problems of poorly drained soil and standing water.

drainage path of another area of your garden, or your roses may end up waterlogged in spite of your efforts.

Remove compacted clay. If the area has been subject to construction trauma (stripped of topsoil, compacted by heavy equipment traffic, and so on), you may have to remove the bad stuff and replace it with a mixture of loamy topsoil, organic matter, and a bit of sand. This is hard work, but it will save you much frustration later.

Lay perforated drain tile. Although this is the most drastic measure, it is a must if you want to plant roses in soils in which water accumulates and stands after a heavy rain. You can save yourself the expense of having someone else install the tile by doing it yourself. To install drainage tile, dig a 2- to 3-foot-deep trench through the planting area and beyond, toward any point lower than the planting bed where the water can flow out. Line the trench with pea gravel, then cover it with perforated drain tile enclosed in a fiber

sock. (The sock prevents soil from infiltrating the tile.) Be careful to slope the tile slightly away from the bed, making the water flow in the desired direction. Cover the tile with another layer of pea gravel. Refill the trench with soil and plant your roses directly on top of it. The tile will do a wonderful job of wicking excess water away from the roots of your roses.

Using Cover Crops

No matter what type of soil you have, you can improve it by adding plenty of organic matter. One of the best ways to do this is to plant a cover crop—or green manure—in the area where you plan to plant your roses next season. Cover crops are fast-growing plants that you turn under the soil after they've grown for several months. All cover crops add organic matter to the soil, improve soil structure, prevent erosion, and smother weeds, but many of them also offer a host of additional benefits. Planting a cover crop requires a bit of foresight and planning, as well as a willingness to accept a somewhat delayed—but decidedly enhanced—gratification.

Cover crops are sometimes called green manures because they afford all the benefits of animal manure in plant (green) form. But think how much easier it is to spread the seeds of a cover crop than it is to spread a ton of manure! But unlike manure, which can introduce weeds to a garden, a cover crop smothers weeds with its quick growth. Some cover crops even suppress the germination of weed seeds. What's more, cover crops that are legumes (like crimson clover) capture nitrogen from the air and transform it into compounds that other plants can use. That's like getting fertilizer for free.

You can plant the area with a single type of cover crop or use a combination of several different types. The type or types of cover crops you should use depends on the time of year, your region, and how long you can wait to plant your future rose garden. Southern gardeners have more options because many cover crops will grow through the winter in Zone 7 and warmer. But even northern gardeners can plant rye or mustard in late winter for a cover crop "quick fix."

A Cover Crop Is a Beautiful Thing

Cover crops benefit your garden by:

Loosening soil. Common vetch, mustard, radish, rape, red clover, and turnip act like "biological plows." Their deep, penetrating roots help break up the soil.

Attracting beneficials. The flowers of clovers, lupines, mustard, phacelia, and vetch provide food for beneficial insects.

Inhibiting weeds. Rye, sorghum, and sudangrass contain natural allelopathic compounds that suppress the germination of weed seeds.

Providing forage for honeybees. The flowers of alfalfa, clovers, mustard, phacelia, and vetch provide nectar and pollen for honeybees.

Fixing nitrogen. Alfalfa clover, fenugreek, lupine, and vetch capture nitrogen from the air and transform it into compounds that plants can use.

Making phosphorus available. Buckwheat and sweet clover extract phosphorus from the soil and make it more available to succeeding plantings.

Buckwheat

Lifting nutrients from the subsoil. All deep-rooted cover crops scavenge nutrients from the subsoil and concentrate them in the topsoil layer.

Providing an edible crop. Radishes, turnips, and spinach can be grown as cover crops. Harvest some of the plants for yourself, then turn under the rest to feed your soil.

Adding Amendments

If you are unable (or too impatient) to plant a cover crop, you can still build deep, rich soil for your roses. Instead of amending each planting hole, prepare the entire bed for rose planting. The roots of your roses eventually will fill the entire area, if you plant them at the recommended spacing of 3 to 4 feet apart. And if you plan to plant your roses in a mixed border, improving *all* of the soil in the bed will benefit not only your roses, but also the perennials and annuals you plant there.

Begin by tilling or spading the area thoroughly. Remove perennial weeds, roots and all. If you have time, water the area, then wait a few weeks for weed seeds to germinate. Till again or hoe to destroy the young weeds in their vulnerable seedling stage.

Now, spread the good stuff: compost, leaf mold—whatever cocktail of decomposed organic matter you can get your hands on. Apply a 6-inch layer to sandy soils and a 4-inch layer to loam and clay soils. In addition, add 2 inches of coarse sand to clay soils. To help the roots of your new roses establish themselves quickly, broadcast bonemeal over the entire area.

After you've added the amendments, till the entire bed again thoroughly or mix your amendments in with a garden fork. Be sure to blend the amendments evenly into the soil below—don't just stir the amendment layer around by itself. If your ground is rocky, remove any big stones, but don't worry about little ones. They actually help improve the porosity and drainage of the soil.

Adjusting Soil pH

Soil pH is a measure of acidity or alkalinity. The relative acidity or alkalinity of your soil helps determine the availability of certain nutrients to plants. For instance, your soil may be rich in iron, but if it has an alkaline pH, the iron will be in a form that some plants can't use. With these conditions, a rose would suffer from chlorosis (yellowing between the leaf veins). To transform the iron into a form that your rose can use, you would need to acidify the soil.

How can you determine the pH of your soil? Endemic weeds may provide a clue (for example,

Monitor Soil pH with an "Indicator Hydrangea"

You can plant a bigleaf hydrangea (*Hydrangea macrophylla*) with your roses to indicate soil pH. In acid soil, the hydrangea's flowers will be blue; in neutral to alkaline soil, they'll be pink. This is especially useful if your soil is naturally alkaline: Pink hydrangeas signal it's time to acidify your soil.

Also, avoid using phosphorus fertilizers on your indicator hydrangea. High levels of phosphorus will prevent the hydrangea from taking up aluminum, which is necessary for blue color. If given too much phosphorus, a hydrangea will bear pink blooms even in acid soil.

dandelions often indicate acid soil), but the only way to know for sure is to test your soil. This is easy to do with a do-it-yourself soil pH test kit; just follow the kit's directions. Or, send a soil sample to a lab for professional testing—pH is always part of a soil analysis. (Contact your local cooperative extension for information on soil-testing kits and soil-analysis labs.)

If your native soil is around neutral (pH 7.0), you don't need to worry about adjusting it. But if your soil is either very acidic (below 6.5) or very alkaline (above 7.5), you'll need to adjust the pH so that the soil in your rose bed will be as close to 6.5 as possible. Follow the recommendations on your soil test when adjusting the pH of your soil.

Preparing the soil may seem like a lot of work, but it's worth its weight in rose petals. You can be sure that your roses will establish quickly, grow like blazes, and flower profusely. Not only that, but they'll be as healthy as they have the genetic potential to be and will be better equipped to withstand any attacks by pests. Now that you've laid the organic groundwork for flourishing roses, you're ready to plant.

If you plant your roses correctly, they may be around for your grandchildren to enjoy.

planting new roses

The moment has arrived.

The delivery truck has just pulled out of your driveway, and you're faced with a large cardboard box. In your mind's eye, you envision the contents: luxuriant shrubs weighed down with fragrant flowers. You open the box and you see…some ungainly, chopped-off canes with a vulnerable-looking tangle of roots—all swaddled in packing material and wrapped in plastic. Not exactly what you had in mind.

The truth is, bareroot roses *are* vulnerable. And understanding what makes them vulnerable is invaluable when planting your roses. As we'll see in this chapter, no matter where you live, timing is everything when planting a bareroot rose. *Dormant, bareroot roses must be planted as early in the season as possible.* And while you can plant containerized roses later in the season, plantings in hot, dry weather are always riskier and require more post-planting maintenance than do plantings in early spring or fall.

In addition to timing, planting at the proper depth is absolutely essential. Perhaps no other aspect of rose culture is as misunderstood—or as disputed—by gardeners as this simple yet critical element. Most roses are grafted—that is, the nursery has spliced the desired variety onto another rose's rootstock. For your rose to thrive, you must plant it deep enough to protect that point of union from both cold and dryness.

Let's take a closer look at the way the rose's anatomy and behavior influence planting.

The Nature of the Rose

Two key aspects of roses affect the way you should plant them. One is anatomical—whether or not the rose has been grafted, as opposed to grown on its own roots. The other factor pertains to the unique way that dormant, bareroot roses behave when breaking dormancy.

Own-Root versus Grafted Roses

Nurseries propagate rose cultivars vegetatively, and the most direct way to do this is to take cuttings of the desired rose variety and root them. This produces what is known as an "own-root rose." If you look closely at an own-root rose, you'll see a mass of roots, as well as a 1- to 4-inch-long "trunk" or main stem with three or more canes radiating from it.

As we discussed in Chapter 2, you should always try to choose an own-root rose over a grafted rose because a rose on its own roots will be hardier, healthier, and easier to grow.

The problem is, most roses are sold as grafted stock. That's because the process of rooting roses is lengthy and can be quite difficult with some varieties. With a grafted rose, the nursery simply splices a cutting of the desired variety onto a hardy and vigorous rootstock, saving time and money.

This process creates the graft union—that mysterious bump on the main trunk of the rose. With a little practice, recognizing the graft union becomes a snap.

The graft union is a slightly swollen area on the main stem of the rose—the region between the canes and the roots. The union may be in line with the trunk or it may seem to come off of the side (as with a bud-grafted or "budded" rose).

Why all the fuss about this little gnarled bump? Because that bump—the graft union—is the most vulnerable spot on your grafted rose. When planting, you must protect it from cold temperatures and from drying sun and wind, as we'll soon explain.

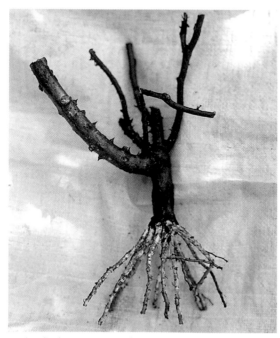

Graft union

With a little practice and experience, you'll be able to distinguish between own-root roses *(left)* and grafted roses *(right)*. Just look for the graft union, a "scar" created in the grafting process.

The Secret Life of Roses

The other key factor affecting planting is the unique way that dormant bareroot roses behave. Rather than being simply dormant, bareroot roses experience dormancy on two levels.

The roots of the rose are in deep sleep—rose REM, you might say. They won't start to stir for at least a week after planting. And even then, it will take a month for them to become fully awake and ready to meet the needs of the rest of the plant.

Meanwhile, the canes of the rose are only lightly dozing. The slightest bit of light, warmth, and air circulation will cause the buds to break into leafy growth and, consequently, begin to draw water and nutrients from the canes and roots.

But because those roots are so puny and sleepy, they cannot keep pace with the demands of the new, aboveground growth. The sad result may be all too familiar: After what seemed like a favorable start, the new shoots suddenly stutter to a stop, wither, and die. And the warmer the weather, the more likely this is to happen. What's more, if the rose has broken dormancy during shipping—as often happens with late orders—getting it established becomes even more dicey.

That's why it's so critical that you order and plant bareroot roses promptly. The earlier you order, the more likely the rose will be shipped at the earliest possible date for your area and the less likely it will have broken dormancy in transit. And the earlier you plant the rose, the less likely the canes will be to sprout before the roots start growing. Your newly planted bareroot rose should have at least a month of cool to cold temperatures to allow the roots to become established before the topgrowth begins.

Exactly *how* early should you plant? As a rule of thumb, you should plant bareroot roses as soon as the ground thaws and becomes workable. If you're in Zone 6 or colder, this may sound scary. (See "Windows of Opportunity" on this page for the ideal planting time for your area.) But for the rose, these conditions are ideal. After planting, a cap of mulch will protect those canes from extreme cold snaps and drying winds, and it will keep the buds dormant while the roots catch up.

Windows of Opportunity

The following ranges represent the best times to plant bareroot roses in each hardiness zone. The colder your hardiness zone, the later you can plant within that time frame. After the final date for your zone, stick to containerized roses.

Zone 3—thaw to May 20

Zone 4—thaw to May 5

Zone 5—thaw to April 20

Zone 6—thaw to April 5

Zone 7—November 20 to March 20

Zone 8 and 9—December 20 to March 5

Preparing to Plant

Now that you know how crucial it is to order and plant your roses early, you may already be headed out the door, rose and shovel in hand. But not so fast! Although you *should* plant your roses the same day that you receive them, you must first take the time to properly inspect and prepare them. These few extra steps can help ensure long-term success.

Inspecting Your Order

As soon as your roses arrive, unpack and inspect them. No supplier will be sympathetic if you call a week after you receive the shipment to report that something's wrong.

First, check to see that you received what you ordered and that the contents match the packing list. Then, examine the roses closely. Look for mold—a small amount of white mold isn't serious, but green mold definitely is cause for plant replacement.

Ideally, the roses should be fully dormant, with their buds tight and no new growth emerging. If you see pale, white to pinkish shoots, all is not lost, but your new roses will need special care. As a precaution, call the supplier immediately to report that the roses are not dormant. This will give you some leverage if you should need to negotiate with the supplier for replacement roses.

If the roses are not dormant, handle them with extreme care. The fragile new shoots can break at the slightest touch, and they are very susceptible to drying out. Cover sprouted roses with a damp cloth or enclose them in a breathable plastic bag, then store them in a cool, dark spot until you can plant them.

The Kindest Cut

Now is also the time to give your roses their first pruning. Begin with the roots, cutting off any that were broken or damaged during shipping. Wipe off any white mold. Then, lightly trim the remaining roots by ½ inch or so to remove any dead tissue at the ends and stimulate new growth.

Next, inspect the canes of the roses. Remove any damaged wood as well as any spindly or awkwardly placed growth. Then cut back the canes. Most rose experts advise cutting back the canes of a new rose to 6 to 8 inches long, but I prefer to leave about 12 inches of cane intact and then mulch the canes after planting. By pruning less drastically, you have a chance of seeing some of those much-anticipated flowers the first year. And mulching makes the more severe pruning unnecessary because it keeps the canes dormant longer.

Pralinage:
The French Mud Bath

Many experts recommend soaking bareroot roses in water or some sort of booster solution before planting. This technique makes perfect sense, as roses become dehydrated during shipment. The problem is, when you remove the roses and carry them outside to

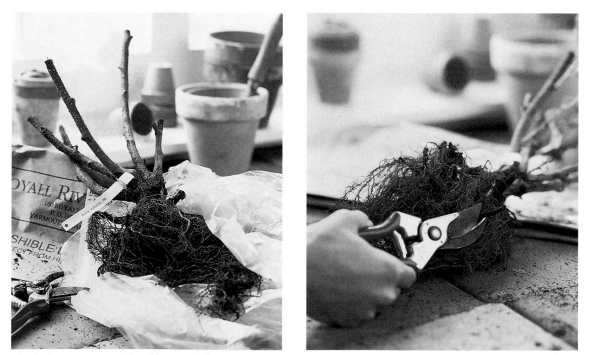

Ideally, bareroot roses should arrive fully dormant *(left),* with no new growth emerging. Before putting them in the ground, cut off any broken roots *(right).*

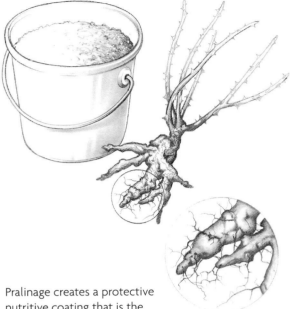

Pralinage creates a protective nutritive coating that is the perfect incubator for new roots.

plant, their roots are liable to dry out quickly, especially on a sunny or windy day.

To circumvent this problem, French gardeners use a centuries-old technique called *pralinage*. Pralinage doesn't require any fancy potions, and it goes beyond rehydrating. Pralinage protects a rose's roots and provides a boost to the plant even after planting.

This Old World trick simply consists of mixing equal parts of garden soil—preferably clay—and aged cow manure (bagged manure is fine) with enough water to make a thick, pourable slurry. Use a bucket that is large enough to comfortably accommodate the roots of your rose.

To make sure the mud bath is the proper consistency, plunge the roots into the slurry and then remove them. The roots should be more or less evenly coated with the mud. If the mud isn't clinging to them, add more soil and manure in equal proportions. When you've got the right consistency, immerse the rose's roots and allow them to soak for about an hour. Then carefully remove the plant and lay it on several layers of newspaper. If you're outdoors, lay it on the ground but out of the sun until the coating dries.

The roots of your rose are now protected with a "whitewash" of nutritive mud. This coating will protect them from drying out while you dig. In addition, the roots will bond better with the surrounding soil after planting, providing a highly nutritive microenvironment for the emerging root hairs—the tiny but important roots that will nourish your rose.

Planting Bareroot Roses

You've inspected the contents of your order and properly pruned and soaked your roses. At last, you're ready to plant! Whether you plant your rose in a prepared bed or in the middle of the lawn, the most important thing is to plant at the proper depth.

How Deep?

Regardless of your hardiness zone, you should plant your roses so that their graft unions are 3 to 5 inches below the surface of the soil. Many rose experts insist that you can plant the graft union at the soil surface or even a couple of inches above it in warm climates, but my experience has taught me otherwise.

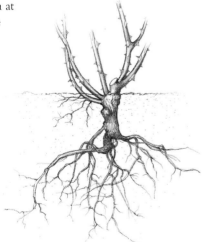

Planting a rose with its graft union 3 to 5 inches below the soil line encourages the canes to form their own roots, greatly enhancing the rose's health and vigor.

Roses on Hold

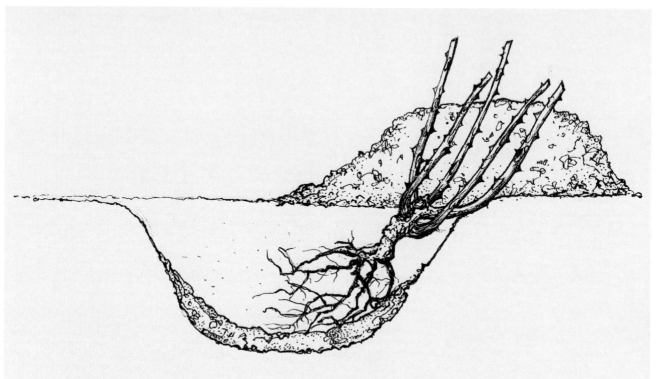

If you can't plant your bareroot roses immediately after pralinage, keep them safe and dormant by heeling them in at a 45-degree angle in a compost-lined trench deep enough to accommodate the roots and part of the length of the canes.

1. Choose a shaded spot, protected from prevailing winds. Dig a trench a bit wider and deeper than necessary to hold the roots and part of the canes of your roses when you lay them in the trench at a 45-degree angle. (Heeling the plants in at an angle will make it easier to remove them at planting time.)

2. Line the bottom of the trench with a 1-inch layer of light, fine-textured compost. A fluffy material such as this is essential to prevent new roots from breaking off when you remove the rose. And the fine texture reduces air spaces around the roots, minimizing the chances that they'll dry out.

3. Lay the roses in the trench at a 45-degree angle, then cover them with more of the compost so that only the tips of the canes are visible. You may use a slightly coarser material, such as ground leaves or straw, to cover the canes, but make sure the graft unions are securely buried in compost. Water thoroughly several times.

4. When ready to plant, water the heeled-in roses again. Remove any coarse mulch and use a garden fork to gently pry the roses out of their trench.

5. Repeat pralinage immediately if new roots are exposed, then plant immediately—don't wait for the coating to dry.

Rain on Your Rose Parade

What do you do if the weather isn't cooperating and you can't plant or heel in (see "Roses on Hold" on the opposite page) your roses right away? You should still inspect your roses, then rewrap them in their packing material and place them in your refrigerator until you can heel them in or plant them. If you think your roses will dry out despite being wrapped in the packing material, pack them in damp peat moss (milled sphagnum), place them in breathable produce storage bags, and keep them in your refrigerator (or a dark place that's around a cool 33° to 40°F).

Many years ago, I began noticing a significant difference in the growth of the potted roses in my nursery. The roses that had their graft unions buried below a couple of inches of potting mix leafed out quickly and thrived. But the roses that had their grafts above the soil sprouted weakly and languished, or just dehydrated and died. Over the years, I've repeatedly observed this phenomenon, not only with bareroot roses planted in pots, but also with roses planted in landscapes.

In colder zones, deep planting protects the graft union from extreme cold. In warmer climates, it protects it from extreme heat and drought. And in all climates, deep planting encourages the canes to form their own roots, which will make your rose even stronger and healthier.

Planting in a Prepared Bed

Assuming you've already prepared the bed according to the recommendations outlined in the last chapter, digging the hole for your new rose will be easy. Gather a plastic tarp, a wheelbarrow, about a cubic foot of compost per rose, and enough moist, damp mulching material to cover most of the canes of your rose. (Composted manure, compost, chopped leaves, or shredded hardwood mulch work best as a mulch to cover your roses.)

Now take a look at your rose. The hole you dig needs to be deep and wide enough to more than accommodate the rose's roots, along with the bottom 3 to 5 inches of the canes. (If you live in Zone 5 or colder, opt for the deeper planting.) In most cases,

this means you'll need to dig a hole that's 18 to 24 inches deep and just as wide. Try to match the shape of the hole to the shape of your rose's roots. Some bareroot roses have most of their roots off to one side. Dig an oval hole or any other shape necessary to comfortably fit your rose's roots. To avoid compacting the fluffy soil in your bed, stand on a plank or piece of plywood while you work.

Excavate the top 12 inches of soil (about a spade's depth) and pile it on your tarp. This soil should be fluffy, highly organic, and enriched due to your previous preparation. Then dig the rest of the hole, placing about half of this heavier subsoil in the wheelbarrow and mixing the rest with the compost on your tarp (the compost/subsoil mixture should be about half compost and half subsoil). If you have heavy clay subsoil, punch the bottom of the hole a couple of times with a fork to ensure good drainage.

Next, shovel a bit of the reserved topsoil (from the top 12 inches on the tarp) into the bottom of the hole to form a cone shape. Lay the handle of a shovel or other tool across the middle of the hole to serve as a guide for measuring depth. Position your rose straight up on the cone of soil, and adjust the height of your cone of soil until the graft is 3 to 5 inches below the bottom edge of your tool handle. Plant own-root roses so that their crowns are 3 inches below this point.

Spread the rose's roots as much as possible, so they radiate from the center of the plant, but *do not* try to force woody roots; they'll break!

Backfill the hole to within about 3 inches of the surface, using first your reserved topsoil from the tarp (for the bottom of the hole) and then the subsoil-compost mix (closer to the top of the hole). Water your rose thoroughly, allowing the hole to fill with water. To settle any air pockets, insert the end of the hose into the soil at three or four different spots in the planting hole. After watering, recheck the depth of your rose, as it may have settled. Adjust its depth (by carefully inserting a spade next to the rose, lifting slightly, and shoving a bit of additional soil beneath it) and rewater if necessary.

Finish filling the hole with the soil-compost mix, then use a bit of soil to create a rim 2 to 3 inches high around the edge of the planting hole. This miniature dam will trap water and direct it down to the thirsty roots of the rose. At this point, water the rose again and check the effectiveness of the basin you've created. If necessary, reinforce any leaks in your dam with additional soil. If you planted your rose on a slope, you'll need to make the soil rim higher on the downhill side of the hole.

Carefully spread the roots of the rose over the cone of soil inside the planting hole. Make sure the graft union is 3 to 5 inches below the tool handle.

Rose Alert!

Now pile the moist mulch inside your dam, leaving only the tips of the canes exposed so that you can see where they are. The mulch will protect the canes from severe cold and, even more important, will trick them into remaining dormant long enough to give the roots a chance to catch up to them.

Check your rose every few days by gently pulling away some of the mulch. When the buds begin to elongate, gradually remove the mulch over a period of 8 to 10 days. Be very careful when removing the mulch: The new growth will be extremely tender and easy to break. Leave a 2-inch layer of mulch around the base of the rose.

Planting in the Lawn

Roses look best when planted in combination with other plants in a bed. But that doesn't mean that you *can't* plant a rose by itself (as a specimen) in your lawn or in some other location where you haven't prepared an entire bed.

In this case, you'll need to improve the soil at planting time. And you'll need to dig a larger hole than you would if planting in a bed. When digging the hole, remove the heavy subsoil at the hole's bottom and any large rocks and haul them away. (Save the sod, though—you can use it later.) Add compost to the remaining excavated soil so that the mix is about half native soil and half compost. If your soil is extremely heavy or mucky, add a couple shovels full of coarse sand. Work lime or sulfur into the mix also, as directed by the results of a soil test or the results of a home pH test kit.

Before you backfill, place some of the saved sod upside down in the bottom of the hole where it will decompose. After you plant, create and maintain a 3-foot-diameter grass-free zone so that grass doesn't compete with your rose. To do this, cut a 1-foot-wide section of additional sod all the way around the perimeter of the planting hole. Turn this "doughnut" of sod upside down over the same area, then cover it with several layers of newspaper and an additional layer of mulch.

Make sure to prevent grass from slowly closing in on your specimen rose. Edge the perimeter of the grass-free zone regularly, and reapply mulch as the old stuff breaks down.

Maintain a 3-foot-diameter grass-free zone around a rose that's been planted in turf. To keep the zone grass-free, reapply mulch such as compost as needed.

Planting a Potted Rose

Planting a rose that's been growing in a container is just like planting a bareroot rose in terms of soil preparation, size of the planting hole, and planting depth. Locating the graft union on a potted rose can be a bit tricky, however. For this reason, be sure to ask the supplier whether the rose is grafted or own-root. If you don't get a decisive answer or the person answering your question seems unsure, assume the rose is grafted.

Unlike other container-grown nursery stock, potted roses should not automatically be planted at the same level they grew at in the pot. Many growers try to economize on the size of pots they use, so the graft is very likely to be at or above the soil line—not a few inches below it.

To determine exactly where the graft is located, run your fingers along the trunk of the rose, beginning at the base of the canes and heading downward. Inspect carefully, gently removing the potting mix from around the trunk if necessary, until you locate the telltale bump of the graft. Just as with a bareroot rose, you must position that spot 3 to 5 inches below the rim of the planting hole.

Before you plant, set the pot in a tub of water for a few hours to soak the rootball and hydrate the plant. You don't need to do any pruning on a container-grown rose, except to remove any dead or damaged areas.

Now, grit your teeth and remove any open flowers. Rose blooms dissipate lots of water from the plant and divert its energy. (You don't need to waste those flowers, though—float them in a crystal or glass bowl in the house.) If it's late in the season and hot weather is approaching, remove any flower buds, as well. This will channel the plant's energy toward establishing the all-important new root growth.

If masses of roots are growing out the bottom of the pot, don't try to pull the plant from the pot. Instead, cut away the plastic pot so that you don't damage the roots. After you free the plant, inspect the root mass. Carefully loosen any circling roots and spread them outward. Use your fingers or a handheld

Post-Planting Care

For the first month or two after planting, be especially vigilant about watering your rose—whether it was container-grown or bareroot. Frequently monitor the soil moisture, especially during dry spells, by sticking your finger down into the soil. If the soil feels dry 1 inch below the surface, that's your signal to water. Never wait for the rose to wilt.

Water deeply and thoroughly to encourage deep rooting. If you water only the top few inches of soil, the rose's roots will develop only in that area.

Do not fertilize your new rose for at least a month after planting. Early fertilization will stimulate more topgrowth than the roots can support, leading to the dreaded "dwindle-and-die" syndrome.

Transplanting without Trauma

It happens in every garden, sooner or later: The planting site that once seemed ideal isn't anymore, and now you must move your rose. Perhaps the rose grew bigger than you thought it would, or maybe you plan to build a new garage on that spot.

Whatever your reason for transplanting, by all means try to do it when the rose is dormant—preferably in late fall. In Zones 7 through 9, you can even move a rose during the winter. Don't try to move

Unlike other containerized plants, container-grown roses must be planted considerably deeper than they were in their pots.

cultivating fork to lightly "frazzle" the root ball, scarifying its surface and breaking a few rootlets in the process. Slightly injuring the small roots this way will stimulate them to grow outward.

You're now ready to plant your pot-grown rose, just as you would a bareroot rose (described earlier in this chapter).

Rose Alert!

Never replace a rose with another rose, unless you're also willing to replace all of the soil that surrounded the roots of the prior occupant. When planted in soil where another rose grew recently, roses usually languish due to a condition known as soil sickness, or specific replant disease. Rose roots seem to secrete substances into the soil that stunt the growth of successor roses no matter how much care they receive. If you don't plan to replace the soil, wait at least 2 years before planting another rose in that location.

a rose in leaf, however, unless it's near the dormant season. In that case, strip all the leaves off of the rose and remove all flowers and flower buds before you transplant.

Before moving the rose, always water it thoroughly. I like to do this the night before transplanting, so that the ground won't be too muddy when I dig up the rose.

Digging the New Hole

Prepare your rose's new home *before* you dig it up. That way, you'll keep the rose aboveground for a minimum of time and lessen the shock of transplant. Do your best to estimate the size of the hole you'll need—it should be a foot wider than the rootball of the transplanted rose and deep enough to accommodate the graft union at that 3- to 5-inch depth.

Preventing Prickles

Moving a dormant rose is much like moving any other shrub, except that roses are prickly! The first step is to bundle the rose's canes with heavy twine. To make the job easier, ask an appropriately clad friend to assist you by grabbing the canes of the rose in a bear hug. You do the wrapping: Attach one end of the twine to the base of a major outside cane, then spiral the twine upward around the outside of the rose, bundling it snugly. Near the top, make a circle with the twine and tie it to itself.

"Ball and Burlap"

"Ball and burlap"—nursery-speak for digging up a shrub or tree—is the next step. Before you dig up your rose, get a piece of burlap or an old sheet and wet it down. The wet burlap will protect the rootball while it is aboveground.

If your rose is small to medium-size, dig a 12- to 18-inch-diameter rootball. The bigger the rose and

the less you prune it back, the bigger you'll need to make the rootball.

Using a well-sharpened spade, dig all around the rootball, and then undercut it. With one hand, use the spade to lever up the ball; with your other hand, place the wet burlap beneath the raised portion of the ball. Keep enough of the cloth outside the rootball to reach around and up to the top of it; bunch the excess beneath the ball. Then, lift the rootball from the opposite side and pull the bunched burlap toward you, encasing the rootball. Tie up the opposite corners of the cloth snugly, like a kerchief, making square knots. You can then use the knotted burlap as a convenient handle to safely lift your rose out of the hole without injuring the rose's roots.

Don't automatically plant your rose at the same depth it grew at before. If the graft union wasn't deep enough at the old site, now is the time to correct this. Use a yardstick to measure the distance between the bottom of the rootball and the graft union. Then measure the depth of the new planting hole. The hole needs to be 3 to 5 inches deeper than the distance between the bottom of the rootball and the graft—if it isn't, make the necessary adjustments.

Remove the burlap or sheet, then carefully place the rose inside the planting hole. Never drop or handle a balled-and-burlapped rose roughly, or you'll crack the ball, severing lots of roots in the process and jeopardizing your plant. Backfill, form a basin, water, and then mulch as described on page 38. Your rose is now safely settled in its new home.

PART II

basic care

No other plant has its care as hotly contested as the rose. Advice varies widely and many questions may seem to have more than one right answer. Taking care of your roses organically doesn't have to remain a mystery, though. It's simply a matter of recognizing what your roses need. For example, on the pages that follow you'll see how you can keep diseases to a minimum by choosing resistant varieties, watering carefully, providing sound nutrition, and practicing safe preventative measures. And once you understand the rationale behind various pruning cuts and times, a task that once may have seemed daunting will suddenly become satisfying.

If you care for your roses keeping in mind what they like best, you'll find that they're simply good garden plants—and not the high-maintenance prima donnas that we've come to know them as.

Watering your roses correctly is one of the simplest ways to minimize disease problems.

watering your roses

Watering may seem like the most obvious thing in the world—certainly not a subject that merits an entire chapter in a book about roses. But after soil preparation, nothing else is as crucial to a successful garden as careful and effective watering. That's especially true for roses, which are extremely sensitive to poor watering practices.

Unfortunately, careless watering is all too common, as my experience working with homeowners and nursery staff has taught me. Most watering mistakes seem to be caused by our impatience: We're just too busy to water. If we're watering by hand, we're sloppy or we don't water our plants for long enough. Or, more often, we install some sort of irrigation system so that we don't have to do the job at all.

But no matter what watering method you use, paying attention to the water needs of your plants is critical. Proper watering can mean the difference between healthy, beautiful roses and sickly plants that fail to live up to your expectations. So in this chapter you'll find tips for watering by hand, as well as for using soaker hoses and drip irrigation—all effective means of quenching your roses' thirst.

An Ounce of Prevention

Correct watering is more important to the organic cultivation of roses than to any other plant. By providing adequate water and delivering it properly, you can prevent or minimize the three major fungal diseases of roses. Two of these diseases—black spot and rust—need to come in contact with a wet leaf surface to infect the plant, and they spread via water droplets. The third disease—powdery mildew—typically infects drought-stressed roses. So how, when, and how much you water play vital roles in the prevention of all three of these rose diseases.

Delivering an adequate supply of water also can protect your roses against the ravages of spider mites and whiteflies, both of which thrive during periods of hot, dry weather.

And, if you're still not convinced that you should pay special attention to your roses' need for water, here's one more incentive: You'll get more blooms! An even, ample supply of ground moisture will stimulate your roses to bloom as prolifically and as often as they are capable of doing. On the other hand, drought-stressed roses will set few or no flower buds.

Once your roses come into bloom, you'll need to be extra vigilant about watering. Roses lose enormous amounts of water through their blossoms (water is lost through each individual petal), and if a plant isn't getting enough water through its roots

at this time, its blossoms will wilt. So the more fully double and larger the blossoms of your rose, the more water it will transpire, and the thirstier your plant will be.

Autumn, a notoriously dry season in many regions, is another time to pay extra attention to watering. Be especially sure that your roses are plump and turgid with moisture just before the ground freezes. Dehydration at this time can result in major damage to canes. In frozen ground, soil moisture gets locked up in ice crystals and is no longer available to the rose's roots. Yet the canes continue to transpire water, making them susceptible to dieback if they aren't hydrated adequately going into winter.

Watering your roses thoroughly and correctly, one elegantly simple technique for successful organic rose growing, will go a long way toward preventing all of these common problems. Using mulch around your roses to help to retain soil moisture will also help prevent moisture-related problems.

Ways of Watering

There are many ways to water roses, ranging from low to high tech. On the low-tech end is watering by hand, using a can or hose. On the high-tech end is the use of sophisticated drip irrigation systems with metered flows zoned on automatic timers. Between the two extremes is a range of intermediate solutions. Let's take a closer look.

Rose Alert!

Roses are especially prone to drying out in the following conditions. Be extra vigilant about watering your roses if they

- were planted less than 2 months ago,
- are just leafing out,
- are in full bloom,

- are exposed to strong winds,
- are experiencing temperatures above 80°F,
- are planted in light, sandy soil,
- are planted on a hill or slope, or
- are planted in containers.

Watering Wisdom

No matter what method you use to water your roses, follow these basic rules:

- Water deeply, and less frequently. Provide 1 inch of water per week, in one or two deep applications, if you haven't had sufficient rainfall. Deep watering encourages deep rooting so that roses can access groundwater during drought. Superficial irrigation causes rose roots to develop just below the soil surface.

- Avoid wetting the foliage. Water on leaves promotes the development of fungal disease and spreads existing disease throughout the plant. Water only the roots of your rose.

- Water in the morning. That way, any water that does splash on the leaves has a chance to dry quickly, minimizing the likelihood of spreading disease.

- Water gently. If you're watering by hand, use a breaker nozzle to deliver a gentle stream. A gentle application minimizes splashing, which spreads disease.

- Water slowly and repeatedly. Slow application allows water to sink into the ground, rather than run off the surface—and go to waste. When watering by hand, make two or three passes with your watering can or hose.

- Water throughout the growing season, until the ground freezes. While in leaf, your roses need water to grow. Later in the season, they need water to withstand the onslaught of winter.

Watering by Hand: Easy Does It

Hand watering is the most time-consuming way to water, but it has a couple of advantages. You may find that this old-fashioned method of watering provides you with some much-needed downtime for reflection. At the same time, your roses will benefit by receiving several minutes of your undivided attention whenever you water.

To paraphrase an old Chinese proverb, the footsteps of the gardener are the best fertilizer. In other words, don't underestimate the importance of getting in there and examining your roses carefully. There simply is no substitute for getting up close and personal with your plants, and that's especially true in an organic garden. Close and careful inspection allows you to discover small problems before they become big ones. Over time, you will become familiar with

the way your roses look when they are healthy—and the way they look when they are not.

As you water, whether with a hose or a watering can, inspect your roses carefully. Look for signs of disease, insects, or other stress, such as spots, discoloration, holes in leaves, curled leaves—in short, anything that looks abnormal. This is also a great time to look for and remove rootstock suckers. Make note of the health of your roses and, if necessary, take the appropriate action.

Using a watering can. When using a watering can, direct the spout at the foot of the plant, without wetting the foliage. Water slowly, a little at a time, letting the moisture sink in before you add more. When you're lugging water by hand, you don't want any to go to waste by running off the surface before the soil can absorb it.

Watering with a hose. If you choose to water by hand with the aid of a hose, follow the basic principles for correct watering (see "Watering Wisdom" on page 47). One of the most important principles involves using a breaker wand for the end of your hose. This will allow you to provide a generous supply of water to your roses without damaging them in the process.

A breaker wand is an angled, metal tube with a fitting for the hose at one end and a fitting for a breaker head at the other end. Like the rose on a watering can, a breaker "breaks" the stream of water into a gentle spray.

Select a wand that's a comfortable length for you. Avoid the models with plastic fittings; they will crack with repeated use and exposure to sunlight. Instead, try to find a breaker wand with brass screw fittings. Also get yourself a brass quarter-turn valve to put on the end of your hose before screwing on the wand. The valve will allow you to regulate the flow and turn off the water whenever you want.

At all costs, avoid watering with a spray nozzle— that pistol-like device that you squeeze to deliver a jet of water. Although spray nozzles deliver relatively little water, the water is under pressure, so you think you're giving your plants more than you actually are. As a result, you stop watering long before you should. In addition, the forceful jet splatters fungal spores all over the place but prevents water from soaking into the ground.

Overhead Irrigation: Why It's Not for Roses

Instead of watering your roses personally, you could leave the job to some sort of irrigation device. If you do, be sure that you *don't* use an overhead irrigation system. For roses, overhead irrigation is definitely the worst watering technique.

Rose First-Aid Kit

Organize a small basket to take with you when you water. Include the items you most frequently use to care for your roses, such as the following:

- pruning shears
- small journal or notebook and pen
- trowel or other weeding tool
- roll of twine or plant twist-ties
- small bottle of diluted kelp or fish emulsion
- small plastic spray bottle of insecticidal soap
- hand lens (or magnifying glass) for identifying hard-to-see pests
- small jar of soapy water for killing beetles or for collecting pest specimens for later identification

Grab your first-aid basket before you head out the door to water your roses. You'll have everything you need to correct any small problems that you spot while watering.

Avoid using overhead irrigation to water your roses. Doing so may cause the blossoms to stick together.

Overhead systems keep the foliage wet for prolonged periods—which is just the ticket for black spot and rust development. By increasing humidity, these systems encourage mildew, as well. In addition, overhead irrigation beats the soil at the base of the roses, causing the spores of fungal diseases to splash onto nearby plants.

Overhead irrigation can also spoil the flowers themselves, just as an extended period of wet weather can. When exposed to these conditions, the buds of some rose cultivars will show color but fail to open because the outer petals stick together (a phenomenon known as "balling"). Blossoms with lots of petals and a globose form are especially prone to this unsightly condition. On other rose cultivars—particularly those with soft-textured petals—the blossoms may open but will mat together and then, unfortunately, rot.

Another problem with overhead irrigation is that it deposits minerals on the foliage of your roses. Whatever makes your water "hard" will end up as a coating on the leaves. If your water contains a lot of iron, for instance, your plants will look as though they're coated with rust—and they will be! Not only is this unsightly, but it also partially blocks sunlight from reaching the leaves.

Finally, the constant drumming of water by overhead irrigation compacts the soil over time. For all of these reasons, avoid exposing your roses to overhead irrigation.

Soaker Hoses: Effective Low-Tech Irrigation

Fortunately, there is more than one way to irrigate a rose. At the low-tech end of the spectrum of possibilities are soaker hoses and "leaky pipe"—porous hoses or perforated tubing that leak water along their length.

A soaker hose is easy to install. You just snake it among your plants, connect the end to a conventional hose, and away you go. The hose terminates in a blind end, forcing water out through the pores. While you could choose to install a soaker hose permanently, below your mulch, most people just lay it on top of the mulch and move it around.

The advantages of a soaker hose are that it's cheap, it's easy to move, and it delivers water without wetting the foliage of your roses. The disadvantages are that the pores in the tube clog easily with minerals and dirt, and there's no way to flush them out. Also, if your roses are spaced far apart, those spaces between them will get watered as well as the root zones of the roses.

A more serious problem is that soaker hoses deliver water very unevenly. Roses at the head of the line receive lots of water, while those at the end get almost none. To

Although a soaker hose is better than overhead irrigation, it delivers water unevenly. To compensate, keep it on top of mulch so that you can move it around frequently.

irrigate all of your roses adequately, you must reverse the direction halfway through the watering. What's more, soaker hose is limited in length, so you can water only a small area at a time.

It doesn't take long for most of us to tire of dragging a soaker hose around. When you reach that point, you're ready to go to the ultimate level in watering: drip irrigation.

Drip Irrigation: The Pinnacle of High-Tech Watering

Modern drip irrigation systems are high-tech in the best sense of the word. We're talking microtubules here, not microchips. Developed in response to the crucial water needs of arid or drought-stricken areas such as Israel and Australia, drip irrigation systems make use of extremely sophisticated engineering.

When it comes to watering roses, it just doesn't get any better than a real, bona fide drip irrigation system. In terms of plant health, soil care, and economies of time and money, drip systems are light years ahead of all other methods of watering. Quick and simple to install, a drip system can be used to evenly irrigate even the most difficult sites, including slopes and irregularly shaped areas, with essentially zero water waste.

A drip irrigation system waters roses efficiently and ecologically, while reducing disease problems.

Drip irrigation is ideal for both new and established plantings. To install dripline, you just lay it on top of the soil, then cover it with mulch. No trenching is required, unless you want to lay an underground supply line to the head of the dripline. And because the lines are so accessible, changing the layout or fixing a leak is easy to do yourself.

Most drip irrigation systems are made of durable, UV-resistant, black polyethylene tubing. They deliver the water through emitters, at rates ranging from ½ gallon to 1 gallon per hour. With some systems, the emitters are built into the tubing, spaced 6 inches to 3 feet apart. On others, you punch in the emitters yourself. If your roses are spaced at irregular intervals and you have no other plants between them, choose a system with insertable emitters so that you can place them to suit your plants.

Another great feature of drip irrigation systems is that they're practically maintenance free. You don't need to clean them because minerals don't build up inside the slick tubing and soil particles can't get inside the emitters. The most sophisticated emitters contain a tiny strainer that is cleaned by an ingenious self-flushing mechanism. What's more, the emitters always stay open, so you don't need to shut down the system for the winter or service it in spring.

Drip irrigation systems require a pressure reducer and filter, both of which are installed at the head of the supply line. (If you're buying your system piece by piece, rather than buying an entire system from an irrigation installer, you'll need to make sure to buy these two vital components.) To maintain even pressure along the length of the line, drip systems use either "turbulent flow" or a pressure-compensating dripline. Turbulent flow (used on less-expensive systems) works fine for shorter runs with less than 10 feet of elevation change. For longer or more steeply sloped areas, use the pressure-compensating type.

You don't need to be a master plumber to assemble and install a drip irrigation system. The joints and fittings are simply designed, and you just seal the joints. With some of the newest systems, you don't even need to do any gluing.

Before you install a drip system, plan it out on paper and check the product specifications. Many factors influence the layout of a drip system. One of

Drip Irrigation Delivers the Goods

Drip irrigation offers many advantages in terms of rose health, savings in time and money, and the environment. Consider these benefits:

- fewer disease problems because foliage stays dry

- no spread of fungal or bacterial diseases due to splashing water

- no discoloration of foliage due to hard-water minerals

- faster, more robust plant growth due to improved and even soil/water/oxygen balance

- deeper root systems due to better percolation of water

- less germination of weed seeds because of minimal soil-surface wetting

- water anytime—day or night (whether or not you're at home)

- virtually maintenance-free—no cleaning or winterizing needed

- consumes 30 to 50 percent less water than other irrigation methods

- lower energy costs due to low-pressure system

- no evaporation of water

- minimal runoff

- preserves soil structure because water does not compact the surface

the most important factors is soil type, because it affects the way that water percolates from the system. On sandy soil, for instance, you should space emitters 15 to 18 inches apart, but on clay soil, an interval of 24 to 36 inches is adequate. The goal is to have slightly overlapping zones of saturation from one emitter to the next.

The slope of the area is another consideration when planning the layout of your system. Concentrate the density of drip lines at the top of the slope, and gradually decrease the number as you go down. Steep slopes may require no lines at all at the bottom because of the cumulative percolation from above.

After you've assembled and installed a drip irrigation system, experiment with the duration and frequency of operation until you come up with a combination that suits your location and climate. During periods of no rainfall, roses typically need 2 to 5 hours of drip irrigation (depending on emitter flow rate) every couple of days in hot weather; every 3 days in warm weather; and every 4 days in cool weather.

If you use an automatic timer, remember to check the soil moisture during periods of extreme weather. You may need to increase the duration and frequency during hot, dry weather or decrease them in cool, rainy periods.

At no time should you operate a drip irrigation system for so long that water runs off the surface of the soil. Remember that too much water can be just as lethal as too little. Strange as it seems, roses (and other plants) sometimes wilt in waterlogged soil. That's because water fills all of the tiny air pockets around the plants' roots, so the roots can't breathe. Without oxygen, a plant can't pump in the water it needs, so it experiences physiological drought—resulting in wilting.

For this reason, don't automatically assume that wilted roses need more water—they could actually be receiving too much. To find out if this is the case, stick your finger below the surface of the soil. If it's already saturated, decrease the duration and frequency of your irrigation.

Feeding your roses an organic diet will help keep them healthy and beautiful all season long.

fertilizing roses organically

If you choose the rugged, disease-resistant roses recommended in Chapter 2 and you plant them according to the advice and instruction in Chapters 3 and 4, your roses will probably do just fine for at least a couple of years without any additional nutrients. After that, they would still live and grow without extra attention, but not as lushly or as quickly as they would if you were to feed them.

You don't have to run out and buy all kinds of fertilizers to feed your roses, though. A simple, well-rounded organic diet of annual applications of compost will encourage any rose to bloom more abundantly and have more luxuriant foliage. (If a soil test shows that you need to make nutritional adjustments to your soil, you can do that organically, as well, with amendments such as fish meal.) Organically nourished roses also will be better able to resist diseases and insect pests. And because well-fed roses are able to store a full load of carbohydrates for the winter, they will emerge from the cold season with plenty of reserves, ready to start growing strong.

What Roses Need

In many ways, fertilizing roses organically is just like feeding any other flowering plant. It starts with your soil: Organic, humus-rich soil is the foundation of any healthy garden. Such a soil, kept free of chemical fertilizers, teems with microbes. The microbes make the nutrients in organic supplements available to plants in usable forms. Rather than providing a drug-like dose of fertilizer salts that quickly wash away (as chemical fertilizers do), annual applications of compost supply nutrients gradually. As the rose uses the nutrients, the microbes' constant activity releases more. In this way, having organic matter in the soil is like having nutrients in the bank.

When it comes to feeding your roses, compost should be your top choice. Compost provides plants with large amounts of carbohydrates, as well as nutrients to feed what soil scientists call the "soil food web." Only organic matter (in the form of compost) can provide nitrogen and all the other nutrients that plants need while at the same time feeding the diverse soil food web that's made up of bacteria, fungi, earthworms, and other soil organisms.

Of course, you should always test the soil in a new garden before planting your roses, to see whether you need to make any nutrient adjustments. (Call your local Cooperative Extension Service for a soil-testing kit or the name of a local soil-testing laboratory.) You'll learn about the specific nutrients you'll be testing for on the following pages. But after making any adjustments, all you'll need to do to keep your roses well fed is add compost each year.

Nutritional Stars: Nitrogen, Phosphorus, and Potassium

Like all plants, roses require all of the "big three" nutrients (also known as the "primary macronutrients"): nitrogen (N), phosphorus (P), and potassium (K).

Job Descriptions for the "Big 3"

Understanding the functions of the primary macronutrients will help you recognize any nutrient deficiencies that might arise.

Nutrient	Function	Signs of Deficiency
Nitrogen (N)	Promotes the growth of lush stems and foliage	Reduced growth; yellow leaves; red-tinged leaves
Phosphorus (P)	Promotes the growth of strong roots and stems, as well as flowering and fruiting	Weak rooting; reduced flowering; weak stems; browning of leaves
Potassium (K)	Promotes vigor and resistance to disease, insects, and cold; also needed for strong leaves and stems	Reduced growth; browning of leaf edges; necrotic (dead) patches on leaves

Soil testing takes the guesswork out of fertilizing. Gather soil samples from several areas, collecting a core at least 8 inches deep from each spot. Label carefully and send them off to a soil-testing lab. (Call your local Cooperative Extension Service for a soil-testing kit or the name of a local soil-testing laboratory.)

Roses need nitrogen for strong, sturdy growth; phosphorus for root growth and winter hardiness; and potassium for abundant flower production.

The NPK numbers on a bag of organic fertilizer express the ratio and percentage of the three major nutrients. For instance, a supplement with a 6-12-6 NPK analysis would contain 6 percent nitrogen, 12 percent phosphorus, and 6 percent potassium (the perfect balance of NPK for roses).

Keep in mind that the three major nutrients behave differently in the soil, and these differences affect how you should supply them to your plants.

Nitrogen—after it is converted to ammonia or nitrate—is very mobile and leaches rapidly from the soil. That's why it's important to provide your roses with a steady supply of *organic* nitrogen, which becomes slowly available to plants through the action of soil microbes.

If a lot of carbon is present in the soil, however, those same microbes will tie up the nitrogen. Wood or bark mulches, for example, provide a huge reservoir of carbon. To break down this carbon, soil microorganisms must pull nitrogen from the soil. They release the

nitrogen, gradually, only after the decomposition is complete. So compost wood chips before you spread them as mulch, to reduce the temporary nitrogen tie-up.

Phosphorus, on the other hand, stays just about where you put it in the soil. Electrical charges tightly bind the phosphorus to soil particles, especially in clay. Phosphorus that isn't within reach of your roses' roots is likely to remain out of reach. If your soil test results show that your soil is low in phosphorus, it's important to place your source of phosphorus in the bottom of the hole when you plant your rose and to continue to supply phosphorus to the plant's root zones.

Potassium leaches regularly from the soil, and soils low in organic matter also tend to be potassium deficient. On the other hand, too much potassium can result in problems with soil balance and pH. Annual applications of compost to the soil, however, should provide just the right amount of potassium and help correct any problems.

Foliar feeding is also a good short-term option for boosting your plant's potassium needs. (See page 60 for details on foliar feeding.)

Supporting Actors: Magnesium, Calcium, and Sulfur

Magnesium, calcium, and sulfur are the "secondary macronutrients." Of the three, magnesium is of special interest to rose growers. Among the benefits it bestows are increased resistance to aphid attacks, more intense flower color, and more vigorous branching from the base of the plant and from lateral buds. These new branches are called "breaks," and they result in a bushier silhouette and more flowers. Too much magnesium can be toxic to roses, though, so check your soil test results before applying it. (Some soils are naturally high in magnesium.)

Calcium builds strong cell walls, which will help your roses resist diseases and insects. Most soils contain adequate calcium, but if a soil test indicates that your soil is deficient in this nutrient and has a *low* pH, apply oyster shell lime or mined limestone. Both fertilizers supply calcium while simultaneously raising

The right amount of magnesium will provide intense, richly saturated colors.

Interveinal chlorosis, caused by a lack of iron, usually occurs in alkaline soils. Rugosa roses are especially prone to this condition.

pH. If your soil is deficient in calcium and has a neutral to *high* pH, apply gypsum, instead.

Before you apply any type of calcium fertilizer, always test your soil to determine exactly how much you need to add. Adding too much of this mineral to your soil can raise the pH and make important micronutrients unavailable. Excessively high calcium also interferes with your plants' uptake of magnesium.

Roses, like all plants, need sulfur to help synthesize protein and starch. Most soils, especially those with plenty of organic matter, contain enough sulfur for roses. Only extremely sandy soils are likely to be deficient. If a soil test indicates a sulfur deficiency, begin correcting the problem by increasing your soil's organic matter. For a more severe deficiency, you could add gypsum (calcium sulfate) or elemental sulfur. Just be aware that using these minerals will lower your soil's pH, which could make macronutrients less available to your roses.

Minor but Essential Players

Roses and other plants need only tiny amounts of boron, chlorine, copper, iron, manganese, molybdenum, and zinc, but these micronutrients (also called trace minerals) are essential for the plants' good growth and health. (Your roses probably will never experience a lack of any trace minerals, though, if you amend the soil with plenty of compost and feed your plants organically. Just make sure your soil's pH remains in the neutral to slightly acid range so that these essential elements remain available to your roses.)

Of all the trace mineral deficiencies that can affect growing roses, you're most likely to notice a lack of iron, which appears as yellowing between the veins of leaves (interveinal chlorosis). Just as hemoglobin is essential to our own blood, iron is essential to chlorophyll, and leaves will turn yellow without it.

If your roses suffer from an iron deficiency (make sure you know your soil's pH), you can treat them with a solution of chelated iron, which is immediately available to plants. Apply it either as a soil drench or as a highly diluted foliar spray (see page 60). Rugosa roses (varieties with crinkled or "rough" leaves) are an exception, however. You should apply iron chelates to them only as a soil drench because their rough leaves can't tolerate any foliar sprays. Before applying iron chelates to any rose, read the label for appropriate dilution rates.

If chlorosis reoccurs, test your soil's pH again. At higher pH levels, iron becomes tied up and unavailable to plants. To free up the iron in alkaline soil and make it available to your roses on a long-term basis, you need to lower the soil's pH level. The best way to do this is to mix elemental sulfur throughout the bed.

A Balanced Organic Diet

Feeding roses organically is a soil-building process. By working lots of compost into the soil, you begin feeding your roses even before you plant them. Compost provides organic matter, as well as a mild dose of nutrients for your roses. Organic matter keeps the soil loose and aerated, while boosting its ability to retain water. And more importantly, organic matter provides food and shelter for the essential soil microbes that break down complex nitrogen- and sulfur-containing compounds into forms that plants can use.

When you add organic matter to your garden, you're actually contributing to the development of a healthy, living soil that will nourish your roses—and all other plants—in an ecologically sound, sustainable, organic way. This soil building is an ongoing process that is never finished.

If you had to choose between using only compost or only organic fertilizers to feed your roses, though, you should always choose compost. Nothing can replace it for building healthy, nourishing soil. You can supplement your roses with light applications of organic fertilizers (see "Solid Foods" on page 58) to encourage faster, healthier growth and more abundant flowers, but the mainstay of your nutrient management should be compost.

The Magic of Compost

Compost is nothing more than thoroughly decomposed organic matter, but it is an absolute must for growing roses organically. Compost helps build the soil and feeds soil life, which in turn helps feed your roses and other plants.

When you make compost, you're simply replicating the natural cycle of decomposition in a concentrated area. You can compost just about any form of organic matter, including most garden and kitchen wastes, grass clippings, leaves, weeds that haven't gone to seed, and shredded prunings. Exceptions include dog and cat manures; meats and fats; and diseased or insect-infested plants—burn or haul away discarded plant matter instead of adding them to your compost pile.

Build your compost pile in the shade, layering the materials as much as possible. Include a mix of both carbon materials (leaves, straw, and shredded prunings) and nitrogen materials (grass clippings, kitchen

The Lowdown on Manure

Although animal manure is a rich source of soil nutrients, it may also contain toxic bacteria—particularly the virulent strain of *Escherichia coli* bacteria—E. coli 0157:H7. If you add fresh animal manure to your compost pile, you run the risk of contaminating it with this strain of *E. coli*. This bacterium lives in the intestines of cows and some other animals and appears in their manure. *E.coli* 0157:H7 is dangerous because it produces a toxin that can cause severe illness, especially in small children, the elderly, and people with compromised immune systems.

Because of this, until scientists learn more about this new strain of *E. coli*, you may want to avoid using raw manure in your home compost pile. The good news, though, is that you don't need manure to make compost. Fresh grass clippings, vegetable scraps, and alfalfa and soybean meals are all examples of alternative sources of nitrogen that you can add to your pile.

Providing your roses with plenty of compost keeps them from going through the "feast or famine" cycle of chemical fertilization. Apply compost at planting time and at least once a year after that.

and yard wastes, and finished compost). Keep the pile moist but protected from rain.

If the pile seems to be breaking down too slowly, you may need to add more nitrogen-containing materials. When the pile looks crumbly and brown and you can't distinguish the individual ingredients from one another, your compost is ready to use.

Solid Foods

Of course, if you don't have access to compost or your soil needs an extra boost, you can choose from a variety of organic fertilizers to help give your roses the nutrition they need.

These organic fertilizers require the action of those microbes we just discussed to make the nutrients available. For that reason, it's difficult—but not impossible—to burn your plants with organic fertilizers easily as you can with soluble synthetic fertilizers. Organic fertilizers have the additional advantage of releasing their nutrients slowly, over a long period of time, so that they remain available to your plants instead of being leached away into groundwater or runoff, as is the case with synthetic fertilizers.

Your goal is to provide an overall NPK ratio of approximately 1-2-1. But as an organic grower, you don't need to worry as much as chemical gardeners do about the precise balance of the fertilizer. That's because most organic fertilizers are very slow-acting, releasing nutrients gradually in response to the action of soil microbes. As long as your roses have an adequate reservoir of phosphorus in the soil, they should be fine.

In addition to these inexpensive meals, a wide variety of excellent, commercially formulated organic fertilizers are available. They are more expensive, though, so you may want to reserve them for correcting specific deficiencies in your soil.

Spoil Your Roses with Compost Mulch

Instead of surrounding your roses with the standard wood chip mulch, pamper them with compost mulch. Research has shown that a mere 1-inch layer of compost applied to the surface of the soil will protect plants against a host of diseases.

Another advantage of mulching with compost is that it does not cause the carbon-nitrogen imbalance in the soil that wood mulch does. Because wood is a high-carbon material, it ties up nitrogen in the soil as it decays, depriving your roses of the nitrogen they need for healthy growth. Compost, on the other hand, poses no such problem. By contributing nutrients, organic matter, and much more to the soil, compost provides just what your roses need for luxuriant growth and bloom.

Adding Organic Fertilizers

Although compost is the best food for your roses, sometimes you might need to make a nutrient adjustment to your soil. The fertilizers listed below are all good sources of organic nutrients—just remember to test your soil before adding any.

Organic Sources of Nitrogen

Because organic fertilizers almost always contain nitrogen in more than one form and because these nitrogen-containing materials break down at varying rates, nitrogen may become available to your roses at different rates. That's why organic fertilizers are characterized as slow, mid-, or fast release—and that's how individual fertilizers can release nitrogen at two different speeds.

The following organic fertilizers are all great sources of nitrogen. Store them in a dry place, and protect them from rodents and other animals.

- Bat and seabird guano (fast release)
- Fish meal (fast and slow release)
- Bloodmeal (midrelease)
- Alfalfa meal (mid- and slow release)
- Feather meal (slow release)

Organic Sources of Phosphorus

Most dry organic fertilizers release their phosphorus at a slow to moderate rate. All of the following fertilizers also contribute significant amounts of calcium to the soil. Be sure to follow recommended rates. Incorporate the fertilizers thoroughly throughout the root zones of your roses.

- Bonemeal
- Fish meal
- High-phosphorus seabird guano
- Shrimp shell meal
- Soft rock phosphate

Organic Sources of Potassium

The following fertilizers are good sources of potassium. Remember to incorporate dry sources into the soil near the roots of your roses. Liquid forms are readily absorbed from foliar feedings, as well as by the roots.

- Fish meal
- Greensand
- Kelp extract

Organic Sources of Trace Minerals

Most organic fertilizers, as well as compost and manure, contain trace minerals, but the following supplements are particularly rich sources of these micronutrients:

- Bloodmeal
- Fish emulsion
- Fish meal
- Greensand
- Ground oyster shells
- Kelp extract
- Kelp meal
- Shrimp shell meal

Liquid Diets

Liquid organic fertilizers are excellent additions to your rose-care program. Because the nutrients in liquid fertilizers are rapidly available, these fertilizers are great for giving plants a boost during periods of stress. Liquid fertilizers are convenient, too. You can apply them either as foliar sprays to the leaves of your roses or as soil drenches to the root zones of your plants.

For roses, kelp extract is like a magic elixir. Not only is it rich in all of the major and minor nutrients and trace elements, but it also contains growth-stimulating factors and compounds that trigger a plant's own immune system, which helps it fight disease. Fish emulsion is an excellent source of nitrogen and a good source of phosphorus and potassium.

Always water your roses *before* you apply liquid fertilizers, and wet down their leaves before applying foliar sprays. In dry soil, even diluted fertilizer solutions can burn plants.

Nourishing Teas

Teas of fertilizing materials (also called infusions) are like nourishing tonics for roses. The brewing process "predigests" the fertilizing ingredient, making it easier for plants to assimilate the nutrients.

Many different ingredients can be used to make teas. In fact, in Europe, a tea made from stinging nettles (*Urtica dioica*) is the most widely used and best-loved organic fertilizer. In concentrated emulsion form, nettles extract is sold in virtually all European garden centers, much as fish emulsion is available in North America. Europeans have enormous respect for the health benefits of nettles for both people and plants, but in the United States, the horticultural benefits of this wild herb are practically unknown.

Stinging nettle is an herbaceous perennial that thrives in rich, moist soils throughout most of the temperate world. As its name suggests, the plant is covered with hairs that produce a burning and itching sensation when they come in contact with bare skin. Nettles are incredibly rich in nitrogen, potassium, magnesium, enzymes, and trace minerals (especially iron), which explains why the tea makes such a fantastic plant tonic. Nettles tea also is an excellent substitute for chelated iron products to treat chlorosis in roses. You can use it either as a foliar fertilizer or a soil drench.

If you don't already have nettles growing on your property or somewhere nearby, you can plant a nettle patch in a rich, moist spot, such as near your compost pile. The easy-to-grow plants tolerate poor drainage and partial shade, and you can cut them as often as four times a season. And in spring, the cooked, young shoots make a delicious pot herb.

Foliar Feeding: An IV for Plants

You may be surprised to know that roses and other plants can absorb fertilizers through their foliage. In fact, foliar fertilization is like feeding your roses through an IV needle—the leaves absorb nutrients almost instantaneously.

You can apply any soluble fertilizer to foliage, as long as it is at an *extremely diluted rate* (typically $\frac{1}{10}$ the rate used for soil applications). Higher concentrations will burn leaves. Check the product label—most liquid and soluble solid fertilizers provide specific rates for foliar application. Spray the solution on the foliage of your roses in early morning (midday sprays can burn a plant's leaves).

Caution: Never apply foliar fertilizers of any kind to rough-leaved rugosa roses. The notches in their leaves retain so much spray that they become burned. Foliar sprays are okay for smooth-leaved rugosa hybrids, however.

Stocking Up on Nettles

If you don't have nettles on your property but you run across a patch in the wild, you can cut them and dry them for future tea-making. (Make sure you have the property owner's permission before harvesting.) Hang the branches in bundles in a well-ventilated, dry location. After the nettles are dry, store them in feed sacks or burlap bags. *Always wear leather gloves when handling fresh or dried nettles.*

Here's how to make a nourishing nettles tea for your roses:

1. Cut the nettles. Wearing gloves, cut the plants at around half their height. Using shears or pruners, roughly chop the plants.

2. Mix with water. Put the chopped plants in a plastic barrel or garbage can. Add 1 gallon of water for every pound of fresh nettles or for every 2 ounces of dried nettles. Use only nonchlorinated water—preferably rainwater—because chlorine inhibits the fermentation necessary to release the nettles' nutrients. Cover the barrel with a lid (nettles tea smells horrible!).

3. Ferment for 1 to 3 weeks. Stir your nettles tea every day. Fermentation will happen faster in hot weather. When bubbles stop appearing when you stir the tea, fermentation has finished.

4. Strain the tea. Do this as soon as fermentation ceases. Store your nettles infusion in clean plastic or glass containers in a cool spot. Dump the dregs onto your compost pile.

5. Dilute before using. For foliar feeding, dilute the tea to a 5 percent solution (½ cup of infusion to 10 cups of water, for example). For a soil drench, dilute it to a 10 percent solution.

In addition to nettles, alfalfa meal and compost also can be used to make fertilizing teas. And you can enhance any fertilizing tea for roses by adding ½ cup of Epsom salts (for the magnesium content) per 5 gallons of water. Apply teas once a month as a soil drench or once a week as a foliar spray. If you use tea as a foliar spray, remember to dilute it by at least a factor of 10.

Timing Is Everything

Roses profit from regular fertilizer boosts in spring and early summer, when they grow and flower prolifically. Later in the season, they need to slow down. From mid-July on in Zones 7 and northward, and from mid-August on in Zones 8 and southward, withhold fast-acting solid and liquid fertilizers. This will put the brakes on your roses' active growth and encourage them to harden off their canes in preparation for winter's cold.

Hardening off is just that—a process through which soft, lush growth becomes woody. At the same time, the roots of plants stock up on carbohydrates. If you continue feeding your roses late into the season, you'll encourage a flush of soft new growth that is sure to be killed by the harsh conditions of winter.

Withhold fertilizer throughout late summer and early fall to help your roses go into the winter in a safe state of dormancy.

No matter what type of roses you grow in your garden, proper pruning and training will ensure that they reach their greatest flowering potential.

pruning and training your roses

Most of the roses that are recommended in this book would grow and flower just fine with very little pruning. But if you're the sort of gardener who likes to get the most from your roses, you'll enjoy pruning and training them a bit more. Some of the most refined techniques will produce plants that appear as though you haven't done a thing to them—vigorous, natural-looking shrubs clothed with vibrant foliage and luxuriant blooms. This sort of result may be the greatest testament of all to your pruning skills.

Other techniques are a chance to show off your artistry. For instance, you might enjoy training roses to form a romantic garland around an outdoor dining area or to grow on pillars to add dramatic vertical accents to your garden.

Regardless of the look you want to achieve, good pruning techniques clearly contribute to the health, vigor, and flowering of your roses. Pruning becomes easy once you understand the rationale behind each technique. Start practicing, and don't worry about mistakes—roses are forgiving plants. Before long, you'll find you get a lot of satisfaction out of pruning your roses.

Pruning Basics

The most fundamental reason to prune your roses is to help them stay healthy by removing dead and diseased wood, as well as competing rootstock suckers. Beyond that, pruning your roses allows you to manage and accelerate their growth for improved vigor, flowering, and overall appearance.

In nature, a rose tends to regularly produce vigorous new shoots from its base. Meanwhile, the shoots that have already flowered gradually weaken and die.

When you prune, you quicken this process, using techniques suited to the habits of the various classes of roses. For instance, you wouldn't prune a damask rose in winter as severely as you would a hybrid tea. If you did, you wouldn't have any flowers the following summer. (This is because damasks bloom only on the previous year's growth and you would have removed all of the blooming wood.)

On the other hand, if you would prune a hybrid tea or floribunda—which flower only on new shoots—with the restrained hand you'd use on an heirloom rose, you'd soon have a gawky, leggy plant with few flowers. Understanding the growth and flowering habits of your roses will allow you to prune them in an informed manner; later in this chapter we'll go into more detail about how to prune specific roses.

First, though, let's look at some techniques and principles that hold true for all types of roses.

The canes of once-blooming shrub roses like these damasks go through a natural cycle of death and regeneration. Pruning accelerates the cycle, with the emphasis on rejuvenation.

Removing Deadwood

The first step when pruning any rose is to remove the deadwood. Deadwood is unsightly, clutters the plant, and can harbor insects and disease. With a little careful observation and practice, recognizing deadwood becomes a snap.

Live rose canes (except for very old canes) are green even in winter. When you scratch the epidermis (the outside layer of the cane), you'll see white to tan or light green tissue below. Canes that have recently died

In areas with mild winters, hybrid tea roses should be severely pruned *(left)*. Without pruning, these roses develop into leggy, unattractive shrubs that flower only at the tops of the plants *(right)*.

Living rose canes *(left)* are green even in winter, and they have light-color tissue below the surface. Recently deceased canes *(center)* are dark outside and below the surface. Canes that have been dead for a year or more *(right)* are silver-gray and snap easily.

are dark brown to black; when you scratch them, the epidermis peels away easily and the tissue beneath it is dark and discolored. Rose canes that have been dead for a year or more are silver-gray and snap easily when bent. They have a tough, woody texture when you prune them.

When pruning out deadwood, don't hold back—be aggressive. If the cane is dead to the ground, cut it as close to the base as possible; don't leave an ugly stump. If the cane has died back only part of the way, cut at least ½ inch below the lowest dead point. Make your cut through clean, live wood. The slightest bit of dead tissue left behind will continue to spread downward into living wood.

Removing Diseased Wood

Pruning out diseased portions of roses helps prevent the spread of infection to the remaining canes of the sick plant, as well as to other roses in your garden. Prompt pruning of infected growth is essential for halting the spread of rust disease, and it may even stop the spread of rosette virus. Cutting out the infected canes is the only way to get rid of some diseases, such as stem canker. (See Chapter 8 for more detailed descriptions of these diseases.)

When cutting out diseased wood from your roses, always disinfect your pruners with ethanol or a bleach

solution before making additional cuts on healthy parts of the same plant or on other plants. Gather up the infected cuttings, then burn or otherwise dispose of them. Don't compost them, and don't leave them lying around where they can infect other plants in your garden.

If you discover stem canker on your roses, cut well below the diseased portion into clean, live wood.

Removing Rootstock Suckers

When rootstock suckers rear their ugly heads, you may think your rose is being taken over by an alien being—and that wouldn't be far from the truth. These canes may bear little resemblance to the others on the plant. Their leaves may be smaller or of a subtly different shape or texture. Their thorns may be prickly, while those on the other canes are spiny—or vice versa. One thing is certain: These "alien" canes are vigorous. The next thing you know, your formerly yellow rose is now blooming red or white, or your red rose has "turned" pink.

What has happened is that the rootstock of your grafted rose (see "Own-Root versus Grafted Roses" on page 32) is sending up its own shoots instead of staying quietly underground and supporting the grafted top, the way it is supposed to. If you don't intervene, the rootstock soon will become a plant of its own and the graft will die off.

While deep planting minimizes the chances of rootstock suckering, you're bound to encounter this phenomenon sooner or later if you grow grafted roses. The biggest danger is that you just won't recognize the suckers. Keep a sharp eye out for shoots that look suspiciously vigorous or different in any way.

The suckers always originate *below* the graft or bud union (see below), usually from the base of the plant but occasionally a short distance away by means of a spreading root. Verify the origin of new shoots by gently clearing away soil from the base of the shoot. If you discover that the growth is emerging from below the graft union (indicating a sucker), use a gloved hand to pull it off of the root. Don't worry if you tear off a piece of root epidermis along with it—the goal is to remove the "eye" from where it sprouted, even if that means being brutal.

If the sucker won't come off without pulling out the entire root, use a pocket knife to cut the sucker off right where it sprouted from, shaving off a piece of root epidermis in the process. Do not simply snip off the sucker with pruning shears—doing so will only encourage more suckers to grow back with renewed vigor.

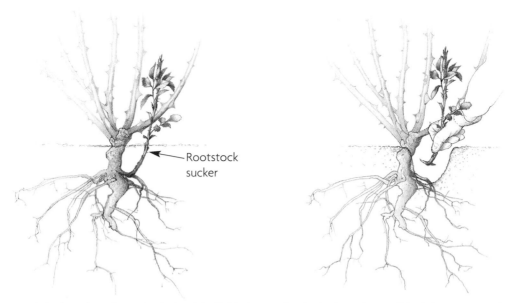

Rootstock sucker

Follow rootstock suckers down to their origin *(left)*, then pull—don't clip—them off *(right)* to prevent them from resprouting.

The Kindest Cuts

If you're pruning a live rose cane (as opposed to removing a dead cane or rootstock sucker), use these simple rules to encourage vigorous, attractive, flowering growth and eliminate the possibility of introducing disease or decay.

■ **Always use first-quality, clean, well-sharpened, and well-oiled pruning shears.** A good, cared-for tool ensures that you slice cleanly through the rose cane, rather than mashing or mangling it. Use heavy lopping shears to cut through very thick or tough, dead canes.

■ **Make pruning cuts just above an outward-facing bud.** This will force a "break," or sprout, to the exterior of the plant and helps keep the interior open, which makes for a healthier, more attractive plant. Remember that the new growth will emerge from the bud just below the cut.

■ **Cut on an angle from just above the bud to approximately ¼ inch below it.** Cutting at a greater distance above the bud will cause decay to set in on the "stump" left behind. Cutting too close to the bud will damage it. Cutting on a slant ensures that rain will shed off the cut surface, minimizing the chances for disease to set in.

■ **Remove weak and spindly growth at ground level or the growth's origin.** Canes that are thinner than a pencil clutter the form of the shrub and rarely develop flower buds. Remove them so that they do not sap energy from flowering wood.

■ **Remove canes that cross or rub against each other.** Crossed growth looks unattractive and prevents air from circulating through your rose, thereby encouraging disease. Canes that rub against each other also can develop abrasions, which allow disease organisms to gain entry.

■ **If more than one sprout emerges from a bud, remove all but the most vigorous sprout.** You can do this with your fingers if you catch the canes when they're first sprouting.

■ **Always burn or otherwise destroy rose prunings.** They are a potential reservoir of disease and should not be composted.

Basic Formative Pruning

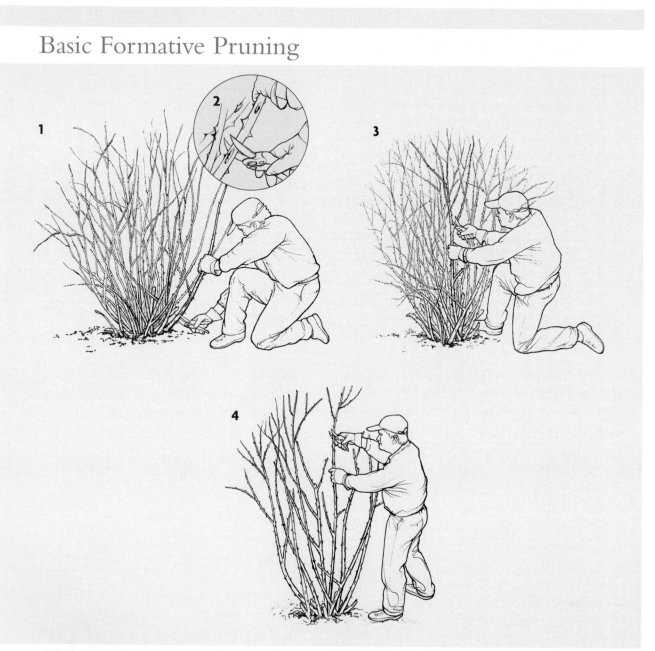

All shrub roses can be pruned by following these four simple steps. Of course, you should modify them to suit the particular flowering pattern of your rose.

1. Prune out all deadwood at ground level or its point of origin. Remove one or two of the oldest, thickest canes at ground level.

2. Make the cut on an angle, above an outward-facing bud.

3. Prune out spindly growth and crossed canes in the interior of the shrub to let in light and air.

4. Prune back the top one-quarter to one-third of the tallest canes to encourage development of flowering wood and to keep the plant from whipping in the wind. Burn or otherwise dispose of the prunings.

Winter Formative Pruning

Pruning roses for form is the subject of much disagreement among opinionated rose experts. Minimalists would have you prune out *only* the deadwood, while maximalists would like you to reduce all roses—regardless of variety—to short stubs every winter. Both approaches, I believe, are too simplistic and arbitrary. First and foremost, you need to prune in accord with the flowering and vegetative habits of the specific rose.

The time to do most formative pruning is during the dormant season, when the danger of prolonged, deep cold has passed. That's late winter to very early spring in Zones 7 and northward and as early as January in Zones 8 and southward. Pruning at winter's end allows you to cut out all winter-damaged wood. And pruning while your rose is dormant makes it much easier to see what you're doing.

First remove any dead and damaged wood. Then, step back to inspect your rose and evaluate what else needs to be done. This is the time to remove spindly and crossed or rubbing canes, as well as inflorescences (faded flower clusters) left from the previous season. The goal is to create a rose with a balanced form and a structure that's open enough to allow light to penetrate and air to circulate throughout the shrub.

On vigorous shrubs, remove one or two of the oldest canes at ground level each year to make room for vigorous new growth that will flower in ensuing years. You can also remove the top quarter to third of the tallest, most vigorous canes to encourage flowering growth to form at the sides of the shrub.

Late winter is also the time to prune hybrid tea and floribunda roses. Cut back into healthy, live wood as described on page 67. Hybrid teas and floribundas need more severe pruning than shrub roses to keep them floriferous and vigorous.

Summer Maintenance Pruning

In summer, the most important pruning activity is "deadheading," or removing spent flowers. Removing these faded blossoms encourages repeat-flowering roses to rebloom quickly instead of putting energy into forming hips. Even on a nonfruiting rose (a rose that doesn't produce hips), prompt deadheading encourages faster rebloom.

A few rose varieties have the unattractive habit of retaining their wilted blossoms rather than dropping their petals. If you have a rose with this trait, remove the spent flowers as soon as possible. These unattractive "mops" are not only unsightly, but they can also harbor disease.

Many rose experts advise making the deadheading cut just above the first leaf that has five leaflets, but your rose will rebloom more quickly and vigorously if you cut back to the third eye (leaf node) below each blossom. If the cane is not long or vigorous enough to support such a cut, then go ahead and cut just above the first five-leaflet leaf.

The only roses that should not be deadheaded routinely are those that produce attractive hips. To enjoy the colorful red and orange fruits of once-blooming species roses and their cultivars, don't deadhead them at all. On fruiting roses that repeat bloom, deadhead only through the first part of the summer to encourage rebloom. Then, from late summer through fall, do not deadhead at all to allow the plant to set hips that will add beauty to your garden throughout the winter.

Summer is also the time to remove diseased canes at the first sign of infection with spot anthracnose or cankers. (See Chapter 8 to learn to recognize the signs of these diseases.) Also snip off leaves infected with black spot and mildew as soon as they appear, to minimize the spread of these diseases. Remember to burn or dispose of all of these clippings promptly, and always disinfect your pruning shears before moving to the next plant or a healthy section of the same plant.

Deadhead your roses to encourage fast rebloom. Make the cuts just above the third eye below the wilted flowers.

Another summer pruning task is to cut back repeat-blooming roses that send up long, vigorous shoots right after their first flowering, as climbers do. Encourage these shoots to develop lateral flowering branches by cutting them back by one-quarter to one-third, just above a leaf in the direction you'd like your rose to branch. If you leave these canes untended, they will continue to shoot skyward and won't bloom until the following season.

Early midsummer—right after bloom—is also the time to do major formative pruning of once-flowering roses. Because they produce their flower buds the previous season, just like a lilac or forsythia, you need to do any necessary pruning immediately after they bloom. That way, you won't remove the flower buds as you would with a winter pruning.

Pruning Once-Flowering Roses

Roses that flower just once a year are not only inherently more hardy and disease-resistant than repeat bloomers, but they also require less pruning. In terms of pruning, these carefree shrubs fall into two major categories: 1) the species or "wild" roses and their varieties, and 2) all other once-flowering roses, including once-blooming ancient roses (albas, centifolias, damasks, and gallicas) and once-blooming modern hybrids, such as 'Constance Spry' [shrub rose].

Species Roses

Most species roses, including their selections and near hybrids, are rugged shrubs that produce delicate single flowers in early spring, followed by ornamental hips later in the season. The hips last through winter, providing spectacular color for the garden and food for the birds. Indeed, some species—such as *Rosa moyesii* and *R. rubrifolia*—are grown more for the beauty of their hips than for their flowers.

Species roses need only the slightest pruning. In late winter, shear off any remaining clusters of hips. If

Beautiful urn-shaped hips are the star attractions of *Rosa moyesii* 'Geranium'. Like other species roses, it needs little or no pruning other than the removal of deadwood.

new shoots appeared from the base of the plant the previous season, cut out one or two of the thickest, oldest canes at ground level. On species that form a main trunk and that do not sprout from the base, remove only the deadwood—do nothing to alter the rose's basic structure. With only minimal pruning, most species roses will develop into arching, fountain-like plants with great character. Just make sure they have enough room to develop so that you don't disfigure them with pruning cuts to control their size.

Other Once-Blooming Roses

Compared to species roses, these tough roses are less likely to set hips and more likely to send up basal shoots. Like species roses, they need very little pruning, other than an occasional shaping.

Cut out deadwood and spindly growth in late winter as you would for any rose. At the same time, cut out one or two of the thickest, oldest canes to encourage more vigorous basal growth.

Refrain from any other pruning of these once bloomers until immediately after their early summer flowering has finished so that you don't remove the coming season's flowering wood. When flowering ceases, cut back the plant's longest canes by one-quarter to one-third, and prune flowering laterals back to 6 to 8 inches long. Your newly shaped rose will now produce flower buds for the following season on the remaining canes.

Pruning Repeat-Flowering Shrub Roses

When it comes to pruning, I like to divide this vast group of roses into two groups: continuous-flowering roses and remontant roses. Continuous-flowering roses, if they are well nourished, bloom pretty much nonstop from early summer through fall. Remontant roses bloom heavily in early summer and then put on a second, lighter flowering in late summer or early fall with a smattering of blooms in between.

Continuous-Flowering Roses

This large group includes many (but not all) modern shrub roses, most of the "English" roses of David Austin, and modern groundcover roses. (Although most rugosa roses and their hybrids also flower continuously, they are pruned more like the species roses. See "Special Case: Rugosa Roses," below, for specifics.)

Continuous-flowering roses flower on both older wood and on vigorous new growth, so their pruning treatment also requires you to take a two-season approach.

In winter, prune continuous-flowering roses by cutting back the longest canes by one-third and reducing laterals to 6 to 8 inches long. Also remove one or two of the thickest, oldest canes, as well as any spindly growth and deadwood.

In summer, after their initial flowering, deadhead them promptly and continue to do so throughout the season. To encourage additional flowering lateral branches to form, cut back by one-quarter any vigorous vertical shoots that have emerged. If the rose forms ornamental hips, stop deadheading in autumn to allow the hips to form.

Special Case: Rugosa Roses

Most rugosas and their hybrids flower continuously, but unlike other continuous bloomers, they need very little pruning. Treat them like species roses by removing an occasional old cane in late winter. During the summer, be on the lookout for any canes that appear to be succumbing to rose borers. Infested canes rapidly turn brown. If you spot any, remove them promptly at the base of the shrub, then destroy the clippings.

'Delicata'

Remontant Roses

This group includes many modern hybrids, such as some of the best of the Explorer series, as well as old-fashioned hybrid perpetuals. For vigorous rebloom on these roses, you'll need to provide them with some encouragement in the form of proper pruning and training techniques.

Prune remontant roses just like you would continuous-flowering roses, with only two differences. First, instead of removing just one or two old canes annually in late winter or early spring, you should remove one-third of the oldest canes each year. Old wood on remontant roses becomes rapidly senescent—the plant equivalent of senile—meaning that the old canes "forget" how to bloom. Cutting these canes out encourages lots of new basal growth, which will be more floriferous.

Second, instead of cutting back the vigorous vertical shoots, train them into an arched, horizontal position.

Arching Roses for Rebloom

You can encourage more generous rebloom of your remontant roses by arching the longest canes and either pegging them or tying them to stakes. To peg the canes, use a U-shape sod staple to secure the longest canes to the ground. If you'd like to propagate your rose at the same time, cover a portion of the cane with soil to encourage rooting. After roots form, simply cut away the new plant from the mother cane.

Or, instead of pegging the canes, just bend the longest canes of your remontant rose outward, then drive short wooden stakes into the ground where they touch. Tie the ends of the canes to the stakes, being careful to avoid the tender tips.

This horizontal position encourages the cane to produce a multitude of flowering laterals. You can train remontant roses horizontally in several ways. (See "Arching Roses for Rebloom" on this page, as well as "Fountain of Bloom" on page 79.)

Pruning and Training Climbers and Ramblers

Both climbing and rambling roses grow very long canes. Differences between the two types are less clear-cut, partly due to their complex breeding. A rambler can easily be used as a climber and (to a lesser extent) vice versa. So don't panic if you notice that one book or catalog calls a certain variety a rambler while another calls it a climber.

For pruning and training purposes, we'll define a climber as a long-caned rose that primarily blooms on the lateral shoots of a scaffold of "mother" canes that persist from year to year. A climber can be once- or repeat-blooming, and its new shoots are strongly vertical. Blooms can occur on old or new wood, or both.

In contrast, a rambler is a long-caned rose that flowers only once per growing season on the previous year's wood. Long, supple shoots, which grow from the base of the plant, bloom from their second year on. Ramblers are sometimes extremely vigorous and can easily clamber into trees or cover a shed.

Naturally, there are exceptions to these general groupings. Some "ramblers" produce few basal shoots and bear blooms primarily on laterals produced on a permanent scaffold of canes. Other roses, called "small climbers" or pillar roses, bloom only on the new, lateral growth produced on old canes.

But don't fret about the murky boundaries between these two groups. Thanks to their vigor, climbers and ramblers are forgiving plants. Even if you can't find a reference on the exact growth pattern of your particular climber or rambler, you should be able to figure out how to prune it just by observing its growth and using old-fashioned trial and error.

Most climbing roses bloom on the lateral branches of their scaffolding canes. The new shoots are strongly vertical. Climbers can be once- or repeat-blooming.

Most rambling roses bloom on the previous year's wood and produce lots of lateral shoots from the base of the plant. Ramblers usually bloom only once each season.

No Visible Means of Support

Thin, stainless steel airplane cable (available at specialty hardware stores and hardware supply houses), strung at 18-inch intervals, is ideal for attaching a rose invisibly to a masonry wall. Masonry eyebolts anchor the cable into the wall, and turnbuckles keep the cable taut. If the span of the cable is more than 6 feet, place eyebolts halfway down its length to support the cable in the middle.

This technique ensures that support will be available wherever you want to anchor your rose, while making a minimum of holes in the masonry. And the stainless steel won't discolor, the way some other materials would.

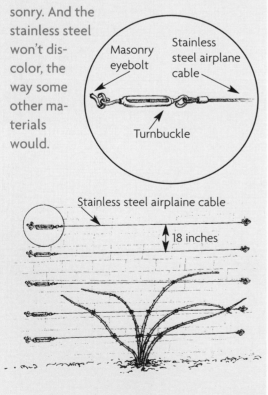

Masonry eyebolt

Stainless steel airplane cable

Turnbuckle

Stainless steel airplaine cable

18 inches

Like remontant roses, climbers and ramblers also benefit from training. By training the canes as horizontally as possible, you can encourage more blooms. In a vertical cane, sap flows freely to the tip of the shoot, sending a hormonal message to the rose to continue producing vegetative (nonflowering) growth. But once the cane arches horizontally—either under its own weight or because you position it that way—the sap flows more slowly, sending the message to produce flowering wood instead of vegetative shoots.

Training is also necessary because climbers and ramblers can't climb a vertical surface without your help—they're not like vines, which have tendrils or other means of climbing. Even the most vigorous ramblers require your assistance in their early years to get headed in the right direction.

A final, less-essential—but still important—reason to train a climber or rambler is to achieve the aesthetic look you want. For example, you might train a climber on a wall of your house to frame a window or cloak a stark corner. If you want those billowing masses of bloom to present a pleasing, balanced picture, you'll need to guide them in the right direction.

Climbing Roses

Because the main scaffolding canes of a climbing rose are long-lived, it's important to develop and train them properly right from the start. At planting time, select three to five of the strongest canes to become the scaffolds. The number of canes you select depends on how you'll train the rose. If you want it to climb a tree, three scaffold canes probably will do. But if you want it to climb the wall of a house, you'll probably want five major canes so that you can train them into a fan shape. If the rose doesn't have enough strong canes to use for scaffolding at planting time, select additional canes during the first growing season or even the second one.

The first year, the only pruning you'll need to do is to remove any new canes that sprout from the base of the rose that you don't want to keep as scaffolds. Nip them as soon as they appear, so your rose can put its energy into producing laterals that will flower next season. But you will need to carefully train your selected canes against their support. Choose their positions carefully because the canes will become too rigid to move easily as they grow heavier and thicker. Remember that the more horizontal their angle, the more quickly they'll develop flowering wood. If you have some vertically positioned rose canes, nip them back a bit during the growing season to encourage them to produce flowering laterals.

In late winter or early spring of the next year (and subsequent years), cut back the lateral branches that flowered the previous year to around 8 to 12 inches long. A good pruning and training practice is to cut back the flowering branches to their juncture with a vigorous branch, then arch that branch backward and attach it to a support (see the illustration below). If you repeat this practice over the years, you'll create a handsome lattice of canes covered with blooms.

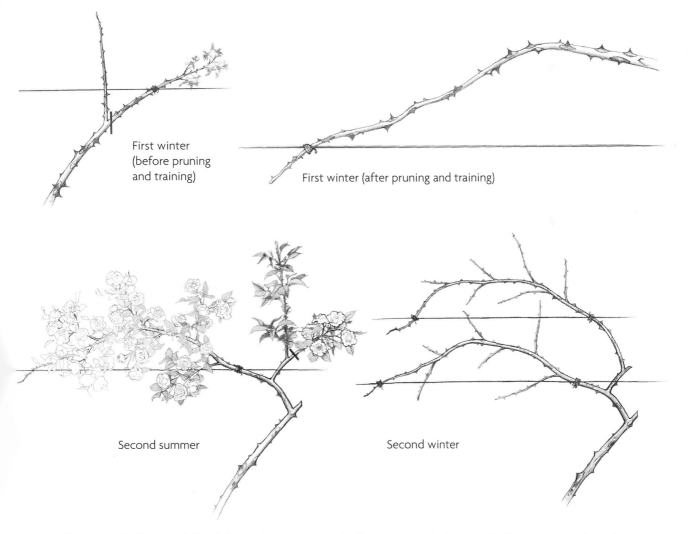

First winter
(before pruning
and training)

First winter (after pruning and training)

Second summer

Second winter

After your climbing rose's first full growing season, cut the flowering terminal shoots back to a vigorous branch. Arch that branch backward and attach it to the support. Repeat this pruning and training pattern in subsequent years to create a beautiful, easy-to-care-for lattice of flowering canes.

Almost any large shrub rose (6 feet tall or more) can be pruned and trained as a climber. The converse is also true: Many small climbers, such as the Canadian Explorer rose 'John Davis' [hybrid kordesii] *(above)*, can be grown as spectacular cascading shrubs.

Rambling Roses

If your rambler is typical, it blooms on the previous year's wood and produces lots of new canes from its base. In this case, prune (in late winter or early spring) all canes that flowered the previous year, cutting them off at ground level. Then fertilize the plants well to encourage lots of new growth.

If you've trained the rambler to climb a wall, you can use less-drastic pruning. Just shorten the laterals that have flowered to around 8 to 12 inches long, and remove an old cane or two every couple of years.

Ramblers left to scramble at will can rapidly become so large and tangled that pruning becomes unfeasible. If that happens, at least try to cut out any deadwood that develops. The easiest way to do this is to make several cuts along the length of the cane.

One way to rein in overgrown ground-covering ramblers is to trim them back to about 18 inches with a string trimmer, using the steel blade attachment. Ground-covering ramblers on level ground can also be mowed with a euonymus mower (a special landscaping mower) set at the highest level.

Because ramblers are so unruly and big, you don't have to cut at any specific place on the plant, especially if you're using the blade on a string trimmer.

Also keep in mind that many ramblers produce magnificent displays of colorful hips through fall and winter. For this reason, refrain from deadheading them during the growing season.

Ramblers, Size XXL

Use the largest, most vigorous ramblers to climb into trees or smother that unsightly shed on your property. Just point these fast-growing roses in the right direction and they'll take care of the rest, growing as much as 15 to 20 feet long in 3 years. Most ramblers bloom later than other types of roses, with bloom beginning toward the end of June. Choose from the following varieties:

- **'Albertine' [hybrid wichurana]**—fully double, salmon-pink blossoms

- **'Alberic Barbier' [hybrid wichurana]**—double, creamy white with a flush of yellow

- **'Bobbie James' [hybrid wichurana]**—gracefully drooping clusters of semi-double, strongly fragrant white flowers

- **'François Juranville' [hybrid wichurana]**—clear pink double with deeper shadings; bronzy foliage

- **'Kiftsgate' [species]**—single, fragrant, creamy white with golden stamens; shiny red hips; can grow to 30 feet

- **'Rambling Rector' [hybrid multiflora]**—large clusters of creamy white semi-double flowers; excellent hips

- **'Veilchenblau' [hybrid multiflora]**—fragrant, violet, semidouble; beautiful mingled with 'Alberic Barbier'

'Veilchenblau'

Ties That Bind

Any material that does not chafe or cut into your rose's canes can be used to attach a climber to its support. Raffia is an excellent, old-fashioned, biodegradable material. Plastic twist-ties are also handy. And garden centers carry many other attachment gadgets, most of which resemble the plastic ratcheting ties that come with garbage bags (which, by the way, also are perfectly suitable for roses).

Always tie roses close to their supports so that their weight won't pull them outward and downward, but leave enough slack so that you can insert at least a couple of fingers between the cane and the tie. Attaching roses too snugly can injure the canes. Make a figure eight between the support and the cane to eliminate possible chafing.

Whatever type of ties you use, check them after a couple of years to make sure that they aren't choking the growing canes. With climbing and rambling roses, check attachments annually to be sure the canes are well supported. A large climber or rambler in full leaf and flower is incredibly heavy. You'll have a tough time tying it back up if it falls away from its support—not to mention the fact that it will become mangled in the process.

Special Effects

If you're a gardener with a flair for drama, here are some techniques that you can use to create spectacular effects with roses. Of course, achieving and maintaining this much style requires some extra effort. But in the process, you'll have lots of fun, wow your friends, and become more adept at pruning and training your roses.

Natural Ties for Roses

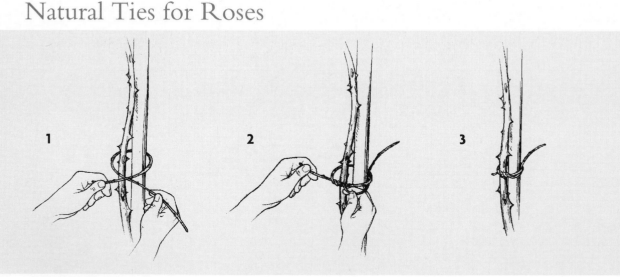

Flexible willow twigs make perfect ties for attaching climbing roses to their supports. They look natural, are strong, and decompose in 2 to 3 years, before they become too tight and choke growing canes.

1. Begin with a 12- to 15-inch piece of willow twig. Loop it around the rose cane and the support, and adjust it so that one end protrudes about 5 inches past the other. Twist the ends together several times.

2. Now insert the long end back through the loop surrounding the cane and support and pull it snug.

3. Trim off any excess. In 2 to 3 years, when the willow ties begin to weaken, apply new ones.

Fountain of Bloom

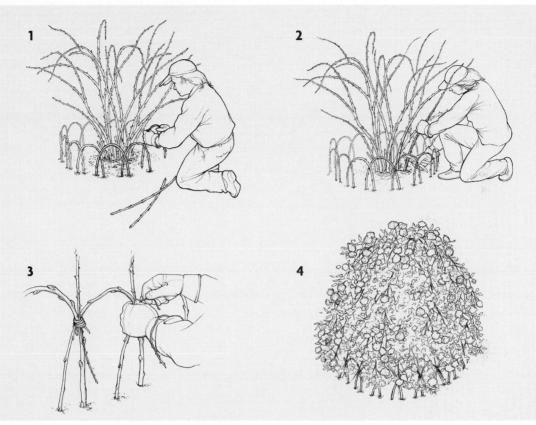

Imagine a spectacular dome of blooming roses, like a fountain of flowers in your lawn. This old-time French technique uses a combination of aggressive renewal pruning and tying to create a breathtaking specimen rose. Once-flowering ancient roses and remontant hybrid perpetuals are the roses best suited to this treatment.

1. Create a miniature fence of overlapping arches around your rose, using approximately 4-foot lengths of willow, bamboo, hazel, dogwood shrub prunings, or another flexible wood. Stick one end of the arch deep into the soil at a 45-degree angle. Thrust the opposite end into the soil to create an arch about 1 foot tall. Continue working, overlapping the arches slightly, to create a minifence with a diameter of 5 to 8 feet around your rose (depending on the eventual size of your rose). Remove the grass inside the circle, then mulch the entire area.

2. Cut all canes that flowered the previous year off at ground level. Keep all of last season's new growth, including the long, nearly unbranched, supple canes that have not yet bloomed. Pull back old mulch and apply a 1-inch layer of compost to the circle around the rose.

3. Bend all remaining canes (last year's new growth) outward and downward. Attach them to the arches of your border with raffia.

4. Enjoy your fountain of flowers later that summer. New canes will come up in the middle of the dome. Repeat Steps 1 through 3 early the following spring, cutting away all the canes that were attached to the arches and attaching the new canes from the center in their place. Don't forget to add compost.

Tower of Flowers

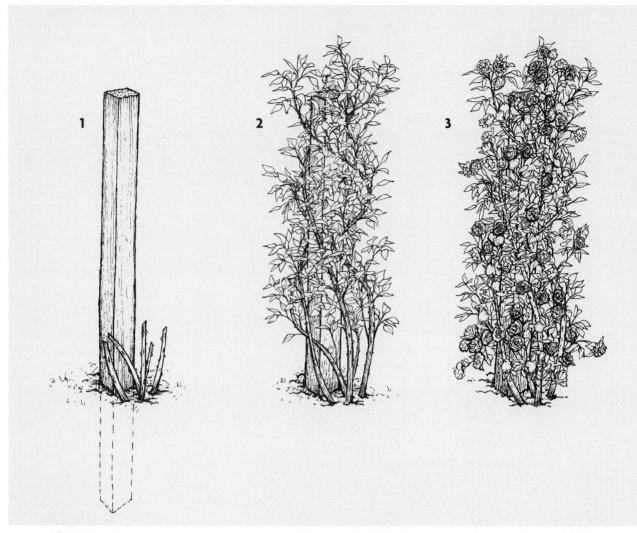

Pillar roses are just small climbers trained on an upright post or obelisk. This easy-to-train form creates dramatic, space-saving, vertical accents for the background of a mixed perennial border. It also looks great in a narrow space next to a wall where you don't feel like fussing with a tall climber.

1. Plant the rose in front of the support. Sink an 8-foot cedar, black locust, or other rot-resistant post (but not treated wood) about 2½ feet into the ground. Plant a small climbing rose close in front of it. (If you're using a decorative metal obelisk, set it over your newly planted rose.)

2. Spiral the canes around the support. Feed the rose generously after new growth appears, then train three or four main canes to spiral around the post in both directions. Spiraling the canes, rather than allowing them to grow straight up, encourages more flowering branches to form.

3. Maintain good form on the pillar. Deadhead, water, and feed your rose routinely. Early each spring, remove any deadwood and cut laterals back to 8 to 10 inches. Reattach the canes as necessary, using eyebolts screwed into the wood and raffia or plastic-coated twist-ties.

Garlands of Roses

Graceful swags of roses cascading between posts, smothered with flowers . . . who could resist? Rose garlands can be used to create a barrier along a walk or driveway, define an outdoor dining area, or add a feeling of privacy to a patio.

Before you create a rose swag, you'll need to do some preliminary construction. If you garden in Zone 5 or colder, make a short swag (as described below), with posts only 3 feet high, so that the roses can thickly cover both the posts and the chain between them. In warmer zones, you can use a taller, 8-foot version of this arrangement to frame an outdoor living area.

1. Install rot-resistant wood (such as cedar or black locust, but not treated wood) or metal posts. Firmly anchor them in place with 3 feet exposed above ground. Connect the posts loosely with lengths of marine rope or heavy chain. Plant roses next to each post. Ramblers are well suited to this technique because of their supple canes. You can use climbers, too, but you'll need to be vigilant about training them before their canes become too rigid.

2. Train two or three rose canes in each direction from the top of the post. Twist the canes around the rope in a gentle spiral and attach them with raffia at regular intervals as they grow.

3. Keep your garland roses well fertilized, watered, and deadheaded for maximum bloom. In late winter, remove deadwood and shorten laterals to 8 inches long.

Careful cleanup is a key to growing
healthy roses organically.

fighting diseases

Let's not beat around the bush: Dealing with diseases is the most frustrating aspect of growing roses. Even if you don't mind hauling out an arsenal of organic products, it's no fun to have to do it.

The good news is that if you implement the practices recommended in the earlier chapters of this book, serious disease problems will rarely, if ever, plague the roses in your garden.

Because your roses are growing in optimal, well-drained soil, they're growing vigorously and are naturally more disease-resistant. Thanks to your careful watering practices, your roses are being spared wet leaves and splashed spores that would give fungal diseases the upper hand. And your informal pruning program also plays an important role in discouraging disease.

Another key to fighting rose diseases is learning to recognize common diseases—and how to prevent conditions that favor them. We'll cover the big four diseases—black spot, downy mildew, powdery mildew, and rust—within this chapter, as well as look at good gardening practices and other preventive measures that will go a long way toward keeping disease at bay.

First, though, we'll start with a quick review of the groundwork we've already laid for rose health.

Promoting Rose Health

By following the four practices listed below, you'll help give your roses an edge when it comes to fighting disease.

Choose disease-resistant varieties. Roses with genetically strong constitutions are much less likely to become victims of disease. On the other hand, no amount of good cultural practice will keep a rose that's truly susceptible to a disease like black spot from becoming infected.

Feed the soil. Careful soil preparation provides a nourishing environment for the roots of your roses. After planting, use organic materials to meet your roses' nutritional needs in a natural and balanced way. Go easy on the nitrogen—excess nitrogen promotes soft, weak growth that is prone to disease.

Water with care. Poor watering techniques promote and spread disease in the rose garden. Move roses out of zones of overhead irrigation and install a drip system, instead. If you water by hand, be sure you do not wet the foliage.

Practice good pruning. Pruning your roses as described in the last chapter will aid greatly in disease prevention. Proper pruning promotes air circulation, which discourages diseases and prevents their spread by removing infected plant parts.

Besides following these basic practices for rose health, you can take additional measures to prevent disease problems, as we'll explain in this chapter. And if rose diseases do show up, don't despair. There are safe, nontoxic remedies that you can use to restore your roses to good health.

Recognizing Rose Diseases

Let's take a look at the various maladies that can affect roses. By understanding the conditions that favor the development of these diseases, you'll be able to do everything possible to prevent them. And if any problems do crop up, you'll be able to recognize their symptoms and quickly respond with the appropriate treatment.

Fungal Diseases

Fungal diseases—black spot, downy mildew, powdery mildew, and rust—are by far the most prevalent rose problems. (For a summary of their characteristics, see "The 'Big 4' Rose Diseases" on the opposite page.) Disease-resistant varieties are your best line of defense. If you grow disease-resistant varieties such as those recommended in this book, no fungal disease will ever seriously threaten your roses. You can further decrease the odds of fungal disease on your roses by feeding your roses adequately, practicing good garden sanitation, and using pruning to ensure good air circulation. The oft-repeated expression "An ounce of prevention is worth a pound of cure" is never truer than in the case of rose fungal diseases.

With so many healthy roses, such as 'Lichtkonigin Lucia' *(above)*, to choose from, there's no reason to waste your time on frustrating, disease-prone roses.

The "Big 4" Rose Diseases

Black spot (*Diplocarpon rosae*)

Symptoms
Irregular black spots surrounded by yellow zones on upper leaf surfaces. Appears on oldest foliage first.

Effects
Defoliation; fewer flowers; severe weakening of the canes; occasional plant death.

Conditions Favoring Development
Wet leaves; hot weather; humidity; poor air circulation.

Transmission
Spores germinate on wet leaves; most often spread by water hitting infected leaves on the ground and splashing onto plant foliage; also spread by tools, clothing, and hands. Occurs nearly everywhere, but not as much of a problem in the dry Southwest.

Treatment
Mulch with compost to create a barrier between your plant and disease spores in the soil. Rose Flora (commercial bacterial treatment); spray baking soda and horticultural oil on a weekly basis before symptoms appear; Remedy (commercial baking soda product); antitranspirants; weekly sulfur applications.

Downy mildew (*Peronospora sparsa*)

Symptoms
Small purple blotches on leaves; leaves turn yellow and drop; infected canes develop purplish black spots.

Effects
Severe and rapid defoliation; infected canes die over winter.

Conditions Favoring Development
Cool, damp climates.

Transmission
Spores spread by wind; overhead watering helps promote the disease.

Treatment
Thoroughly coat the entire plant with antitranspirants.

(continued)

The "Big 4" Rose Diseases—continued

Powdery mildew (*Erysiphe* spp.)

Symptoms
Patches of fuzzy white or gray "powder" on leaves and stems of new growth in spring and fall.

Effects
Curled, rippled leaves, or leaves that "fold closed" along the midrib; new growth and flower buds fail to develop; increased susceptibility to black spot; weakening of the canes; increased winterkill.

Conditions Favoring Development
Drought; warm days and cool nights; humidity; shade; poor air circulation.

Transmission
Spores germinate on dry leaves; spores carried by wind; also spread by tools, clothing, and hands. Widespread problem, but especially prevalent on the Pacific coast.

Treatment
Spray baking soda and horticultural oil on a weekly by schedule; apply skim milk solution on weekly basis; antitranspirants; weekly sulfur applications.

Rust (*Phragmicium* spp.)

Symptoms
Orange pustules on undersides of leaves; leaf surface turns yellow; black pustules appear in fall as overwintering structure of fungus.

Effects
Leaves turn yellow, then brown; defoliation; overall deterioration and plant death in susceptible cultivars.

Conditions Favoring Development
Warm, wet weather; poor air circulation; cultivar susceptibility.

Transmission
Spores germinate on wet leaves and spread by water droplets, as for black spot. More prevalent in southern and northwestern United States.

Treatment
Baking soda and horticultural oil on weekly basis and after each rain; sulfur applications on weekly basis.

If rosette virus occurs in your roses, destroy any wild *Rosa multiflora* plants existing on your property. This overly vigorous oriental rose species harbors the mite that spreads the virus. The multiflora rose was introduced as a hedging plant by the USDA in the early part of the 20th century and has spread to become a noxious weed throughout much of the eastern and central United States. Roses grown on *R. multiflora* rootstocks, however, are *not* more susceptible to rosette virus than roses grown on other rootstocks.

Bacterial Diseases

A couple of bacterial diseases also may crop up among your roses. The one you're most likely to see is stem canker, which causes brown lesions or dead areas on rose canes. Fortunately, canker rarely occurs on vigorous, hardy roses.

Marginally hardy plants that have just come through a tough winter are quite susceptible, as are very old roses that have been neglected and that harbor lots of dead wood. The good news is that canker is easy to control: Just remove the infected canes an inch or more below the margin of the lesion, and destroy the clippings.

Crown gall, another bacterial disorder, is much less common. It causes rough, irregular, swollen areas just above the graft union of the plant and is always introduced through a wound or by contaminated pruning shears. Roses that are planted deep enough almost never suffer from this malady. If the disease does appear, it is difficult to control. You can try to pare away the damaged tissue with a sharp knife. If this fails to solve the problem, you'll need to destroy the plant. Do not replant roses in the same spot.

Viral Diseases

Viral diseases are much less prevalent than fungal disorders in roses. Mosaic virus and rosette virus are the two you're most likely to encounter—one is tolerable, but the other can be deadly.

If you suddenly notice irregular wavy yellow lines, mottling, or other bizarre blotching patterns on the leaves of your rose, a mosaic virus is probably to blame. Mosaic is transmitted by infected rootstock during propagation, and unfortunately, there's absolutely nothing you can do about it once it occurs.

Stem canker, a bacterial disease, is easily controlled by cutting out the infected canes well below the lesion.

In general, yellow, orange, and truly crimson roses are inherently more prone to black spot than roses with pink and white blooms. Reds that are really very dark pinks, such as the magenta and cerise old roses, are not susceptible to this unsightly disease.

(To avoid this problem in the future, seek out a grower who guarantees that his plants are propagated on virus-free stock.)

Although mosaic virus reduces the vigor of plants, it isn't fatal and does not spread in the garden. Because of this, you don't need to destroy an infected rose unless it becomes very unsightly.

Rosette virus, on the other hand, is usually fatal and definitely contagious. You'll recognize it because it looks as though the rose's new growth has mutated in some bizarre way. The shoots will be red-tinged and gnarly, thickly cloaked with rubbery prickles, and they will break easily.

You might be able to save a rosette-infected plant if you cut out all of the diseased canes as soon as you spot them. If symptoms reoccur, however, you'll need to destroy the rose immediately so that your other roses don't become infected.

Vexing Viruses

Rose viruses are less common than fungal diseases, but they can be just as deadly. Here's how to recognize and prevent them.

Rose common mosaic

Symptoms
Light green to yellow mottling in wavy lines, rings, or blotches, most apparent on new growth; puckering of leaf, sometimes in oak-leaf pattern.

Effects
Reduced vigor; reduced number and size of flowers; not fatal.

Transmission
Infected rootstocks; not contagious.

Prevention
Buy certified virus-free stock.

Treatment
None.

Rose rosette (witch's broom)

Symptoms
Thick clusters (rosettes) of stubby, soft, brittle stems, extra prickly, with rubbery thorns; elongated leaflets; aberrant growth that's burgundy or lime green in color.

Effects
Distorted growth (gnarled or curled); weakening; death.

Transmission
Microscopic mite (*Phylocoptes fructiphilus*) harbored by *Rosa multiflora*.

Prevention
In winter, remove all previous leaflets and petioles; spray with dormant oil.

Treatment
Destroy the plant immediately.

Rose yellow mosaic

Symptoms
Like common mosaic, but more extensive and brighter chlorosis; "vein clearing" in which leaf veins appear yellow

Effects
Reduced vigor; reduced number and size of flowers; not fatal

Transmission
Infected rootstocks and grafts; not contagious

Prevention
Buy certified virus-free stock

Treatment
None

Plant a Medicine Chest for Your Roses

Why not dedicate an out-of-the-way spot on your property to growing medicinal plants for your roses? Stinging nettle (*Urtica dioica*), horsetail (*Equisetum arvense*), and Russian comfrey (*Symphytum* × *uplandicum*) are all vigorous plants that tolerate poor drainage and partial shade. (Because they are so vigorous, you should make sure to plant them where they won't invade other garden beds.) Having a patch of these therapeutic plants will ensure a steady supply that you can use to fertilize and treat your roses. Dry the surplus for future use, or add leftover plants to the compost pile.

Preventive Measures

Many factors influence the occurrence of rose diseases. Weather patterns, region, air circulation, and (on grafted roses) the type of rootstock used all play a role. Rust, for instance, is much more common in the South and Northwest than in the Midwest or Northeast. And if your neighbor's roses have black spot, the problem is much more likely to show up on your roses, too. (Check with your local Cooperative Extension Service if you're not sure which diseases are problematic in your growing area.) But no matter how many factors seem to be working against your roses, you still can do much to prevent or minimize disease problems.

Good watering practices are absolutely fundamental to preventing fungal diseases, as discussed in Chapter 5. Overhead watering is not a good idea for roses because wet foliage provides the perfect environment for the germination of black spot and rust spores, while splashing water does more to spread black spot than any other factor. Mildew, on the other hand, typically occurs when drought follows a period of heavy rainfall. Keep your roses evenly and adequately watered to minimize mildew problems.

Finally, remember that good air circulation can also help prevent fungal diseases. If possible, plant your roses where they will receive regular breezes. And don't forget to prune the plants to allow air to circulate through them.

Good Garden Practices

The most important preventive measure you can take can be summed up in two words: good sanitation. Infected foliage on the plant, dead leaves on the ground, and mulch all harbor disease spores. To stop the cycle of disease, remove diseased foliage from plants at the first sign of infection. In the case of mildew, cut off infected shoots and buds, put them in a plastic bag, and dispose of the bag immediately. Afterward, wash your pruners and your hands. Also, meticulously rake up fallen leaves.

At the end of the growing season, strip off any foliage still on your rose plants, then dispose of the debris; don't compost it. After your roses go dormant, rake up all of the mulch around them and dispose of it.

pH-Based Preventives

Black spot spores need a near-neutral pH to germinate, so anything you can do to lower the pH on the surface of your roses' leaves will help prevent the disease from becoming established. Before air pollution control laws, black spot was less common in urban areas because acid rain (caused by sulfur-containing pollutants dissolved in rainwater to make acids) inhibited the germination of black spot spores.

We don't want to go back to the days of air pollution, of course, but you can manipulate pH to your advantage against black spot fungus. For instance, a solution of skim milk applied to rose foliage will do a pretty good job of inhibiting black spot. The theory is that as the milk "spoils" on the leaf surface, lactic acid and casein are produced. Lactic acid lowers the pH, while the casein helps bind the milk solution to the leaves.

To use skim milk as a fungal preventive in your garden, spray a solution of 9 parts water to 1 part skim milk on the foliage of your roses once a week. Begin as soon as the leaves have fully opened and continue until the leaves begin to drop in autumn.

At the other end of the pH range, sodium bicarbonate prevents fungal diseases by *increasing* the pH on the leaf, making it more alkaline. To use baking soda as a fungal preventive, mix 1 tablespoon per gallon of water. Add a tablespoon of oil—either a light horticultural oil or regular vegetable oil—along with a squirt of mild dish soap to help the liquid stick to the leaves. Spray in the early morning. If the weather is humid or the threat of disease is high, spray every 5 to 7 days. Spray both sides of the leaf thoroughly at the first sign of disease.

Sulfur is another preventive that works on the pH principle by acidifying the leaf surface and preventing the germination of fungal spores. Be aware, though, that sulfur does not kill the fungus—it merely prevents new fungus from growing. For this purpose, be sure to buy a sulfur product made for foliar application, not "soil sulfur," which is much less soluble. Sulfur is caustic, so wear protective clothing and follow the recommended precautions on the product label when applying it. Do not apply when temperatures are over 85°F. Sulfur also adversely impacts some beneficial insects and mites, so consider it a last resort in your disease management program. (Don't mix sulfur and baking soda together; they'll neutralize each other.)

Horsetail (*Equisetum arvensis*) makes an excellent mild fungicide and foliar fertilizer for roses.

Plant-Based Preventives

One way to help your roses resist foliar diseases is to supply them with adequate potassium, which is essential for strong cells. Bimonthly foliar feedings of potassium-rich kelp extract strengthens the leaves of roses, thereby reducing their risk of fungal diseases. But kelp appears to boost plant health by doing more than merely supplying nutrients (see "Vaccinate Your Plants with Kelp," below).

Horsetail (*Equisetum arvensis*), which is rich in silica as well as calcium, iron, magnesium, molybdenum, potassium, and sulfur, also can be used to

Vaccinate Your Plants with Kelp

Scientific research is finally catching up to what organic gardeners have observed for decades: Kelp extract works wonders for plant health! Researchers are finding that plants mount an innate chemical defense when attacked by a disease organism. Unfortunately, that defense is often too little, too late. That's where kelp comes in. Recent laboratory studies of algal (kelp) extracts have found that they contain a compound that stimulates plants' immune systems. So treating your roses regularly with kelp extract is like vaccinating them against fungal and bacterial diseases.

Glossy Leaves Foil Fungi

Rose varieties that have glossy leaves, such as 'Palmengarten Frankfurt' have more than just their good looks going for them. Glossy-leaved roses have a waxy coating on the surface of their leaves, and fungal spores have trouble penetrating it. That's why glossy-leaved roses are more disease-resistant than matte-leaved roses. In general, the thinner the leaves of the rose and the more dull the leaf surface, the more likely the rose will succumb to fungal infection.

'Palmengarten Frankfurt'

prevent rose diseases. European gardeners have long used infusions of horsetail against mildew and rust. Because of its mild nature, horsetail is best used as a preventive measure (it can also help protect roses against insects by strengthening their leaves).

You can buy the dried herb at health food stores, or grow the plants yourself. The plants are most potent when harvested near the end of summer. Dry them in a dark, dry, well-ventilated place. When the herb has dried, crush it and store it in an airtight container until you're ready to use it.

To prepare a horsetail infusion, simmer 1 pound of dried horsetail leaves in 1 gallon of rainwater or distilled water over low heat for an hour. Allow the liquid to cool for 12 hours or overnight. Filter and dilute it to a 20 percent solution for use as a foliar spray. Spray your roses weekly with the infusion, early in the morning, just after the dew dries. Store the unused portion of the horsetail infusion in a plastic or glass container in a cool, dark place.

How about a mild, medicinal mulch for your roses? The antifungal properties of Russian comfrey (*Symphytum* × *uplandicum*) leaves will help your roses fight disease. And because comfrey leaves are large, they'll cover up any fungal spores that have dropped to the ground or onto existing mulch, acting as a protective barrier. Just lay fresh comfrey leaves on the ground, and you have an instant mulch.

Disease Barriers

To infect rose leaves, germinating fungal spores must penetrate the surface of the leaves with their hyphae, or rootlike structures. Because of this, you can prevent fungal penetration by coating the leaves of your roses with a barrier of film. Nontoxic, pine-resin–based antitranspirants—the kind sold in garden centers to prevent desiccation of evergreens during the winter—are excellent for this purpose.

Antitranspirant products cover rose foliage with a waxy coating that acts as a barrier against germinating fungal spores, much like the natural barrier on glossy-leaved roses (see "Glossy Leaves Foil Fungi" above). You can use an antitranspirant—whether the rose is actively growing or dormant. And the products help roses in other ways, too. If you use an antitranspirant in summer, you'll need to water a bit less often because your roses will lose less water through their leaves. If you spray your roses with an antitranspirant in late fall, you'll not only protect them against fungal infections the following spring, but you'll also minimize winterkill caused by desiccation.

When applying any spray to rose leaves, whether a preventive or treatment, remember to spray the undersides as well as the top surfaces of leaves. Sprays can only protect the areas that they come in contact with.

A richly diverse landscape encourages beneficial insects and birds, resulting in fewer pests on your roses.

preventing insect pests

Having lots of insects in

your garden doesn't have to mean you have pests on your roses. In fact, having more insects can mean *fewer* pests. During 10 years of growing more than 100 rose varieties, I have never had to spray to control insect pests. Japanese beetles—the only real pest on my roses—have been easily controlled with hand-picking.

I'm convinced that the reason for this fairly pest-free situation is that I grew hundreds of varieties of ornamentals, fruits, herbs, and vegetables for a farmers' market, and this diversity of plants was surrounded by natural meadow and forest. In short, my property provided a rich variety of foods and habitats for beneficial insects and birds, which kept the pests in check.

You'll find that the greater the diversity of plants in your landscape, the fewer pest problems your plants will have. By inviting nature into your yard, pests on your roses will rarely be a concern.

Inviting Beneficial Insects into Your Garden

We gardeners tend to think of insects as bad news. But on the contrary, there's a whole world of insects out there that can actually benefit your garden—insects that would welcome the chance to be invited in.

These beneficial insects are unrelated, other than by virtue of their value to gardeners. They work in different ways. Some, such as lady beetles, hover flies, lacewing larvae, and assassin bugs, are full-fledged hunters that pounce upon and devour their prey. Others, such as parasitic wasps, are more devious: They lay their eggs in a pest's body or egg, and when the eggs hatch, the larvae develop inside the pest or egg, killing it.

Provide the proper conditions, and these natural predators will hang around and dine on the harmful insects that would otherwise eat your roses and other garden plants.

Planting for Beneficials

Most beneficial insects have an appetite for more than just other insects. At one or more stages in their lives, they also need nectar, pollen, or some other form of food provided by plants. Beneficials are most attracted to plants that have lots of small flowers (florets) or many small flower parts, such as members of the composite family (such as asters, coreopsis, and sunflowers), the carrot family (dill, Queen-Anne's lace, and many other herbs), and the cabbage family (alyssum, cresses, mustards, and a variety of wildflowers).

You don't need to plant a garden specifically for helpful bugs, but keep in mind the types of plants they prefer. Then mix those plants—including annuals, perennials, and herbs—throughout your landscape to benefit not only your roses, but the rest of your garden, as well.

Roses in mixed borders are less prone to devastating insect attacks than those in solid beds of roses. There are several reasons for this. In a monoplanting, pests can spread easily from one plant to the next. In a highly mixed planting, pests have a harder time zeroing in on roses because the blend of aroma

Having pollen and nectar plants in your garden will entice beneficial bugs to take up permanent residence.

Beneficial Herbs

Herbs not only provide fragrance and flavor for your home and kitchen, but they also attract a wide range of beneficial insects to your garden. The following herbs are most attractive to good bugs, especially to the tiny and highly effective parasitizing wasps:

- Angelica (*Angelica archangelica*)
- Chervil (*Anthriscus cerefolium*)
- Cilantro (*Coriandrum sativum*)
- Dill (*Anethum graveolens*)
- Fennel (*Foeniculum vulgare*)
- Lovage (*Levisticum officinale*)
- Parsleys (*Petroselinum* spp.)
- Sweet cicely (*Myrrhis odorata*)
- Valerian (*Valeriana officinalis*)

chemicals from many plants masks those of the roses. In addition, the beneficial insects that prey upon pests are likely to be more abundant in a border where there are many types of plants available to provide plenty of food and shelter.

Buying Beneficials

If you don't want to wait for beneficials to show up in your garden on their own, you can buy them. Many companies sell a wide range of beneficial insects in egg, larval, and adult forms. (See "Recommended Reading and Resources" on page 264 for commercial sources of beneficial insects and other biological pest controls.) Beneficial insects can be quite expensive, though, so be sure you have both plant and pest food sources available before the insects arrive. Without food, adult insects tend to fly away. (Also make sure you'll be at home—and not away on vacation—when the beneficials arrive, so you can release them in your garden as soon as possible after receiving them.)

Beneficials are more likely to stick around if you hatch the eggs yourself. Just be aware that you may need to fuss a bit to maintain the temperature and humidity levels necessary for hatching.

Annual Attraction

Beneficial bugs are highly attracted to most annual flowers grown for cutting, including the following:

- Blue-lace flower (*Trachymene coerulea*)
- Calendula (*Calendula officinalis*)
- Chinese aster (*Callistephus chinensis*)
- Cosmos (*Cosmos bipinnatus*)
- Mexican sunflower (*Tithonia rotundifolia*)
- Pincushion flower (*Scabiosa atropurpurea*)

- Stocks (*Matthiola* spp.)
- Sunflowers (*Helianthus* spp.)

Natural-Born Killers

When you see bugs on your roses, don't panic. Learn to recognize the most common beneficial insects so that you can separate the good from the bad.

Beneficial Insect	Rose Pest Controlled	Comments
Braconid and chalcid wasps (BRACONIDAE and CHALCIDIDAE)	Wide range of caterpillars.	Parasitize caterpillars by laying eggs in their bodies; very small; adults usually go unnoticed.
Ground beetles (CARABIDAE)	Slugs, snails, and a wide variety of other pests.	Large beetles that forage at night, hiding in litter during the day.
Hover or flower flies (*Syrphus* spp.)	Aphids and other soft-bodied insects.	Larvae are predatory (one larvae can eat as many as 400 aphids); adults must consume pollen to reproduce.
Lady beetles (*Hippodamia convergens; Coleomegilla maculata*)	Aphids, mites, scale, thrips, and other soft-bodied insects; eggs of many pests.	A single lady beetle may consume 5,000 aphids during its life. Both larvae and adults are predatory. Adult lady beetles also feed on pollen and nectar. Lady beetles are found in most areas—don't purchase them because commercial beetles collected from the wild tend to disperse instead of staying put.
Lacewings (*Chrysopa* spp., *Chrysoperla* spp.)	Aphids, scale, spider mites, thrips, whiteflies.	Only larvae are predatory; adults feed on nectar and pollen.

Beneficial Insect	Rose Pest Controlled	Comments
Minute pirate bug (*Orius* spp.)	Aphids, mites, small caterpillars, thrips	If purchased, place on roses with paintbrush; pollen-rich flowers and herbs are necessary for survival.
Praying mantids (MANTIDAE)	Wide variety of pests and their eggs; also eats beneficials except ladybugs, which are bitter.	Learn to recognize egg cases; place them off the ground, near roses.
Predatory mites (*Galendromus occidentalis; Phytoseiulus persimilis*)	Spider mites, two-spotted mites, and others.	Help control pest mites prevalent during hot weather.
Spined soldier bug (*Podisus masculiventris*)	Wide variety of pests.	Harpoons victims, injects paralyzing venom, and sucks out their body contents; both nymphs and adults are predatory and feed over a 30-day period.
Thrips predator (*Amblyseius cucumeris*)	Rose thrips.	Predatory mite feeds on the young stages of thrips.
Whitefly predator (*Delphastus pusilius*)	Spider mites; all stages of whiteflies.	Beetle will consume several hundred whiteflies per day; both larvae and adults are predatory.

Bringing Birds to the Aid of Your Roses

Birds are an incredible asset to your garden, consuming vast amounts of a wide variety of pest insects. (They avoid beneficial lady beetles because of their bitter taste.) Do everything you can to encourage birds to take up residence around your roses. Provide lots of perching and shelter sites nearby in the form of evergreen and deciduous trees and shrubs.

To provide food and shelter for your avian allies through the winter months, plant hedges of roses that bear hips, as well as other berried shrubs and trees like beautyberry, coralberry, crabapples, hawthorns, hollies, snowberry, and viburnums. Hang small bags of suet from your shrub roses to attract birds that will demolish any insect eggs overwintering in the roses.

If you include a bird feeder in your garden, place it where plant-toxic sunflower hulls won't fall among your plants.

Finally, don't forget the importance of water when attracting beneficial life to your rose garden. A small pool will draw not only birds, but also frogs, toads, insects, and other creatures that can help keep your roses pest-free while enriching your life with theirs.

Rogues' Gallery

Occasionally, despite the presence of beneficial insects and birds, a large outbreak of pest insects may occur on your roses. When that happens, don't despair. There are plenty of organic pest-control measures you can take, as we'll soon discuss.

Before you take any action, however, be sure you know which pest you're fighting so that you use the most effective controls. Keep in mind that pest identification sometimes means learning to recognize the pest's damage, which may be more visible than the pest itself.

Pests cause damage to roses in two ways: they either pierce the plant's tissue and suck out the juices and nutrients or they chew the plant's foliage or flowers. Let's take a closer look at both types of rose pests so that you can identify the problem and act quickly and effectively against it.

Sucking and Chewing Pests

The damage of sucking pests—especially very tiny ones, like rose midges, or highly mobile ones, like whiteflies or leafhoppers—can be difficult to identify. Sucking pests can cause leaves or buds to become deformed, chlorotic, spotted, or brown, so the effects sometimes are mistaken for disease. (See "Nasty Little

Hummingbird Hub

Do all you can to attract hummingbirds to your garden. Besides sipping nectar from flowers, hummingbirds consume large numbers of aphids and other small insects. You can attract these charming visitors (and reduce aphids on your roses) by planting plenty of tubular flowers, such as bellflowers, cardinal flower, delphinium, honeysuckle, and penstemons.

Unfortunately, highly fragrant roses attract Japanese beetles. If Japanese beetles are known to be a big problem in your area, consider growing scentless roses, such as 'William Baffin' (*above*).

Suckers" on page 100 for a quick guide to sucking pests, their damage, and what control measures you can take.)

Chewing insects tend to be larger than sucking insects, and therefore they're easier to identify. Their damage is hard to miss, too: holes in leaves or flowers. Leafcutter bees, for example, chew large, C-shaped holes in leaves, while Japanese beetles chew holes in flowers and foliage. Cane borers, larval insects, leave flowers and leaves alone but use their heavy-duty chewing mouthparts to tunnel into rose canes near the ground. Their damage is hard to spot until suddenly the entire cane and its leaves turn crisp and brown. This effect perplexes many gardeners, as the rest of the plant continues to flourish. (For a quick guide to pests that chew roses and what to do about them, see "Nasty Little Chewers" on page 101.)

Spotting Little Monsters

A magnifying glass can be invaluable for identifying seemingly invisible pests, such as the two-spotted mite. If you see damage but can't seem to find the cause, check out the undersides of the leaves with a good-quality 10X lens. If you're still uncertain about what's bugging your roses, take a sample of the damage—and the insect, if you can find it—to your local Cooperative Extension Service for identification.

Nasty Little Suckers

Pests that suck the life from roses are sometimes difficult to identify. Learn to recognize their characteristic damage so that you won't be fooled into thinking you're seeing disease. (For details about using the suggested control methods, see "The Organic Arsenal" on page 102.)

Pest	Description	Damage	Controls
Mealybugs (PSEUDOCOC-CIDAE)	Small (less than ¼") insects covered with cottony-looking material.	Leaves wilt or become deformed; defoliation.	Wipe off pests by hand with a soft cloth; parasitic wasps; dormant and horticultural oils.
Rose aphid (*Macrosiphum rosae*)	Soft-bodied green insects (about ⅛" long or less).	New growth becomes deformed; sugary liquid exuded ("honeydew") attracts ants; sooty mold may grow.	Wipe affected growth with soft cloth, or wash off with a strong spray of water. Lady beetles, lacewings, and other beneficials; diatomaceous earth; insecticidal soap; horticultural oil.
Rose midge (*Dasineura rhodophaga*)	Very tiny white larvae feed inside growing tissue.	Deformed and blackened buds.	Cut off and destroy infested terminals as often as they appear.
Rose scales (*Aulacaspis rosae* and other soft and armored scales)	Tiny (⅛") "oysters" form circular, white scaly patches on canes.	Yellow or brown spots or streaks on leaves, resembling virus; encrustations on bark; plant eventually dies.	Remove nearby blackberry and raspberry plants, which host scale. Spray dormant oil on canes before buds break in spring; horticultural oil; parasitic wasps.
Whiteflies (ALEYRODIDAE *Homoptera*)	Clouds of tiny white "particles" fly up when foliage is disturbed.	Wilting, chlorosis, loss of leaves, stunted growth.	Predatory and parasitic insects; insecticidal soap, yellow sticky traps.

Nasty Little Chewers

Most chewing pests are relatively easy to spot. To minimize the extent of their damage, try to take action as soon as you've identified the culprit. (For details about using the suggested control methods, see "The Organic Arsenal" on page 102.)

Pest	Description	Damage	Controls
Cane borer	Larvae of beetle tunnel into rose cane; sawdust at point of entry.	Cane above tunnel abruptly wilts and dies.	Cut out and destroy affected canes well below tunnel.
Caterpillars (many species)	Single or numerous small "worms," usually on undersides of leaves.	Holes in foliage.	Remove by hand; spray BTK (*Bacillus thuringiensis kurstaki*) on undersides of leaves; parasitic wasps; insecticidal soap.
Cucumber beetles (spotted: *Diabrotica undecimpunctata*; striped: *Acalymma vittatums*)	¼" chartreuse beetle, striped or spotted with black; very mobile.	Deep holes in flower buds.	*Beauvaria bassiana* (a naturally occurring fungal disease).
Japanese beetle (*Popillia japonica*)	Large (⅓") coppery green beetles on blossoms.	Holes in flowers and foliage.	Hand pick beetles and drop them into soapy water to kill them; applications of soil nematodes; inoculate soil with milky spore disease to kill larvae.
Leafcutter bee	Solitary bee, ¼"–¾" long.	Large, characteristically C-shaped, smooth-edged holes in leaf margins.	Leafcutter bees are beneficial insects that require no control; their damage is very short-term and not harmful to the health of roses.

The Organic Arsenal

Being an organic gardener doesn't mean that you must learn to live with pest-damaged roses, as some would have you think. As previously discussed, roses that are integrated into a diverse organic garden will suffer fewer pest infestations than roses grown in a landscape with a limited variety of plants and where pesticides routinely wipe out beneficial insects.

As with rose diseases, keen observation and early intervention are potent weapons against pests. If pests do get out of hand, you still have an arsenal of safe, organic techniques at your disposal. For best results, use a combination of methods.

Repellents

If pests threaten your roses, begin with repellent techniques. Repellents work by hiding or masking the presence of roses with a strong scent or by literally repelling the insect with a repugnant or irritating smell or taste.

Most organic repellent products contain citrus oils, garlic, or hot pepper—either alone or in combination with each other or with a waxy substance to help

Thymes make ideal groundcovers around roses. They repel insect pests without competing for nutrients.

spread and adhere the repellent to leaves. Hot pepper wax repels a wide range of pests, including aphids, leaf hoppers, scale, spider mites, thrips, and whiteflies.

Strongly scented herbs, such as artemisias, basil, garlic, tansy, and thyme, can mask the scent of insect-attracting compounds produced by roses. To use these herbs as repellents, plant them around your roses as a groundcover, or use their clippings as mulch.

Physical Removal

Squashing or removing eggs, larvae, and adult insects can be a very effective control tactic. Pest larvae also are easy to remove or crush because they're slow moving, as are adult Japanese beetles. Drop larvae and adult beetles into a container of soapy water for a quick, non-toxic death, then dump them onto the compost pile.

A jet of strong water is another simple but effective way to remove many rose pests, including aphids and spider mites.

Traps and Lures

Traps and lures are especially effective against fast-flying pests like thrips. Commercially sold traps attract pests with a specific color (or are physically placed in the path of pests); insects then become tangled in a sticky substance on the trap. You also can make your own traps by painting yellow or blue plastic or cardboard with a commercially available sticky trapping compound called Tanglefoot. (Use traps with caution because they also capture beneficial insects.)

Lures use a particular scent to draw pests into an inescapable box or bag. The scent may be either that of a target plant or, for male insects, the sexual pheromone emitted by the female insect.

Germ Warfare

Microbiological controls introduce a deadly disease to the pest insect but don't harm people or animals. The best-known control of this type is *Bacillus thuringiensis* (or BT), a bacterium that kills the pest caterpillars of butterflies and moths. BT is sold under many different trade names and includes various strains for specific pests. For caterpillar pests on your roses, use the *kurstaki* strain (BTK). Sunlight hastens the breakdown of BT, so try to spray it on the undersides of leaves to lengthen its effect.

A relatively new microbial control is *Beauvaria bassiana* JW-1. This fungal disease kills cucumber beetles, which can devastate roses. *Beauvaria* also controls aphids, caterpillars, psyllids, and whiteflies. Use with caution, however, because it is less selective than BT and can affect beneficial insects.

Safe Insecticides

Organic insecticides are relatively safe to use, but they do kill both pests and beneficials. That's why you should use them only as a last resort. (See "Organic Insecticides: The Last Line of Defense" below.) Apply them only to pest-affected plants and, for best effect, apply them directly to the pest. (Most of these products must come in contact with the pest to kill it.) Spray in the evening, when fewer beneficials are around. Reapply after rain if necessary.

Organic Insecticides: The Last Line of Defense

These insecticides are safe for organic gardeners but still should be used with caution, as they are toxic to beneficial as well as pest insects. They're listed from least to most toxic.

Insecticide	How It Works	Application	Target Pests
Diatomaceous earth	Dehydration (cuts insects' exoskeletons; must come in contact with insect).	Dust or spray; mix with soft water and add 2 tablespoons isopropyl alcohol per quart (or liter) of solution.	Mealybugs; sawfly larvae; spider mites.
Insecticidal soap	Membrane penetration, paralysis, starvation (must come in contact with insect).	Spray; mix with soft water; apply early, late, or on overcast days to avoid burning foliage; repeat every few days.	Soft-bodied insects such as aphids; leafhoppers; mealybugs; mites; psyllids; thrips; whiteflies.
Horticultural oil	Suffocation (must come in contact with insect).	Foliar spray.	Aphids; mealybugs; mites; psyllids; sawfly larvae; scale.
Dormant oil	Suffocation (must come in contact with insect).	Spray during dormant season in late fall or early spring, before bud swell.	Aphids; mealybugs; scale; numerous other insect eggs.

PART III

remarkable roses

Now that you know the fundamentals of growing roses, you have to face the hard part: deciding which ones to grow. Whether you're just getting started growing roses or are looking to expand your collection, here are the roses that I've found to be the best bets for organic gardens. I've grown all but a few of these myself, and I've based the decision to recommend them to you on a combination of my own experience, the advice of other experts, and a desire to present you with a balanced selection of shrubs of different sizes and landscape uses, plus the best climbers and ramblers I've come across.

So, pull up a comfortable chair, and immerse yourself in page after page of gorgeous roses for your organic garden. Dream about which roses you just have to have—and how you'll incorporate them into your landscape. And then, turn your dreams into reality.

You'll have the most success growing roses without chemicals if you start by choosing varieties that are best for the organic garden.

chapter 10

a gallery of roses

While most rose books focus on an exhaustive listing of rose varieties, what I want to do here is simply recommend a sampling of roses that I think are the best for growing organically. In no way should you imagine that these are the *only* roses that can be grown in an organic garden. But with a limited number of pages at my disposal, I had to devise my own standards for choosing which roses I would recommend. I'll be the first to say that there were plenty of judgment calls involved. Because I believe that *all* horticultural information should be read with at least a small grain of salt, let me just supply you with the saltshaker right now.

Remember that all roses perform differently in various regions of the country, in different parts of the same state, and even in different spots on your very own property. So many factors play into the health and vigor of roses. I've done my best to bring you the top all-around performers.

Making the Cut

In choosing the roses for this gallery, I considered many factors that I tried to weigh objectively. However, from time to time, I softened my rigidity to take into consideration some stark realities. For example, I included a couple of representatives from the Towne & Country series of landscape roses simply because they are becoming so widespread and they are so heavily marketed in the United States. I wanted you to at least have an idea of which of this group would be the best to choose and so that you wouldn't put down this book saying to yourself, "Well, what about those Towne & Country roses?"

In general, I have weighted disease resistance most heavily in my choices, since rose fungal diseases—especially black spot—are the biggest stumbling blocks to growing roses organically. After disease resistance, I considered hardiness. I wanted gardeners in the northern USDA Plant Hardiness Zones to be able to satisfactorily grow as many of these roses as possible. However, realizing that heat tolerance can be a problem to some rose growers in the South, I also included a few varieties just for them.

After health and hardiness, I weighted the rose according to its ability to repeat bloom, knowing that most gardeners, having been "raised" on tea roses, expect a rose to bloom its heart out from spring to fall. If the rose was not a repeat bloomer, it had to bear a good crop of hips after flowering or be otherwise so outstanding that it merited inclusion.

Finally, I got around to considering the sheer good looks of the roses. I tried to offer you a list that is as balanced as possible in terms of color, keeping in mind that red and yellow roses (as well as peach and orange ones) are genetically more prone to black spot than pinks and whites are. I considered fragrance, as I love fragrant roses and believe fervently that their heavenly perfume is one of the major reasons for growing them. (However, this bias didn't prevent me from including a few roses with no fragrance at all, on the strength of their other attributes.)

I organized the gallery according to the function and size of the roses. Having consulted scores of rose books during my professional gardening career, I know that the first thing I have to consider when choosing a rose is how I'm going to use it, not whether it's a gallica or a rugosa. For example, do I need a large shrub to use in the background of a mixed border, or am I looking for a rose to use as a possible groundcover for a dry slope? Or do I need a climbing rose to soften a severe, blank wall where there is little horizontal space?

Be aware that both the eventual size of any given rose, as well as its ability to resist disease, can vary enormously from region to region and even from microclimate to microclimate. Depending on where you live, a rose may grow to be bigger, or remain smaller, than the size I give for it in this gallery. That's because, in addition to being genetic, size is a function of hardiness. A rose will suffer more and more dieback as you move it north. On the other hand, as you move a rose south, it enjoys a longer and longer growing season, giving it more time to store carbohydrates—which is why it grows bigger than it would farther north. Likewise, a rose I list as very resistant to black spot may become diseased in your garden. It's unlikely, but it could happen. That's because disease is not only a result of genetics, but also of other factors, such as weather patterns and gardening practices.

That said, I want you to read this gallery knowing that it is a somewhat subjective listing. I am not the Goddess of Roses sending earthward tablets inscribed with Rose Law. I am merely another gardener, one who happens to have grown a lot of roses and who feels qualified to share that experience. So use this gallery as a guide, knowing that its recommendations are based on lots of experience and research but are subject to your own gardening trial and error. Only you can truly decide which are the best roses for your particular garden.

A note on the organization of the individual gallery entries: Below each cultivar name is the parentage of the rose, if it's known, in parentheses. After the parentage, you'll find the name of the person who formally introduced the rose, followed by the country and date of introduction.

Recommended Small Shrub and Groundcover Roses

All the roses in this section will remain below 3 feet tall in most regions. Use them when space is limited, for low massing, near the front of mixed borders, or as groundcovers where applicable.

'Aspen' (also called 'Gwent')

(Parentage undisclosed) ■ Poulsen, Denmark, 1995

Class: Shrub
Hardiness: Zones 4–10
Size: 1½' × 3'
Uses: Hanging baskets, containers, groundcovers
Shade: Not tolerant
Flowering: Continuous

Bloom Color: Sunny yellow
Fragrance: Light
Black Spot: Moderately susceptible
Mildew: Slightly susceptible
Pruning: Deadhead, remove deadwood, winter maintenance

A strong rebloomer, 'Aspen' sports semidouble, sunny yellow flowers throughout the season. And while its glossy, dark green leaves are more susceptible to black spot than those of other modern groundcover roses, 'Aspen' seems less prone to the disease than most other yellow roses.

The compact, prostrate plants are excellent as a groundcover for small areas. 'Aspen' also looks handsome in a large pot or hanging basket, where its canes can cascade over the edges.

'Charles Albanel'

('Souvenir de Philémon Cochet' × seedling) ■ Svejda, Canada, 1982

This outstanding rose is hardy almost to polar regions and is practically immune to disease. It blooms heavily from late May through June, then repeats off and on until frost, bearing semidouble flowers with ruffled petals and pretty golden stamens. Its large, dark red hips add interest to the winter landscape and provide food for foraging birds.

One of the shortest roses, 'Charles Albanel' makes an excellent groundcover or low hedge.

Class: Hybrid rugosa
Hardiness: Zones 2–10
Size: 1½' × 3'
Uses: Mixed borders, groundcovers, low hedges, wildlife plantings
Shade: Not tolerant

Flowering: Repeat
Bloom Color: Crimson pink
Fragrance: Moderately fragrant
Black Spot: Not susceptible
Mildew: Not susceptible
Pruning: Remove deadwood

'Coral Cluster'

(Sport of 'Orleans Rose') ▪ Murrell, United Kingdom, 1920

AT A GLANCE

Class: Polyantha
Hardiness: Zones 5–10
Size: 1½' × 2½'
Uses: Mixed borders, containers, low hedges
Shade: Tolerant
Flowering: Continuous

Bloom Color: Coral pink
Fragrance: None
Black Spot: Slight susceptibility
Mildew: Slight susceptibility
Pruning: Deadhead, remove deadwood, winter maintenance

'Coral Cluster' is an excellent small rose that should be grown more often. Typical of the dwarf polyantha roses in vogue before floribundas, this dainty, old-fashioned charmer bears clusters of small, delicately cupped, semidouble blooms continuously from June to frost. Its bloom color is a remarkable soft coral pink that fades to near white. Like all true polyanthas, 'Coral Cluster' is not fragrant, but remember that this also makes the plants much less attractive to Japanese beetles.

The small, medium green, glossy leaves are slightly susceptible to disease, but any disease that does occur usually isn't enough to interfere with the overall health of the plant. To reduce the chance of disease, prune the dense, twiggy plants in late winter to open up their interiors. In the landscape, grow 'Coral Cluster' in borders, hedges, or containers; for a sublime combination, pair it with lavender-blue blooms.

(*Note:* Photo not available)

'Corylus'

(*R. nitida* × *R. rugosa rubra*) ▪ Le Rougetel, United Kingdom, 1988

Although 'Corylus' was bred by a passionate amateur, its quality compares to that of roses introduced by the world's most prominent rose breeders. Like other species crosses, this exquisite rose is exceptionally healthy and hardy. The plants seem to bloom constantly all summer, bearing large, single flowers of a luminous light pink. Big, savory, cherry red hips follow.

But 'Corylus' would be beautiful even if it never flowered. Its apple-green foliage, although lightly crinkled like its rugosa parent, has the willowy grace of its nitida parent. In autumn, the leaves turn rich gold and bronze red.

Use 'Corylus' either in a cultivated garden setting (as a groundcover, low hedge, or in a mixed border) or in a naturalized planting for wildlife. It's an especially lovely counterpoint to ornamental grasses. 'Corylus' needs almost no pruning and is easy to root from softwood cuttings.

Class: Shrub
Hardiness: Zones 3–10
Size: 2½' × 3'
Uses: Mixed borders, groundcovers, massings, wildlife plantings
Shade: Tolerant

Flowering: Continuous
Bloom Color: Medium silvery pink
Fragrance: Very fragrant
Black Spot: Not susceptible
Mildew: Not susceptible
Pruning: Remove deadwood

AT A GLANCE

'Dart's Dash'

(Unknown rugosa parentage) ▪ Darthuis Nursery, Holland, date unknown

AT A GLANCE

Class: Hybrid rugosa
Hardiness: Zones 3–10
Size: 3' × 4'
Uses: Mixed borders, ground-covers, low hedges, wildlife plantings
Shade: Not tolerant

Flowering: Continuous
Bloom Color: Bright magenta purple
Fragrance: Very fragrant
Black Spot: Not susceptible
Mildew: Not susceptible
Pruning: Remove deadwood

'Dart's Dash' is an undeservedly obscure rugosa. Like the more commonly planted (but less-impressive) 'Hansa' [hybrid rugosa], it has richly saturated, deep magenta–purple flowers and a heavy, sweet fragrance. But while 'Hansa' is very tall and leggy and flowers mostly in June, 'Dart's Dash' is compact and bushy, cloaked with foliage, and in flower continuously from late May until frost. It bears clusters of pointed, scrolled buds that open into ruffled semidouble flowers to reveal beautifully contrasting golden stamens. As on other rugosas, the rich green foliage is heavily crinkled and the stems are thorny.

Don't deadhead this rose, as it will produce enormous, ornamental scarlet hips all season. (They're excellent for jams, teas, and, of course, feeding birds.) In autumn, the flowers, hips, and bright fall foliage combine to create a spectacular finale to the growing season.

'De Montarville'

(A15 × L76) ▪ L'Assomption, Canada, 1998

Like other recent releases from the Canadian Agricultural Station's Explorer series, 'De Montarville' is a healthy, hardy rose that resembles traditional floribundas and teas in its bloom, habit, foliage, and reduced thorniness. The plants are often sold on their own roots, adding to their hardiness and vigor.

The deep cerise red buds of 'De Montarville' open to medium pink, fading unevenly but not un-

attractively to a paler pink with age. As the semidouble flowers open, the edges of the petals reflex back, giving each petal a pointed appearance, as seen on some hybrid teas. In autumn, the matte, medium green foliage turns warm yellow. Take preventative measures against black spot to avoid the occasional mild outbreaks that are possible with this rose.

Class: Shrub
Hardiness: Zones 3–10
Size: 3' × 3'
Uses: Mixed borders, low hedges
Shade: Not tolerant
Flowering: Continuous
Bloom Color: Medium pink

Fragrance: Lightly fragrant
Black Spot: Slightly susceptible
Mildew: Not susceptible
Pruning: Deadhead, remove deadwood, little winter maintenance

AT A GLANCE

'Dornröschenschloss Sababurg'

(Parentage unknown) ▪ William Kordes Söhne, Germany, 1993

This rose's name—'Dornröschenschloss Sababurg'—may be a mouthful, but its meaning is quite lovely: Sleeping Beauty's castle, referring to the roses that she fell asleep among. With big, solid, clear pink blossoms

that are fully double, this rose is just as romantic as its name. As the blossoms open, the edges of the beautiful, cupped petals fold back, much like those of tea roses. When fully open, the petals swirl like those of ancient roses.

'Dornröschenschloss Sababurg' provides excellent cut flowers, has gorgeous foliage, and is extremely healthy. Its only fault may be that it is slightly less hardy than many of the other shrubs in this size category; otherwise, 'Dornröschenschloss Sababurg' is everything you could wish for in a rose.

Class: Shrub
Hardiness: Zones 5–10
Size: 3' × 3'
Uses: Mixed borders, cut flowers, low hedges
Shade: Slightly tolerant
Flowering: Continuous

Bloom Color: Clear pink
Fragrance: Moderately fragrant
Black Spot: Not susceptible
Mildew: Not susceptible
Pruning: Deadhead, remove deadwood, winter maintenance

'Goldmarie 82'

(['Arthur Bell' × 'Zorina'] × ['Honeymoon' × 'Dr. A. J. Verhage'] × [seedling × 'Sunsprite']) ▪ William Kordes Söhne, Germany, 1984

There's some confusion about the name of this rose because a different rose with this name, 'Goldmarie', was introduced in 1958 by the same breeder and still sometimes shows up in gardening catalogs and garden centers. Make sure you get the '82' version because it is much healthier. 'Goldmarie 82' has clusters of plump, pointed buds that open into semidouble sunny yellow flowers with wavy petals.

Short and bushy, this makes an excellent container rose. In a mixed border, try it with dark blue veronicas (*Veronica* spp. and hybrids) and white shasta daisies (*Leucanthemum* × *superbum*).

For a yellow rose, 'Goldmarie 82' is phenomenally healthy; its green, glossy foliage seems to ward off fungal diseases. But like all floribundas, it requires more severe pruning than many shrub roses. In late winter, remove spindly canes from the interiors of plants to promote more vigorous flowering and reduce the chances of disease.

Class: Floribunda
Hardiness: Zones 5–10
Size: 2' × 2'
Uses: Beddings, mixed borders, containers, cut flowers
Shade: Not tolerant
Flowering: Continuous

Bloom Color: Clear lemon yellow
Fragrance: Moderately fragrant
Black Spot: Not susceptible
Mildew: Not susceptible
Pruning: Deadhead, remove deadwood, cut back by half in late winter

'Goldmarie 82'

'Grüss an Aachen'

'Grüss an Aachen'

('Frau Karl Druschki' × 'Franz Deegen') ▪ Geduldig, Germany, 1909

To know this rose is to love it. Borne in clusters, the refined flowers of 'Grüss an Aachen' have all the romance of the old roses. Deep salmon buds open to reveal creamy, peach-pink blossoms that are excellent for cutting. The petals, which have the texture of heavy silk, resemble seashells around a swirled and quartered glowing heart.

While 'Grüss an Aachen' isn't especially vigorous, it is relatively healthy by modern standards. Use preventative measures to avoid black spot on the slightly glossy, deep green foliage.

The upright, bushy form of 'Grüss an Aachen' is perfectly suited to growing in a large pot on a patio. In a border, this petite but tough rose will thrive and flower even in light shade.

Class: Floribunda
Hardiness: Zones 5–10
Size: 1½' × 1½'
Uses: Mixed borders, containers, cut flowers
Shade: Tolerant
Flowering: Continuous

Bloom Color: Creamy peach pink
Fragrance: Slightly fragrant
Black Spot: Slightly susceptible
Mildew: Not susceptible
Pruning: Deadhead, remove deadwood, cut back by half in late winter

'Immensee'

('The Fairy' × seedling of *R. wichuriana*) ▪ William Kordes Söhne, Germany, 1983

The innovative house of Kordes broke new ground in 1983 with the introduction of this first modern groundcover rose. Since then, 'Immensee' has stood the test of time, offering vigorous, low but wide-spreading growth thickly cloaked with highly glossy, fine-textured foliage that is ornamental even when the plant is not in bloom. One heavy bloom occurs in June, when the prostrate canes of 'Immensee' foam with masses of small, single, mother-of-pearl blossoms that are blushed with pale pink and ornamented with prominent golden stamens. Small, shiny, dark red hips follow later in the year.

Although its most obvious use is as a groundcover, 'Immensee' also can be trained up a tree or around a pillar.

Class: Shrub
Hardiness: Zones 4–10
Size: 1½' × 6'
Uses: Groundcovers, pillars, wildlife plantings, tree ramblers
Shade: Not tolerant

Flowering: One profuse flowering in June
Bloom Color: White with pink tints
Fragrance: Slight
Black Spot: Not susceptible
Mildew: Not susceptible
Pruning: Remove deadwood

'Lexington'

(Parentage undisclosed) ■ Poulsen, Denmark, 1993

Class: Shrub
Hardiness: Zones 4–10
Size: 2½' × 3'
Uses: Mixed borders, containers, massings
Shade: Not tolerant
Flowering: Continuous

Bloom Color: Soft yellow
Fragrance: Moderately fragrant
Black Spot: Moderately susceptible
Mildew: Slightly susceptible
Pruning: Remove deadwood, winter maintenance

'Lexington', one of the many new Towne & Country series roses introduced by Poulsen of Denmark, bears attractive clusters of small, semidouble, soft yellow flowers that fade to ivory at the edges. The blossoms have a light, fruity scent reminiscent of wild roses, but its exact parentage remains a highly guarded trade secret.

In the mixed border, the soft yellow of 'Lexington' blends nicely with pinks and pale blues but doesn't stand up well to brighter, more saturated colors. A big advantage that 'Lexington' shares with other Towne & Country roses is that it is usually sold on its own roots, which substantially increases its hardiness. Marketing literature claims that it will "grow through" any bouts of disease, but given its yellow color, a preventive regimen against black spot is definitely warranted.

'Max Graf'

(*R. rugosa* × *R. wichuriana*) ■ Bowditch, United States, 1919

Discovered in Connecticut by James Bowditch, 'Max Graf' is a vigorous and completely healthy rose that blooms once, over a period of about 5 weeks, in early summer. Its single flowers have golden stamens and satiny petals of clear bright pink that fade to white just at the center. The foliage is bright green and glossy. 'Max Graf' roots as it spreads to form a beautiful low, layered groundcover.

'Rote Max Graf' ('Red Max Graf') [hybrid kordesii] is similar, except that the flowers are a brilliant scarlet with white at the center, and its new growth is bronzy red before turning bright apple green. Once-flowering like 'Max Graf', it still is valuable because it is the hardiest, healthiest true red groundcover rose available in the United States.

(*Note:* 'Max Graf' is genetically linked to a huge number of healthy modern groundcover and landscape roses by its lone offspring, *R.* × *kordesii*.)

Class: Hybrid rugosa
Hardiness: Zones 4–10
Size: 2' × 8'
Uses: Groundcovers
Shade: Not tolerant
Flowering: Once per year

Bloom Color: Clear pink
Fragrance: Strongly fragrant
Black Spot: Not susceptible
Mildew: Not susceptible
Pruning: Remove deadwood

'Mystic'

(Parentage undisclosed) ▪ Poulsen, Denmark, 1994

AT A GLANCE

Class: Shrub
Hardiness: Zones 4–10
Size: 2½' × 2½'
Uses: Mixed borders, containers, massings
Shade: Not tolerant
Flowering: Continuous

Bloom Color: Salmon pink
Fragrance: Lightly fragrant
Black Spot: Slightly susceptible
Mildew: Slightly susceptible
Pruning: Deadhead, remove deadwood, winter maintenance

'Mystic', one of the earlier Towne & Country introductions, is valued for its cupped, semidouble, salmon pink flowers, which are borne in fairly dense clusters. Like most roses of this series, 'Mystic' is often sold on its own roots (rather than grafted onto another rootstock)—a big advantage because own-root plants are more vigorous and hardy. In addition, the glossy, deep green foliage has good disease resistance for its color class (yellow/orange/salmon).

This rose's extremely compact, bushy growth makes it well suited to growing in containers. 'Mystic' looks especially nice when surrounded by periwinkle-blue 'Blue Gown' dalmatian bellflower (*Campanula portenschlagiana* 'Blue Gown').

'Palmengarten Frankfurt'

(Parentage unknown) ▪ William Kordes Söhne, Germany, 1988

'Palmengarten Frankfurt' wins hearts with its dense clusters of bright pink, fully double flowers produced continuously, all summer long. The flowers fade as they age, adding a subtle but pretty shading to them. Supremely robust and disease-free, 'Palmengarten Frankfurt' has deep green, extremely glossy foliage that appears varnished (the key to its disease resistance). Its graceful, arching habit remains low and tidy over the years.

For best effect in the landscape, allow 'Palmengarten Frankfurt' to drape over the edge of a wall or container, or use it as a groundcover or in a mixed border. Pair it with richly saturated colors, such as the deep blue of 'Sunny Border Blue' veronica (*Veronica* 'Sunny Border Blue'), the lemon yellow of 'Moonbeam' threadleaf coreopsis (*Coreopsis verticillata* 'Moonbeam'), or the brilliant magenta of prairie poppy mallow (*Callirhoe involucrata*). If you garden in Zone 7 or south, this rose is also outstanding when grown as a tree form or standard.

Class: Shrub
Hardiness: Zones 4–10
Size: 2' × 4'
Uses: Mixed borders, containers, groundcovers
Shade: Not tolerant
Flowering: Continuous

Bloom Color: Bright, deep pink
Fragrance: Lightly fragrant
Black Spot: Not susceptible
Mildew: Not susceptible
Pruning: Deadhead, remove deadwood, light winter maintenance

AT A GLANCE

'Paulii'

(*R. arvensis* × *R. rugosa*) ▪ Paul, England, before 1903

Class: Shrub
Hardiness: Zones 4–10
Size: 1½' or 3' (see below) × 10'
Uses: Groundcovers, wildlife plantings
Shade: Tolerant
Flowering: Once per year, in June
Bloom Color: Pure white

Fragrance: Very fragrant
Black Spot: Not susceptible
Mildew: Moderately susceptible
Pruning: Remove deadwood, also needs occasional renewal pruning or mowing after bloom

In June, 'Paulii' blooms with starry, single flowers of pure, crystal white, wafting a sweet, clovelike fragrance. The narrow petals converge on a cluster of bright yellow stamens for a fresh and fragile appearance. A slope covered in 'Paulii' resembles a bed of apple-green foliage covered with a light snow of fallen stars. An abundant crop of dark red hips follows the flowers.

This rose isn't fussy about soil and makes an excellent groundcover, especially for slopes and other difficult sites. With its extremely thorny canes, it would also make an impenetrable barrier planting. (*Note:* Grafted plants of 'Paulii' grow into wide-spreading mounds up to 3 feet tall; on their own roots, the plants grow much closer to the ground and, in true groundcover fashion, root as they go.)

'Pink Bassino'

(Seedling of *R. wichuriana* × 'Robin Redbreast') ▪ William Kordes Söhne, Germany, 1993

'Pink Bassino' is a delightful rose that couples the visual appeal of wild roses with the stalwart rebloom of the best modern roses. In June, 'Pink Bassino' bears dense sprays of single, apple-blossom pink flowers with white centers and prominent golden yellow stamens. It holds its charming, bowl-shaped flowers close to its foliage. After the initial, heavy flush of bloom, flowering repeats continuously (but less abundantly) throughout the summer.

With its upright, wide form and dense growth, 'Pink Bassino' is equally suited to use as a low hedge or in a mixed border. It has the glossy, disease-resistant foliage characteristic of other Kordes roses, and the bronze-red new growth matures to a shiny medium green.

Class: Shrub
Hardiness: Zones 4–10
Size: 2' × 4'
Uses: Mixed borders, groundcovers, low hedges
Shade: Not tolerant
Flowering: Continuous

Bloom Color: Light pink
Fragrance: Lightly fragrant
Black Spot: Not susceptible
Mildew: Not susceptible
Pruning: Deadhead, remove deadwood, winter maintenance

'Paulii'

'Raubritter'

'Raubritter'

('Daisy Hill' × 'Solarium') ▪ William Kordes Söhne, Germany, 1936

No other rose has the same cascading form or lush, globose flowers as 'Raubritter'. Its pure pink blossoms are so cupped that they're almost round. And while the flowers are heavily double, they don't spoil in wet weather. This shrub's arching canes become so thickly cloaked with blossoms that they look as though they're weighted down with the flowers, adding to the plant's sumptuous appeal.

Categorized as both a groundcover and a small climber, 'Raubritter' makes an excellent cascading groundcover for a sloped area, or it can be grown as a graceful, arching shrub. Although its dark, matte, gray-green foliage is susceptible to mildew, the disease usually appears *after* flowering and the plants recover quickly. To reduce the chances of mildew, water 'Raubritter' regularly and deeply.

Class: Shrub
Hardiness: Zones 5–10
Size: 3' × 6'
Uses: Mixed borders, small climbers, cut flowers, groundcovers
Shade: Tolerant
Flowering: One profuse flowering in early summer

Bloom Color: Pure pink
Fragrance: Moderately fragrant
Black Spot: Not susceptible
Mildew: Moderately susceptible
Pruning: Remove deadwood, prune after flowering or not at all

'Rosalina'

('The Fairy' × seedling) ▪ William Kordes Söhne, Germany, 1992

Rated by many large-scale rose producers as one of the most outstanding shrub roses for its health, hardiness, and constant flowering, 'Rosalina' has a spreading but upright form that is thickly cloaked with bright, apple green, wrinkled foliage. Its single, cupped blossoms are bright mauve pink, abruptly fading to white at the base of the petals near the cluster of golden stamens. The individual petals are heart-shaped, adding to this rose's simple charm.

Like all rugosas, 'Rosalina' needs adequate drainage and slightly acid soil, but it is very tolerant of salt, wind, and drought. It makes an outstanding focus of color in a mixed border, a stunning low barrier hedge, and a great continuously flowering groundcover, especially for an exposed or difficult site. To enjoy the showy red hips through fall and winter, stop deadheading in late summer.

Class: Hybrid rugosa
Hardiness: Zones 4–10
Size: 2½' × 4'
Uses: Mixed borders, groundcovers, low hedges
Shade: Not tolerant
Flowering: Continuous

Bloom Color: Mauve pink
Fragrance: Somewhat fragrant
Black Spot: Not susceptible
Mildew: Not susceptible
Pruning: Remove deadwood, light winter maintenance

'Rose de Rescht'

(Parentage unknown) ■ A pre-1840 hybrid with strong Damask leanings, rediscovered in Iran by Nancy Lindsay, United Kingdom, 1940

Class: Damask (Portland)
Hardiness: Zones 4–10
Size: 3' × 2'
Uses: Mixed borders, containers, cut flowers, low hedges, culinary, potpourris
Shade: Tolerant

Flowering: Repeat
Bloom Color: Fuchsia red
Fragrance: Extremely fragrant
Black Spot: Slightly susceptible
Mildew: Not susceptible
Pruning: Deadhead, remove deadwood, light winter maintenance

This excellent rose offers strong rebloom, combined with the good looks and fragrance of old roses. Its fuchsia, pompomlike blossoms have a distinct button eye and open from clusters of fat buds packed with more than 40 petals each. The perfume is sweet and heavy, making 'Rose de Rescht' ideal for use in the kitchen or in potpourri.

Rugged 'Rose de Rescht' has a tidy, upright, bushy habit perfect for planting in a container, where it can add old rose charm to a patio or poolside. If rebloom becomes less strong as the plant gets older (a common trait with this rose), prune back the plant by half after its initial bloom, then feed it generously. Occasionally black spot occurs, but the disease usually isn't severe enough to hurt the plant.

'Rose du Roi'

('Portland Rose' × *R. gallica* var. *officinalis*) ■ Lelieur, France, 1815

'Rose du Roi' ("the king's rose") was originally known as 'Rose Lelieur' but was renamed at the request of Louis XVIII of France. By any name, its flowers *are* fit for a king: The bright mauve-fuchsia blooms are intensely perfumed and, when fully open, reveal a button eye at the center. As with all Portland damasks, the blooms are borne on short stalks and are framed snugly against the foliage.

Compared to its cousin 'Rose de Rescht' [Portland], this rose has lighter green and more pointed leaves and is a bit less tidy in habit. A rugged rose, 'Rose du Roi' flowers heavily in early summer, then repeats throughout the summer and into autumn. Every 3 to 5 years, prune the plants back by half after their first flowering to encourage rebloom.

Class: Portland
Hardiness: Zones 4–10
Size: 3' × 3'
Uses: Mixed borders, cut flowers, low hedges, culinary, potpourri
Shade: Not tolerant
Flowering: Repeat

Bloom Color: Mauve fuchsia
Fragrance: Extremely fragrant
Black Spot: Slightly susceptible
Mildew: Not susceptible
Pruning: Deadhead, remove deadwood, light winter maintenance

'Schneezwerg' (also called 'Snowdwarf')

(R. rugosa × a polyantha rose) ▪ Lambert, Germany, 1912

Class: Hybrid rugosa
Hardiness: Zones 3–10
Size: 3' × 3'
Uses: Mixed borders, containers, low hedges, wildlife plantings
Shade: Tolerant
Flowering: Continuous

Bloom Color: Pure white
Fragrance: Very fragrant
Black Spot: Not susceptible
Mildew: Not susceptible
Pruning: Deadhead until late summer, remove deadwood

'Schneezwerg' is a ruggedly hardy, willing bloomer with medium-size, pure white, double blossoms that open almost flat to reveal a cluster of creamy yellow stamens. It is strongly fragrant and sets generous crops of deep red hips, much loved by birds, throughout the growing season. Cooler autumn temperatures bring this rose into strong rebloom, even when the hips are present.

Because of its plentiful, glossy, dark gray-green foliage, 'Schneezewerg' makes an excellent low hedge. Although it can reach 4 feet tall, expect it to remain at less than 3 feet for several if not many years without pruning. 'Schneezewerg' is easy to root from softwood cuttings and also can be propagated from suckers. Deadheading will increase the frequency of flowering, but for hips through fall and winter, stop removing the faded blossoms toward the end of the season.

'Snow Pavement'

(Parentage unknown) ▪ Baum, Germany, 1984

This worthy rose is one of a series developed by German breeder Karl Baum. A low-growing, spreading shrub that suckers handsomely, 'Snow Pavement' is constantly in bloom from late May until frost, bearing fragrant, semidouble flowers with beautiful golden stamens. Despite its name, the blossoms are not snow white but a very pale lilac pink—the color of whipped cream mixed with a few drops of blackberry juice.

Like the other roses in this series, 'Snow Pavement' is extremely hardy and healthy. Its low, spreading form makes an outstanding groundcover for slopes. ("Pavement" is a German translation for "groundcover.")

Other recommended 'Pavement' roses include: 'Pierette' [hybrid rugosa] (bright mauve-pink blooms); 'Purple' [hybrid rugosa] (deep cerise purple); 'Scarlet' [shrub] (magenta); and 'Showy' [shrub] (bright candy pink).

Class: Hybrid rugosa
Hardiness: Zones 3–10
Size: 2½' × 4'
Uses: Mixed borders, groundcovers, low hedges
Shade: Not tolerant
Flowering: Continuous

Bloom Color: White flushed with palest mauve pink
Fragrance: Very fragrant
Black Spot: Not susceptible
Mildew: Not susceptible
Pruning: Winter maintenance

'The Fairy'

('Paul Crampel' × 'Lady Gay') ■ Bentall, United Kingdom, 1932

Class: Polyantha
Hardiness: Zones 5–10
Size: 2' × 4'
Uses: Mixed borders, containers, cut flowers, groundcovers, low hedges
Shade: Tolerant

Flowering: Continuous
Bloom Color: Medium pink
Fragrance: None
Black Spot: Slightly susceptible
Mildew: Slightly susceptible
Pruning: Deadhead, remove deadwood, winter maintenance

'The Fairy' is enjoying a much-deserved renaissance after languishing for decades in the shadow of modern floribunda roses. This hard-blooming little rose bears profuse clusters of small, fully double, sweet pink blossoms from early June until frost. Unfortunately, the flowers aren't at all fragrant, but this is an advantage if Japanese beetles plague your area. The cut flowers make a delightful addition to bouquets of perennials and other roses.

A versatile landscape plant, 'The Fairy' is equally well suited to use as a hedge or groundcover, or as a stunning addition to a mixed border. For a very romantic-looking accent on a deck or poolside, grow a single plant in a whitewashed pot.

Although 'The Fairy' tolerates partial shade, it's much healthier in full sun. Don't be afraid to prune out some of the weakest growth to open up the interior of the plant and encourage stronger blooming.

'Topaz Jewel' (also called 'Yellow Dagmar Hastrup')

('Golden Angel' × 'Belle Poitevine') ■ Moore, United States, 1987

One of the only moderately hardy, repeat-blooming yellow roses in this size group, 'Topaz Jewel' has loosely double flowers that are a pleasing bright primrose yellow. When fully open, the flowers reveal golden stamens at their centers. The semiglossy foliage of 'Topaz Jewel' is reddish as it unfolds.

Don't be lulled into a false sense of security, however, just because this rose has one rugosa parent. Its foliage is smooth—not wrinkled, like that of typical rugosas—and so it is much more prone to black spot. You'll definitely need to practice black spot prevention, and perhaps treatment, to keep it looking good. Also keep in mind that 'Topaz Jewel' is viciously thorny, so be sure to wear thick gloves when pruning it.

Class: Hybrid rugosa
Hardiness: Zones 5–10
Size: 3' × 3'
Uses: Mixed borders
Shade: Not tolerant
Flowering: Continuous
Bloom Color: Primrose yellow

Fragrance: Moderately fragrant
Black Spot: Moderately susceptible
Mildew: Not susceptible
Pruning: Deadhead, remove deadwood, winter maintenance

'Tumbling Waters'

(Parentage undisclosed) ▪ Poulsen, Denmark, 1998

Class: Shrub
Hardiness: Zones 4–10
Size: 2' × 3'
Uses: Containers, groundcovers
Shade: Not tolerant
Flowering: Continuous
Bloom Color: Pure white
Fragrance: Strongly fragrant

Black Spot: Not susceptible
Mildew: Not susceptible
Pruning: Remove deadwood, occasionally use hedge clippers to remove spent flower heads and 25 to 30 percent of the terminal growth to renew

One of the most charming of the new Towne & Country landscape roses, 'Tumbling Waters' has dense clusters of fragrant, snow white, semidouble flowers with visible golden stamens. While many white roses are actually ivory or blushed with pink, this one is pure white, creating a crisp, refreshing look in the garden. Deeply fringed calyces (the leaflets that enclose the buds) add to the charm of the blossoms, setting them off against a background of green lace.

'Tumbling Waters' has an arching habit that looks especially pretty cascading over a retaining wall. Like many low-growing groundcover roses, this one can be renewed with pruning in late winter about every third year. Use hedge clippers or a weed eater with a metal blade, then rake out the clippings.

'White Pet' (also called 'Little White Pet')

('Felicité Perpetue' sport) ▪ Henderson, United States, 1879

'White Pet' deserves to be more widely grown. Although it functions and looks like a dwarf polyantha, it is actually a sport (or branch mutation) of the even less well known *R. sempervirens* 'Felicite Perpetue', or evergreen rose. From early summer to frost, 'White Pet' bears clusters of pink buds that open into double, ivory-white flowers flushed with pink. The pompon-shaped blossoms have scalloped petals, giving the spreading shrub a dainty, old-fashioned appearance.

As a groundcover, 'White Pet' provides an elegant alternative to the somewhat overplanted 'The Fairy'. It looks especially pretty when planted near the little white blossoms of willowy white gaura (*Gaura lindheimeri*).

The dark green foliage of 'White Pet' persists late into the year and is disease resistant. Thin the interior of the dense, twiggy shrubs occasionally.

Class: Polyantha
Hardiness: Zones 5–10
Size: 2' × 2½'
Uses: Beddings, mixed borders, containers, groundcovers, low hedges
Shade: Tolerant

Flowering: Continuous
Bloom Color: White-tinged pink
Fragrance: Barely perceptible
Black Spot: Slightly susceptible
Mildew: Slightly susceptible
Pruning: Deadhead, remove deadwood, winter maintenance

Recommended Medium Shrubs

Medium shrub roses range in height from 3 to 5 feet and vary in form and character. Choose from these roses when you require a rose of substantial but not overwhelming height.

'AC Marie-Victorin'

('Arthur Bell' × [*R. kordesii* × 'Max Graf' O.P.]) ▪ L'Assomption, Canada, 1999

Semidouble with 38 petals, this rose has peach-color buds that open to apricot pink, then fade to pink. Clusters of shiny, orange-red hips follow the flowers.

    'AC Marie-Victorin' is remarkably resistant to disease, considering its peachy color (a trait almost always linked to black spot). The foliage is medium dense, dark green, and glossy, turning warm gold to red in autumn.

Class: Hybrid kordesii
Hardiness: Zones 3–10
Size: 5' × 4'
Uses: Mixed borders, wildlife plantings
Shade: Not tolerant
Flowering: Continuous

Bloom Color: Peach to pink
Fragrance: Lightly fragrant
Black Spot: Not susceptible
Mildew: Not susceptible
Pruning: Deadhead, remove deadwood, winter maintenance

AT A GLANCE

'Alfred de Dalmas' (also called 'Mousseline')

(Parentage unknown) ▪ Portemer, France, 1855

'Alfred de Dalmas' couples all the romance of the old roses with strong rebloom from June through October. Its refined, lightly double blossoms are a creamy mother-of-pearl pink with peachy undertones. When fully open, the cupped flowers reveal sunny yellow stamens. Pink-tinted "mossed" buds give it an incomparably old-fashioned—almost lacy—look.

    'Alfred de Dalmas' is not very thorny, and its tidy canes are well covered with lush, medium green foliage. In the perennial garden, 'Alfred de Dalmas' is complemented beautifully by a foreground of 'Nana Alba' lavender (*Lavandula angustifolia* 'Nana Alba') and a backdrop of milky bellflower (*Campanula lactiflora*).

AT A GLANCE

Class: Moss
Hardiness: Zones 4–10
Size: 3' × 2'
Uses: Mixed borders, containers, cut flowers
Shade: Tolerant
Flowering: Continuous

Bloom Color: Blush pink
Fragrance: Very fragrant
Black Spot: Slightly susceptible
Mildew: Not susceptible
Pruning: Deadhead, remove deadwood

'Alfred de Dalmas'

'Ballerina'

'Autumn Damask'
(also called 'Rose des Quatres Saisons')

(Parentage unknown) ■ Middle East, Ancient

AT A GLANCE

Class: Damask
Hardiness: Zones 4–10
Size: 4' × 3'
Uses: Mixed borders, cut flowers, hedges, culinary, potpourris
Shade: Not shade tolerant
Flowering: Repeats

Bloom Color: Clear pink
Fragrance: Extremely fragrant
Black Spot: Slightly susceptible
Mildew: Slightly susceptible
Pruning: Deadhead, remove deadwood, prune after flowering

Before the introduction of China roses to Europe, 'Autumn Damask' was the only repeat-flowering rose. Its blooms are the very definition of rose pink, with a wonderful, clear tone devoid of lavender. The buds open from lacy calyxes to fully double blossoms of up to 40 petals each, sometimes showing a glimpse of stamens within. Its fragrance is one of the most intense of all roses.

This rose's growth habit is a bit sprawling and uneven, but charming nevertheless. The downy, gray-green foliage is a bit more disease-prone than other damasks, but the plant's overall vigor is rarely affected (as you might expect from a rose that's been cultivated since before the Roman Empire). Don't let the ancient character of 'Autumn Damask' limit the way you use it in your garden. It looks just as wonderful with ornamental grasses as it does in a traditional mixed border or a cottage garden.

'Ballerina'

(Parentage unknown) ■ Bentall, United Kingdom, 1937

An outstanding rose, 'Ballerina' bears clouds of single pink flowers in huge sprays from June until frost. The slightly cupped flowers are a bit more than an inch across and a clear medium pink with striking white centers and golden yellow stamens. Its bright, medium green foliage has good disease resistance.

Versatile 'Ballerina' makes a stunning floral hedge, as well as a refined, constantly blooming container specimen. Like all hybrid musks, it can take the heat of the South very well. To sustain its prodigious bloom, feed and water it regularly. If you need to control its size, cut it back hard right after its first flush of bloom.

Class: Hybrid musk
Hardiness: Zones 4–10
Size: 4' × 3'
Uses: Mixed borders, containers, hedges, massings
Shade: Tolerant
Flowering: Continuous

Bloom Color: Medium pink/white
Fragrance: Slightly fragrant
Black Spot: Not susceptible
Mildew: Not susceptible
Pruning: Deadhead, remove deadwood, winter maintenance

AT A GLANCE

'Belle de Crécy'

(Parentage unknown) ▪ Hardy, France, 1829

A classic gallica, 'Belle de Crécy' has very double (40 petals each) flowers of a deep, rich cerise shadowed with violet, which fade through slate and lilac as they age. When fully open, the cupped and quartered blossoms often reflex to show a button eye with a little bundle of stamens. The fragrance is sweet and intoxicating. In very rainy weather, the flowers may fail to open. If this happens, just tease open the buds with your fingers.

Like most gallicas, 'Belle de Crécy' has slim canes and few thorns. And like the rest of its tribe, it is prone to mildew, so be sure to keep it evenly watered and avoid planting it in the shade or in areas with poor air circulation. Since this rose flowers just once per season, prune it, if necessary, right after it has finished blooming. If you need to control its suckering growth, remove the weakest shoots.

AT A GLANCE

Class: Hybrid gallica
Hardiness: Zones 3–10
Size: 4' × 3'
Uses: Mixed borders, cut flowers, culinary, potpourris
Shade: Not tolerant
Flowering: Once per season

Bloom Color: Deep cerise/purple
Fragrance: Extremely fragrant
Black Spot: Not susceptible
Mildew: Moderately susceptible
Pruning: Remove deadwood, prune lightly after flowering

'Belle Story'

(['Chaucer' × 'Parade'] × ['The Prioress' × 'Iceberg']) ▪ Austin, United Kingdom, 1984

One of the earlier David Austin introductions, this English rose has semidouble, chalice-shaped blooms that open to reveal reddish gold stamens. The extremely large flowers have good substance and are a luminous peachy, shell pink. They have a spicy fragrance (known as "myrrh," in the rose world) that not everyone finds pleasant.

With its open, almost leggy form, 'Belle Story' looks best in a mixed border, with perennials in front of it. Its peachy color complements just about every color, except mauve pink.

The medium green, pointed leaves are moderately susceptible to mildew, so keep this rose evenly watered. It's also quite susceptible to rust, so avoid planting it at all if rust is a problem in your area.

AT A GLANCE

Class: Shrub
Hardiness: Zones 5–10
Size: 4' × 4'
Uses: Mixed borders, cut flowers
Shade: Not tolerant
Flowering: Continuous

Bloom Color: Peachy shell pink
Fragrance: Very fragrant
Black Spot: Slightly susceptible
Mildew: Moderately susceptible
Pruning: Deadhead, remove deadwood, winter maintenance

'Belle Story'

'Camaieux'

(Parentage unknown) ▪ Vibert, France, 1830

Class: Hybrid gallica
Hardiness: Zones 4–10
Size: 3' × 3'
Uses: Mixed borders, containers, cut flowers, low hedges, culinary, potpourris
Shade: Not tolerant
Flowering: Once per season

Bloom Color: Light pink streaked with dark mauve
Fragrance: Extremely fragrant
Black Spot: Not susceptible
Mildew: Not susceptible
Pruning: Remove deadwood, light winter maintenance

'Camaieux' (which in French means "like a painting executed in variations of a single color") is one of the most distinctive roses you can grow. True to its name, the blossoms are clear light pink, delicately streaked with darker shades of candy pink and mauve. The very large, full flowers (more than 40 petals each) have a charmingly irregular form and a heady, intense fragrance. Adding to its character, the edges of the petals are often serrated, making them appear frilly.

'Camaieux' grows quickly into a handsome arching shrub, thickly cloaked with foliage and almost thornless. Surround this outstanding rose with perennials that bloom either earlier or later than it does—you'll want to view its striking flowers without any distractions nearby.

'Cardinal de Richelieu'
(also called 'Cardinal Richelieu' and 'Rose van Sian')

(Parentage unknown) ▪ Laffay, France, 1840

Gallicas are known for their rich colors, but this rose displays some of the most sumptuous hues of all. Its perfectly round buds open into very double flowers of violet purple, with a surprising white eye at the center. As they age, the blooms become more violet and, finally, tinged with slate gray. The flowers, which are borne in profusion, are breathtaking in fresh bouquets and excellent for drying.

In the garden, pair 'Cardinal de Richelieu' with soft golds, such as mulleins (*Verbascum* spp.) and yarrows (*Achillea* spp.). In Zone 8 and southward, it will tolerate light shade. Remove the weakest canes at ground level in late winter. Do all other pruning immediately after flowering has finished to allow next year's buds to form unimpeded.

Class: Hybrid gallica
Hardiness: Zones 4–10
Size: 4' × 3'
Uses: Mixed borders, cut flowers, culinary, potpourris
Shade: Not tolerant (except in Zones 8–10)

Flowering: Once per season
Bloom Color: Purple with white centers
Fragrance: Very fragrant
Black Spot: Not susceptible
Mildew: Slightly susceptible
Pruning: Remove deadwood, winter maintenance

'Charles de Mills'

(Parentage unknown) ▪ Old cultivar

Class: Hybrid gallica
Hardiness: Zones 4–10
Size: 4' × 4'
Uses: Mixed borders, cut flowers, culinary, potpourris
Shade: Not tolerant
Flowering: Once per season

Bloom Color: Deep carmine purple
Fragrance: Extremely fragrant
Black Spot: Not susceptible
Mildew: Slightly susceptible
Pruning: Remove deadwood

A very old rose of obscure origin, 'Charles de Mills' was grown by Empress Josephine at her palace at Malmaison. Often described as the best of the gallicas, this rose has heavily double flowers with more than 40 petals each. The color is a deep, rich carmine shaded with purple and violet. When fully open, the large flowers are flat and quartered with petals reflexed to reveal a green button eye. The fragrance is heavy, sweet, and complex, making this rose wonderful for culinary uses.

'Charles de Mills' is a vigorous grower and less prone to mildew than many gallicas. Its deep green, matte foliage and carmine blooms look stunning with silver-leaved plants such as 'Berggarten' common sage (*Salvia officinalis* 'Berggarten') and strong blue violets such as bellflower (*Campanula latifolia* var. *macrantha*). Remove its weakest canes at ground level in late winter; do any other pruning immediately after flowering.

'Danaë'

('Trier' × 'Gloire de Chédane-Guinoisseau') ▪ Pemberton, United Kingdom, 1913

'Danaë' is one of the healthiest repeat-blooming yellow roses available. It bears generous sprays of small, semidouble, egg-yolk yellow flowers that fade to buff yellow and finally to creamy white before wilting. Sprays of 'Danaë' make charming additions to rose bouquets—their delicate look and light fragrance help balance the heaviness of other blossoms.

The canes are generously covered with glossy, apple green, narrow leaves, making the plants well suited to mixing with other shrubs and perennials in borders. In warm climates it grows taller and can be used as a small climber. Deadhead it regularly to encourage rebloom.

Class: Hybrid musk
Hardiness: Zones 5–10
Size: 4' × 4'
Uses: Mixed borders, cut flowers, massings
Shade: Tolerant
Flowering: Continuous

Bloom Color: Medium yellow
Fragrance: Lightly fragrant
Black Spot: Slightly susceptible
Mildew: Not susceptible
Pruning: Deadhead, remove deadwood, winter maintenance

'Delicata'

(Parentage unknown) ▪ Cooling, United States, 1898

This obscure rugosa deserves to be planted more often. Its large, semidouble, rosy pink blossoms are sweetly fragrant and have tissue-paper–like petals that are loosely arranged around sunny yellow stamens. Tomato-red hips follow the blossoms and often appear simultaneously with them.

'Delicata' is a bushy plant thickly covered with shiny, crinkled, medium green leaves that turn rich gold, orange, and even wine-color in fall. It seems more tolerant of dampness than most rugosas, but it will do even better in well-drained, slightly acid soil and full sun (the preferred site for rugosas). (*Note:* 'Delicata' was one of the first roses I grew, and it thrived despite my inexperienced hand and unimproved, heavy clay soil.)

Class: Hybrid rugosa
Hardiness: Zones 3–10
Size: 3' × 3'
Uses: Mixed borders, low hedges, wildlife plantings
Shade: Tolerant

Flowering: Repeat
Bloom Color: Clear pink
Fragrance: Very fragrant
Black Spot: Not susceptible
Mildew: Not susceptible
Pruning: Remove deadwood

'Felicia'

('Trier' × 'Ophelia') ▪ Pemberton, United Kingdom, 1928

Many authorities consider 'Felicia' the very best of Pemberton's hybrid musk roses. I have found it to be one of the healthiest peachy-pink roses available. The very shapely, fully double blossoms are medium pink through salmon in color, and they fade to near white just before wilting. 'Felicia' bears its largest and most intensely colored blossoms during the cool days of autumn. If you don't deadhead, you'll get sprays of big red hips (but fewer repeat flowers).

'Felicia' has plentiful, shiny, medium green foliage. Like most hybrid musks, it thrives on pruning and will reward you with more vigor and flowers. In addition to shaping the plants in late winter, cut them back by a quarter right after flowering, then feed them generously. Shapely 'Felicia' can be used as a specimen or in a mixed border, where it pairs nicely with lavender blue, such as 'Souvenir d'Andre Chaudon' catmint (*Nepeta* 'Souvenir d'André Chaudon').

Class: Hybrid musk
Hardiness: Zones 5–10
Size: 4' × 4'
Uses: Mixed borders, containers, cut flowers, hedges, specimens
Shade: Not shade tolerant
Flowering: Continuous

Bloom Color: Medium to salmon pink
Fragrance: Moderately fragrant
Black Spot: Slightly susceptible
Mildew: Not susceptible
Pruning: Deadhead, remove deadwood, winter maintenance

'Felicia'

'Félicité Parmentier'

(Parentage unknown) ▪ Parmentier, France, 1835

Class: Alba
Hardiness: Zones 3–10
Size: 4' × 3'
Uses: Mixed borders, cut flowers, hedges, culinary, potpourris
Shade: Tolerant
Flowering: Once per season

Bloom Color: Creamy, pale pink
Fragrance: Extremely fragrant
Black Spot: Not susceptible
Mildew: Not susceptible
Pruning: Remove deadwood, prune after bloom

This lovely, romantic-looking rose bears small clusters of very double, pale pink flowers with more than 40 tightly swirled petals that reflex to form a perfect rosette. The layered arrangement of the petals makes this rose's flowers among the best for drying. Its distinctive fragrance—lemony, intense, and sweet—is one of the most powerful of all roses.

'Félicité Parmentier' is tidy, narrow, and upright in form, making it a good candidate for tight spots in the landscape. With its healthy, dark, gray-green foliage, it looks pretty even when not in bloom. The plants need little pruning; do any that's necessary right after it flowers so that you don't remove next year's flower buds.

'Ferdinand Pichard'

(Parentage unknown) ▪ Tanne, France, 1921

'Ferdinand Pichard' is one of the few hybrid perpetual roses that is both beautiful and robust. For an old rose, it has very large flowers—often nearly 4 inches across. The cupped, double blossoms are white or blush pink striped with deep fuchsia, softened by speckles and striations. As the blossoms age, the pink portions assume soft purple tones, while the white often turns pale pink. The flowers have a rich, fruity fragrance that is like a blend of rose and raspberry.

A vigorous, bushy shrub, this rose has pointed, soft gray-green foliage that is easy to recognize even when the plant is not in flower. Pegging (tying down) the canes will almost double the blooms. To encourage rebloom, deadhead promptly and feed regularly. In Zones 7 and southward, give 'Ferdinand Pichard' partial shade.

Class: Hybrid perpetual
Hardiness: Zones 5–10
Size: 5' × 4'
Uses: Mixed borders, cut flowers, specimens
Shade: Tolerant
Flowering: Repeat

Bloom Color: White or light pink, striped with deep fuchsia
Fragrance: Extremely fragrant
Black Spot: Somewhat susceptible
Mildew: Not susceptible
Pruning: Deadhead, remove deadwood, winter maintenance

'Fimbriata'

(*R. rugosa* × 'Mme. Alfred Carriére') ■ Morlet, France, 1891

Class: Hybrid rugosa
Hardiness: Zones 3–10
Size: 4' × 4'
Uses: Hedges, mixed borders, cut flowers
Shade: Tolerant
Flowering: Repeats

Bloom Color: White with pink blush
Fragrance: Very fragrant
Black Spot: Not susceptible
Mildew: Not susceptible
Pruning: Deadhead, remove deadwood

Resembling dianthus in form, the white, semidouble blossoms of 'Fimbriata' have shaggy, narrow petals with fringed ends—just like garden pinks. The plant is bushy and thickly covered, right to the ground, with bright, apple green rugose (crinkled) leaves.

'Fimbriata' is a strong rebloomer, but deadheading will encourage even stronger rebloom. (For hips through fall and winter, stop deadheading near the end of the season.) The only other pruning you'll need to do is to remove deadwood. The casual, old-fashioned look of 'Fimbriata' is perfect for cottage gardens. Pair it with other cottage-garden favorites like hollyhocks, bellflowers, and, of course, dianthus.

'Frau Dagmar Hartopp'
(also called 'Frau Dagmar Hastrup' and 'Fru Dagmar Hastrup')

(*R. rugosa* seedling of unknown parentage) ■ Hastrup, Denmark, 1914

This rose is popular around the world by any name. The single flowers seem almost oversize for the small plant, resembling gigantic apple blossoms. The luminous light pink petals are wavy and have a distinctive, sweet and spicy fragrance reminiscent of cloves. Enormous, tomato red hips—excellent for tea, jam, and cut arrangements—follow the flowers.

This rose's naturally rounded, bushy form needs absolutely no pruning, other than the removal of deadwood. Like all true rugosas, 'Frau Dagmar Hartopp' is drought-, salt-, and wind-tolerant, and it prefers a slightly acid soil. In fall, 'Frau Dagmar Hartopp' mounts an outstanding show of foliage color, with orange, yellow, and deep purple tones often melding on the same bush. It's not unusual to see it in full autumn color, laden with hips, and still flowering!

Class: Hybrid rugosa
Hardiness: Zones 3–10
Size: 3' × 3'
Uses: Mixed borders, low hedges, naturalizing, wildlife plantings
Shade: Not tolerant

Flowering: Continuous
Bloom Color: Pale silvery pink
Fragrance: Very fragrant
Black Spot: Not susceptible
Mildew: Not susceptible
Pruning: Remove deadwood

'Frau Karl Druschki'
(also called 'F. K. Druschki', 'Reine des Nieges', 'Snedronningen', 'Snow Queen', and 'White American Beauty')

('Merveille de Lyon' × 'Mme. Caroline Testout') ■ Lambert, Germany, 1901

Class: Hybrid perpetual
Hardiness: Zones 4–10
Size: 5' × 3'
Uses: Mixed borders, cut flowers, specimens
Shade: Not tolerant
Flowering: Continuous

Bloom Color: Pure white
Fragrance: None
Black Spot: Slightly susceptible
Mildew: Not susceptible
Pruning: Deadhead, remove deadwood, winter maintenance

The most popular white rose during the first half of the 20th century, 'Frau Karl Druschki' has elegant, high-centered buds that open into very large, globose, cupped flowers. Its very pure white blossoms are among the elite white roses that show no trace of pink, yellow, or cream. The foliage is glossy, leathery, and dark green, and its thorns are substantial.

My main reservation about this shrub—other than its lack of fragrance—is its stiff demeanor: It always looks as though it's standing rigidly at attention. But the beauty and size of the flowers, coupled with the extreme hardiness and disease-resistance of the plant, make up for its faults. Plant this rose with some white butterfly bush (*Buddleia davidii*) and white gaura (*Gaura lindheimeri*) to soften its rigid line.

'Frontenac'

(Hybrid tea line × *R. kordesii* line) ■ Ogilvie, Canada, 1992

'Frontenac' is typical of the more recent efforts of the Canadian Agricultural Experiment Station to breed hardy, healthy roses that offer a different look from their earlier rugosas. Although it may not be overwhelming in its beauty, it is attractive and almost always in flower. The semidouble, bright, medium pink flowers open flat to reveal yellow stamens. The blossoms are borne in dense clusters, literally covering the plant with flowers during its June bloom period. Rebloom is strong and constant, if not heavy.

The bushy plant is well covered with bright, medium green foliage, and it needs little pruning other than to remove deadwood. 'Frontenac' roots easily from softwood cuttings.

Class: Shrub
Hardiness: Zones 3–10
Size: 3½' × 3½'
Uses: Mixed borders, hedges
Shade: Not tolerant
Flowering: Continuous

Bloom Color: Medium pink
Fragrance: Slightly fragrant
Black Spot: Slightly susceptible
Mildew: Slightly susceptible
Pruning: Deadhead, remove deadwood, winter maintenance

'Frau Karl Druschki'

'Henry Hudson'

('Schneezwerg' seedling) ▪ Svejda, Canada, 1976

Class: Hybrid rugosa
Hardiness: Zones 3–10
Size: 4' × 4'
Uses: Mixed borders, low hedges
Shade: Not tolerant
Flowering: Continuous

Bloom Color: White
Fragrance: Very fragrant
Black Spot: Not susceptible
Mildew: Not susceptible
Pruning: Deadhead, remove
   deadwood

This early introduction from the Canadian Explorer series has stood the test of time. 'Henry Hudson' has fat, rounded pink buds that open into flat, scalloped, white blossoms that show a tuft of golden stamens. Cooler weather often gives the flowers a pink blush. The fragrance is pronounced and spicy, redolent of cloves. Unfortunately, this rose neither bears hips nor drops its petals cleanly after wilting. Regular deadheading makes it more attractive and promotes quicker and stronger rebloom.

'Henry Hudson' is thickly covered with apple green, deeply crinkled, rough leaves that resist fungus superbly. It is an ideal hedge plant, with a compact, rounded form that needs no pruning. (Don't mix it with other rugosas in a hedgerow, though—its distinctive form doesn't blend well with other varieties.) This rose is also lovely in a mixed border, especially with willowy plants such as ornamental grasses.

'Hunter' (also called 'The Hunter')

(*R. rugosa rubra* × 'Independence') ▪ Mattock, United Kingdom, 1961

Although many rosarians write off this rose, I consider it one of the best red roses for organic gardeners. While most truly red roses are notoriously susceptible to black spot, 'Hunter' shrugs off this disease and is hardy as nails to boot. Its big, fully double flowers are deep crimson, well formed, and modestly fragrant. They completely cover the shrub in June and again in early fall, with a continuous smattering of blossoms between these two main bloom periods.

'Hunter' is covered with shiny, medium green, slightly narrow leaves, and it has a bushy, compact habit that requires little to no pruning. I've planted this rose in a narrow strip of soil between a sidewalk and street where it receives no spraying, little attention, and brutal heat. Even in this tough spot, it continues to bloom magnificently every year, eliciting unceasing admiration from passersby.

(*Note:* Photo not available)

Class: Hybrid rugosa
Hardiness: Zones 4–10
Size: 4' × 3'
Uses: Mixed borders, containers, hedges
Shade: Tolerant
Flowering: Continuous

Bloom Color: Crimson
Fragrance: Lightly fragrant
Black Spot: Slightly susceptible
Mildew: Not susceptible
Pruning: Deadhead, remove deadwood,
   winter maintenance

'J. P. Connell'

('Arthur Bell' × 'Von Scharnhorst') ▪ Svejda, Canada, 1987

AT A GLANCE

Class: Shrub
Hardiness: Zones 3–10
Size: 4' × 4'
Uses: Mixed borders, cut flowers
Shade: Not tolerant
Flowering: Repeats
Bloom Color: Yellow

Fragrance: Lightly fragrant
Black Spot: Moderately susceptible
Mildew: Not susceptible
Pruning: Deadhead, remove deadwood, winter maintenance

Bred in Canada, 'J. P. Connell' is a fairly hardy yellow rose that suffers winter dieback only in Zones 3 and 4. Its high-centered buds open into lightly fragrant, lemon yellow, double blossoms that fade almost to white. This rose's intial pale coloring tends to become more intense as the plant becomes established.

Unfortunately, this rose is slow to establish and carries the susceptibility to black spot characteristic of so many yellow roses (though not to the degree of many hybrid teas and floribundas). To minimize problems, put it on a black spot prevention regime.

'Jacques Cartier'

(Parentage unknown) ▪ Moreau-Robert, France, 1868

This delightful rose, sometimes classed as a hybrid perpetual, has very double flowers of a deep, clear pink, fading to lighter pink at the margins. The petals are recurved and lightly quartered and have a pleasingly uneven look reminiscent of a peony flower. Their fragrance is richly sweet.

'Jacques Cartier' is rugged, easy-to-grow, and much more disease resistant than the better known

'Comte de Chambord' [Portland]. It repeats vigorously, especially if it is dead-headed and pruned right after the first flush of bloom. Because it tolerates heat well, it is one of the best repeat-flowering old roses for the South. With its tidy, upright habit, 'Jacques Cartier' makes an excellent hedge.

(*Note:* While 'Jacques Cartier' is widely used today, the American Rose Society has determined that the original and correct name of this cultivar is 'Marquise Bocella', a hybrid perpetual raised by Desprez in 1842.)

Class: Portland
Hardiness: Zones 4–10
Size: 3' × 2'
Uses: Mixed borders, cut flowers
Shade: Tolerant
Flowering: Continuous

Bloom Color: Clear pink
Fragrance: Extremely fragrant
Black Spot: Slightly susceptible
Mildew: Not susceptible
Pruning: Deadhead, remove deadwood, winter maintenance

AT A GLANCE

'Jens Munk'

('Schneezwerg' × 'Frau Dagmar Hartopp') ▪ Svejda, Canada, 1974

AT A GLANCE

Class: Hybrid rugosa
Hardiness: Zones 2–10
Size: 5' × 3'
Uses: Mixed borders, hedges, wildlife plantings
Shade: Not tolerant
Flowering: Continuous

Bloom Color: Clear lavender pink
Fragrance: Very fragrant
Black Spot: Not susceptible
Mildew: Not susceptible
Pruning: Remove deadwood

One of the earliest introductions from the Explorer series, 'Jens Munk' represents some of Dr. Svejda's finest work with rugosas. The large, lavender-pink flowers are delightfully fragrant, and the pretty, wavy petals drop cleanly to form large, tomato red hips.

Stalwart 'Jens Munk' is heavily cloaked in small, bright green, extremely crinkled leaves that appear to be immune to disease. It is hardy in the most severe climates and, like all rugosas, is wind-, salt-, and drought-resistant, too. With a compact and tidy habit, 'Jens Munk' is an extraordinary hedge plant, but it looks just as lovely toward the back of a mixed border. Its extreme thorniness also makes it well suited for use as a barrier plant or bird shelter. For a colorful combination in a dry, windy spot, combine it with spreading junipers.

'Léda'

(Parentage unknown) ▪ Early 1800s

This very old rose has unique coloring, which explains its alternate name, 'Painted Damask'. The very double flowers are white (blushed pink in cool weather) with a thin edge of crimson. The central petals reflex to form a very pronounced button eye, while the remaining petals seem to frame the entire blossom in crimson. The blossoms have the rich, attar-of-rose fragrance characteristic of this group.

Ordinarily, 'Léda' is a tidy shrub that grows about as wide as it is tall; in rich soil, however, it can become arching and exuberant. The foliage is typical damask: downy, gray green, and disease-resistant. If cut back fairly hard after flowering and fed generously, 'Léda' sometimes will rebloom, with the second crop of flowers arriving in autumn. Pair 'Léda' with crimson-flowered perennials such as rose campion (*Lychnis coronaria*) and knautia (*Knautia macedonica*) to echo the edges of its petals.

Class: Damask
Hardiness: Zones 4–10
Size: 3' × 4'
Uses: Mixed borders, containers, cut flowers, hedges, specimens, culinary, potpourris
Shade: Not tolerant
Flowering: Once-flowering; can repeat in autumn

Bloom Color: Pale pink to white edged in crimson
Fragrance: Extremely fragrant
Black Spot: Not susceptible
Mildew: Not susceptible
Pruning: Remove deadwood, prune after flowering

AT A GLANCE

'Jens Munk'

'Louise Odier'

(Seedling of 'Emile Courtier') ▪ Margottin, France, 1851

AT A GLANCE

Class: Bourbon
Hardiness: Zones 5–10
Size: 5' × 4'
Uses: Mixed borders, small climbers, specimens
Shade: Tolerant
Flowering: Continuous

Bloom Color: Rose pink
Fragrance: Extremely fragrant
Black Spot: Somewhat susceptible
Mildew: Not susceptible
Pruning: Deadhead, remove deadwood, winter maintenance

This regal rose personifies old rose elegance. Its deeply cupped, rose pink blossoms resemble fully double camellias in structure. The outer petals reflex back, the middle petals are neatly layered, and the innermost petals are swirled and quartered. Borne on long stems, the highly fragrant flowers are superb for cutting.

The canes of the arching shrub have a few maroon-color thorns and are lightly covered with soft, almost olive green foliage. To minimize black spot, practice preventive measures, including good sanitation and careful watering. 'Louise Odier' is a fabulous addition to the mixed border, where its richly saturated pink mingles well with strong blues and violets, as well as clear yellow. Try it with 'Sunny Border Blue' veronica (*Veronica* 'Sunny Border Blue'), catmint (*Nepeta subsessilis*), and Ozark sundrops (*Oenothera macrocarpa*).

'Moje Hammarberg'

(Parentage unknown) ▪ Hammarberg, Sweden, 1931

'Moje Hammarberg' is, in my opinion, one of the all-time great roses—I can't figure out why it isn't better known. The richly fragrant blooms are an intense mauve fuchsia to purple, opening from clusters of scrolled, pointed buds to fully double blossoms that nod slightly on their thin, short stems. These are followed by enormous orange-red hips the size of cherry tomatoes—the biggest hips on any rugosa.

This rugosa's habit—compact and stocky—is equally attractive and never seems to need pruning. Deeply crinkled, bright green foliage cloaks the canes to the ground and turns a soft gold in autumn. 'Moje Hammarberg' is excellent either in a mixed border or as a large-scale groundcover, and it looks positively stunning with golden yellows such as 'Summer Sun' false sunflower (*Heliopsis helianthoides* 'Summer Sun').

Class: Hybrid rugosa
Hardiness: Zones 3–10
Size: 4' × 4'
Uses: Mixed borders, groundcovers, low hedges, wildlife plantings
Shade: Tolerant

Flowering: Continuous
Bloom Color: Mauve fuchsia to purple
Fragrance: Very fragrant
Black Spot: Not susceptible
Mildew: Not susceptible
Pruning: Remove deadwood

AT A GLANCE

'Nur Mahal'

('Château de Clos Vougeot' × hybrid musk seedling) ■ Pemberton, United Kingdom, 1923

Class: Hybrid musk
Hardiness: Zones 5–10
Size: 5' × 4'
Uses: Mixed borders, cut flowers, hedges, specimens
Shade: Tolerant
Flowering: Continuous

Bloom Color: Carmine rose
Fragrance: Lightly fragrant
Black Spot: Not susceptible
Mildew: Not susceptible
Pruning: Deadhead, remove deadwood, winter maintenance

A virtually unknown hybrid musk, this healthy rose bears generous sprays of exquisite flowers on strong stems from summer until frost. The semidouble blossoms are a bright carmine-rose pink that is never gaudy. Looking like a layered petticoat, the distinctive, wavy petals cup around the soft golden stamens, as though covering them in modesty. The fragrance is a characteristic fruity musk. ('Nur Mahal' was named for the wife of an Indian emperor who, according to legend, discovered how to make attar of roses.)

The foliage of 'Nur Mahal' is glossy, dark green, and extraordinarily disease-free. Feed this rose regularly to keep the blooms coming. Due to its heat tolerance, it is a good rose for the South.

'Penelope'

('Ophelia' × 'Trier') ■ Pemberton, United Kingdom, 1924

'Penelope' bears sprays of large, semidouble, creamy pink blossoms that fade rapidly to almost white. Each petal has a bracket-shaped edge, imparting an extra dose of daintiness to the flowers. At the center of each blossom is a very large cluster of golden stamens. Prompt deadheading keeps the flowers coming throughout the summer.

This rose's glossy, narrow leaves are somewhat prone to mildew, so be sure to water it evenly as hot, dry weather begins. Prune out any mildewed shoots immediately and dispose of them. With its graceful, arching habit, this rose looks pretty when draped over the edge of a wall. Feel free to cut generous sprays to grace bouquets. Like all hybrid musks, 'Penelope' thrives on pruning.

Class: Hybrid musk
Hardiness: Zones 5–10
Size: 5' × 4'
Uses: Mixed borders, cut flowers, hedges, specimens
Shade: Tolerant
Flowering: Continuous

Bloom Color: Pale pink to white
Fragrance: Moderately fragrant
Black Spot: Not susceptible
Mildew: Moderately susceptible
Pruning: Deadhead, remove deadwood, winter maintenance

'Petite de Hollande'

(Parentage unknown) ▪ Holland, c. 1800

AT A GLANCE

Class: Centifolia
Hardiness: Zones 4–10
Size: 4' × 3'
Uses: Mixed borders, containers, cut flowers, culinary, potpourris
Shade: Not tolerant
Flowering: Once per season

Bloom Color: Warm pink
Fragrance: Very fragrant
Black Spot: Slightly susceptible
Mildew: Not susceptible
Pruning: Remove deadwood, prune after flowering

A charmer of a rose, 'Petite de Hollande' bears clusters of three to five, 1½-inch, pomponlike flowers of a warm pink color that is more intense at the center. The perfumed, fully double flowers have scalloped, cupped petals that reflex in the center to form a tight button eye. Flowering is very profuse, weighing down the canes of this rose even though it's a compact grower.

'Petite de Hollande' is rather stout in form, with soft, gray-green foliage that beautifully complements its warm pink flowers. Little pruning is needed, but if you feel you must prune, do it immediately after flowering so that you don't remove any flower buds for the next year. 'Petite de Hollande' is wonderful in a container, where its flowering canes will cascade gracefully over the edges of the pot. Its sprays of buds and blossoms also dry very well for use in everlasting arrangements.

'Petite Lisette'

(Parentage unknown) ▪ Vibert, France, 1817

Dainty and refined in all respects, 'Petite Lisette' has profuse, compact sprays of almost miniature (1-inch), medium pink flowers scented with a classic old-rose perfume. For their diminutive size, they have exquisite form, opening very flat, with the central petals reflexed to form a button eye. The outer edge of the blossom is so even that it looks as though it has been trimmed with scissors. Adding to their Victorian look, the buds are enclosed in deeply incised, lacy calyces.

The compact size and small, soft, gray-green leaves of 'Petite Lisette' are in proportion to its flowers. Lovely in the middle of a mixed border, 'Petite Lisette' is complemented by extra-compact 'Nana' lavender (*Lavandula angustifolia* 'Nana') in the foreground. The blossom sprays also dry nicely.

Class: Centifolia
Hardiness: Zones 4–10
Size: 3' × 3'
Uses: Mixed borders, containers, cut flowers, culinary, potpourris
Shade: Tolerant
Flowering: Once per season

Bloom Color: Medium pink
Fragrance: Very fragrant
Black Spot: Slightly susceptible
Mildew: Not susceptible
Pruning: Remove deadwood, prune after flowering

AT A GLANCE

Rosa gallica officinalis
(also called 'Apothecary's Rose')

(Parentage unknown) ▪ Ancient

AT A GLANCE

Class: Species
Hardiness: Zones 4–10
Size: 3' × 3'
Uses: Mixed borders, hedges, wildlife plantings
Shade: Tolerant

Flowering: Once per season
Bloom Color: Bright magenta
Fragrance: Extremely fragrant
Black Spot: Slightly susceptible
Mildew: Slightly susceptible
Pruning: Remove deadwood

This very ancient rose goes by several names, including 'Apothecary's Rose'. Early pharmacists, who used roses for medicinal purposes, valued it because its petals retain their fragrance when dried. The ruffled petals of the semidouble flowers are a bright magenta that contrasts brilliantly with the golden yellow stamens. Water this rose well through the summer and you'll have a show of graceful, urn-shaped, red hips in autumn.

Although 'Apothecary's Rose' is somewhat open and coarse in its habit, it is worth growing for its fragrance, toughness, and lovely hips. Its historical interest makes it just as well suited to the herb garden as the flower border.

'Rugosa Magnifica'

(Parentage unknown) ▪ Van Fleet, United States, 1905

Think of 'Magnifica' as a new and improved 'Hansa' [hybrid rugosa]—bushier and with a slightly brighter, lighter blossom color and much better repeat bloom. Its blossoms are semidouble, showing golden stamens nestled among tissue-paper–like petals that are an intense mauve-magenta color. Big orange-red hips follow the flowers.

'Magnifica' is covered with shiny, crinkled, bright green leaves that are essentially immune to disease. This is an extremely dense shrub, spreading wider than tall, with fat, bushy growth, making it an excellent hedge, screen, and bird habitat. It affords excellent four-season interest with good fall foliage color and persistent, brightly colored hips into the winter.

Class: Hybrid rugosa
Hardiness: Zones 3–10
Size: 4' × 5'
Uses: Mixed borders, hedges, wildlife plantings
Shade: Tolerant
Flowering: Continuous

Bloom Color: Bright mauve magenta
Fragrance: Very fragrant
Black Spot: Not susceptible
Mildew: Not susceptible
Pruning: Remove deadwood

AT A GLANCE

'Soupert et Notting'

(Parentage unknown) ▪ Pernet Père, France, 1874

This little-known but extraordinary moss rose is capable of strong rebloom if given the proper care. The buds and stem terminals are covered with a brownish green moss that releases a piney fragrance when touched. These buds open into small, very double, cupped blossoms of a deep, warm, rose pink. The flowers are intensely fragrant.

'Soupert et Notting' is quite compact, not reaching much taller than 3 feet, with proportionately small, gray-green leaves. For strong repeat bloom in autumn, deadhead promptly and prevent mildew by watering deeply and evenly through the dry summer months. Prune it lightly and fertilize immediately after the initial flowering.

Class: Moss
Hardiness: Zones 4–10
Size: 3' × 2'
Uses: Mixed borders, containers, cut flowers, culinary, potpourris
Shade: Not tolerant
Flowering: Repeats

Bloom Color: Deep pink
Fragrance: Extremely fragrant
Black Spot: Slightly susceptible
Mildew: Moderately susceptible
Pruning: Deadhead, remove deadwood, prune after June flowering

'Tuscany Superb'

(Probable sport of 'Tuscany') ▪ W. Paul, United Kingdom, 1848

Compared to its ancient predecessor 'Tuscany', 'Tuscany Superb' is slightly more vigorous, better formed, and better foliated. Its large, semidouble blossoms are an incomparable, deep magenta red verging on purple—a color not found in any other rose that I know of—enhanced by an extraordinarily prominent boss of golden stamens. The loosely arranged petals have a velvety appearance that is soft and luminous at the same time. The flowers on this rose are also powerfully fragrant and wonderful for cooking or cosmetic uses.

'Tuscany Superb' has deep green foliage and slender canes that sucker easily but not aggressively. Prune the plant lightly after flowering, and remove the weakest canes at ground level in late winter.

Class: Hybrid gallica
Hardiness: Zones 4–10
Size: 4' × 3'
Uses: Mixed borders, cut flowers, culinary, potpourris
Shade: Not tolerant
Flowering: Once per season

Bloom Color: Deep magenta red
Fragrance: Extremely fragrant
Black Spot: Not susceptible
Mildew: Not susceptible
Pruning: Remove deadwood, prune after flowering

'Tuscany Superb'

Recommended Large Shrubs

The roses listed here are at least 5 feet tall, with a couple approaching 12 feet or more in southern parts of the United States. Choose from these large shrubs when you want shrubs with presence—whether for use as specimens, for a large hedge, or for the back of a mixed border.

'Abraham Darby'

('Yellow Cushion' × 'Aloha') ▪ Austin, United Kingdom, 1985

AT A GLANCE

Class: Shrub
Hardiness: Zones 5–10
Size: 6' × 4'
Uses: Mixed borders, small climbers, cut flowers
Shade: Not tolerant
Flowering: Continuous

Bloom Color: Apricot pink
Fragrance: Very fragrant
Black Spot: Moderately susceptible
Mildew: Not susceptible
Pruning: Deadhead, remove deadwood, winter maintenance

While most of the Austin roses are susceptible to disease and not very hardy, 'Abraham Darby' is an exception. Its huge, extremely double flowers are the richest apricot pink imaginable. The intensely fragrant blossoms are cupped and swirled into quarters, like the blossoms of an old rose.

Like all flowers of this color, 'Abraham Darby' looks wonderful when planted with lavender blues such as those of Siberian catmint (*Nepeta siberica*) and balloon flower (*Platycodon grandiflorus*).

'Alba Maxima'
(also called 'Jacobite Rose' and 'White Rose of York')

(Parentage unknown) ▪ Europe, pre-1500

Another historic alba rose, 'Alba Maxima' bears fully double, intensely fragrant blossoms in such profusion that the clusters weigh down the branches. The foliage is dark blue-green, setting off the pure white of the flowers to perfection. A good bloomer in partial shade, 'Alba Maxima' looks wonderful with Bowman's root (*Gillenia trifoliate*) and white-variegated hostas.

Class: Alba
Hardiness: Zones 4–10
Size: 6' × 5'
Uses: Mixed borders, hedges, specimens
Shade: Tolerant
Flowering: Once per season

Bloom Color: Pure white
Fragrance: Extremely fragrant
Black Spot: Not susceptible
Mildew: Not susceptible
Pruning: Remove deadwood, prune after flowering

AT A GLANCE

'Abraham Darby'

'Alba Semi-plena'

(Parentage unknown) ▪ Europe, pre-1600

AT A GLANCE

Class: Alba
Hardiness: Zones 4–10
Size: 8' × 5'
Uses: Mixed borders, cut flowers, hedges, specimens
Shade: Tolerant
Flowering: Once per season

Bloom Color: White
Fragrance: Extremely fragrant
Black Spot: Not susceptible
Mildew: Not susceptible
Pruning: Remove deadwood, prune after flowering

This little-known alba bears profuse clusters of white blossoms that have a sweet, ethereal fragrance. The charming flowers, which consist simply of a double row of petals around a boss of yellow stamens, are followed by the best show of hips among the alba tribe.

'Alba Semi-plena' is covered with very attractive, gray-green leaves that are impervious to disease. The tallest of the albas, it has robust, arching canes that thrust upward to make an imposing shrub. 'Alba Semi-plena' blooms willingly in partial shade and looks absolutely elegant at the edge of a woodland. Because of its tall habit and superb hardiness, this rose can be trained into a tree form, affording even northern gardeners the experience of a rose standard (usually impossible because their top-grafts are cold susceptible).

'Belle Poitevine'

(Parentage unknown) ▪ Bruant, France, 1894

Carefree 'Belle Poitevine' bears clusters of scrolled and pointed buds that begin to open as early as the end of May in most regions. Its large, semidouble blossoms are clear pink and reveal a cluster of creamy yellow stamens at their hearts. Hips are formed sporadically, but rather than wait for their appearance, you may prefer to deadhead the blossoms to encourage quicker rebloom.

'Belle Poitevine' has wonderfully thick, deeply crinkled foliage. In fall, the bright, medium green leaves turn an array of colors—soft gold, orange, and wine purple—all on the same plant. The plants are stout and bushy, and they make an excellent screen or hedge.

Class: Hybrid rugosa
Hardiness: Zones 3–10
Size: 6' × 5'
Uses: Mixed borders, hedges, specimens
Shade: Tolerant
Flowering: Repeats

Bloom Color: Clear pink
Fragrance: Moderately fragrant
Black Spot: Not susceptible
Mildew: Not susceptible
Pruning: Deadhead, remove deadwood

AT A GLANCE

'Blanc Double de Coubert'

(*R. rugosa* × 'Sombreuil') ■ Cochet-Cochet, France, 1892

Class: Hybrid rugosa
Hardiness: Zones 3–10
Size: 5' × 4'
Uses: Mixed borders, hedges, wildlife plantings, specimens
Shade: Tolerant

Flowering: Repeats
Bloom Color: Pure white
Fragrance: Extremely fragrant
Black Spot: Not susceptible
Mildew: Not susceptible
Pruning: Remove deadwood

One of the few pure white roses, 'Blanc Double de Coubert' has blossoms that do not have even a hint of pink or cream. The double blossoms consist of slightly rumpled, tissue-paper–like petals and are intensely fragrant, wafting their scent into the air surrounding the shrub.

In fall, the bright green, crinkled foliage turns rich gold to purple and is accented by a scattering of scarlet hips. In my gardens, this rose has been somewhat slow to establish, so don't be surprised if it takes a while to reach its full height. Like many rugosas, 'Blanc Double de Coubert' needs no real pruning. Given time, it forms a broadly rounded shrub that makes an excellent specimen.

'Blush Noisette'

(Seedling of 'Champneys' Pink Cluster') ■ Noisette, United States, 1825

One of the more tender roses in this book due to its China rose heritage, 'Blush Noisette' is nevertheless an excellent and robust rose for the South and can be grown as far north as Zone 5 with winter protection or in a sheltered spot. It bears long, elegant clusters of dainty, semidouble, pale lavender to blush pink flowers from early summer until frost.

Its bright green foliage is quite healthy for a rose that puts out so much new growth. Grow 'Blush Noisette' as a large cascading shrub or train it as a climber or pillar rose. Trained against the east side of a house, 'Blush Noisette' will present you with a solid wall of bloom. To accelerate rebloom, deadhead it often.

Class: Noisette
Hardiness: Zones 5–10
Size: 7' × 5'
Uses: Mixed borders, climbers, cut flowers, specimens
Shade: Tolerant
Flowering: Continuous

Bloom Color: Pale lavender pink
Fragrance: Moderate
Black Spot: Slightly susceptible
Mildew: Slightly susceptible
Pruning: Deadhead, remove deadwood, winter maintenance

'Celestial'

(Ancient rose of Europe) ▪ Date unknown

Class: Alba
Hardiness: Zones 3–10
Size: 6' × 4'
Uses: Mixed borders, cut flowers, hedges, culinary, potpourris
Shade: Tolerant
Flowering: Once per year

Bloom Color: Soft pink
Fragrance: Extremely fragrant
Black Spot: Not susceptible
Mildew: Not susceptible
Pruning: Remove deadwood, prune after flowering

'Celestial' is an exquisitely beautiful shrub with semidouble to double blossoms that are colored the very definition of perfect pink. The flowers have a sort of translucent beauty, perhaps due to the light-transmitting quality of the petals, the purity of their color, and the elegant poise with which they're arranged. Moreover, their fabulous looks are matched by their superb perfume.

Yet despite its refined and beautiful appearance, 'Celestial' is one of the hardiest roses you can grow. The plant naturally grows into a shapely, graceful, and arching shrub without any pruning assistance whatsoever, and the gray-green leaves are never diseased. The color combination of the foliage and flowers is extremely beautiful. Like all albas, 'Celestial' is very shade-tolerant.

'Celsiana'

(Parentage unknown) ▪ Europe, pre-1750

The semidouble, delicate pink flowers of this lovely damask have an innocence and purity that the more double-flowered members of its tribe lack. Even the large stamen cluster of this rose is pale yellow, adding to the fragile effect. The fragrance, however, is not especially light—it's pure attar of rose and it wafts intoxicatingly into the air. Its blossoms are borne in generous clusters all along the canes, and they fade nearly to white as they age or are exposed to extreme heat.

Despite the fragile loveliness of the flowers, 'Celsiana' is not a delicate plant. Even if you neglect it, this rose will be around for your grandchildren to enjoy. The plant grows into a tall and regal shrub with little or no pruning. For a bushier shrub, cut it back judiciously and lightly right after it flowers.

Class: Damask
Hardiness: Zones 4–10
Size: 6' × 4'
Uses: Mixed borders, cut flowers, culinary, potpourris
Shade: Not tolerant
Flowering: Once per year

Bloom Color: Pale pink
Fragrance: Extremely fragrant
Black Spot: Not susceptible
Mildew: Not susceptible
Pruning: Remove deadwood, prune after flowering

'Celestial'

'Champneys' Pink Cluster'

(*R. chinensis* × *R. moschata*) ▪ Champneys, United States, 1802

This wonderful rose represents the most important American contribution to the development of old roses. Around the turn of the 19th century, John Champneys, a rice grower in South Carolina, was given a start of 'Parson's Pink China' by his neighbor, Philippe Noisette. Champneys crossed this rose with *R. moschata,* then shared the seedlings of his cross with Mr. Noisette. Noisette, in turn, sent both plants and seeds of the cross to his brother Louis, a propagator in Paris, who recognized them as a breakthrough and continued to work with them. The original hybrid became known as 'Champneys' Pink Cluster'.

'Champneys' Pink Cluster' bears long, elegant sprays of fully double, pale shell pink blossoms that are intensely fragrant. The petals are delicate and arranged in a pretty scalloped fashion. The leaves are elongated, dark green, and very healthy—especially for such a strongly repeating rose. This is one of the most beautiful large shrubs or climbers that gardeners in warmer parts of the country can grow. Gardeners in Zone 5 can grow this rose in a sheltered spot, but it won't reach the height that it will farther south.

Class: Noisette
Hardiness: Zones 6–10
Size: 15' × 8'
Uses: Mixed borders, climbers, cut flowers, specimens
Shade: Not tolerant
Flowering: Continuous

Bloom Color: Blush pink
Fragrance: Very fragrant
Black Spot: Not susceptible
Mildew: Not susceptible
Pruning: Deadhead, remove deadwood, winter maintenance

'Cornelia'

(Parentage unknown) ▪ Pemberton, United Kingdom, 1925

'Cornelia', my favorite hybrid musk rose, bears graceful sprays of coral pink blossoms from June until frost. Its bright coral-red buds open into smallish blossoms of a lighter but still intense color, with shades of yellow at the center, fading to pure pink at the edges. When fully open, the double flowers display clusters of cheery yellow stamens. The fragrance of the flowers is a characteristic fruity musk.

This rose's disease-resistant foliage is narrow, shiny, and leathery, and it has a red tinge that combines wonderfully with the color of its blossoms. The canes are almost thornless. With its graceful, arching growth habit, 'Cornelia' looks superb cascading over a wall.

Class: Hybrid musk
Hardiness: Zones 4–10
Size: 5' × 5'
Uses: Mixed borders, cut flowers, hedges
Shade: Tolerant
Flowering: Continuous

Bloom Color: Coral pink
Fragrance: Moderately fragrant
Black Spot: Not susceptible
Mildew: Not susceptible
Pruning: Deadhead, remove deadwood, winter maintenance

'Cornelia'

'Duplex'

'Duplex'
(also called 'Wolly-Dodd's Rose', *R. pomifera duplex*, or *R. villosa duplex*)

(Species sport of *R. pomifera*) ▪ Rev. Wolly-Dodd, United Kingdom, c. 1900

This very little-known rose—a chance garden hybrid of the Asian counterpart (*R. villosa*) of the European Dog Rose (*R. canina*)—has all the charm, grace, and ruggedness of many of the species roses. Semidouble flowers of clear pink are loosely arranged around a cluster of golden yellow stamens. It reblooms intermittently throughout the summer but sets few fruits compared to the species, *R. pomifera*.

One of the shapelier species roses, its deep blue-green foliage is lightly fragrant and free of disease. Use 'Duplex' (and the species, *R. pomifera*) at woodland edges, for naturalizing, and for informal hedges.

Class: Miscellaneous old garden rose
Hardiness: Zones 4–10
Size: 5' × 4'
Uses: Hedges, specimens
Shade: Tolerant
Flowering: Repeats

Bloom Color: Clear pink
Fragrance: Moderately fragrant
Black Spot: Not susceptible
Mildew: Not susceptible
Pruning: Deadhead, remove deadwood

'Elmshorn'

('Hamburg' × 'Verdun') ▪ William Kordes Söhne, Germany, 1951

Stalwart 'Elmshorn' is very free-flowering (what my grandmother called a "thrifty" rose), blooming continuously from June until frost. It bears dense, enormous clusters of vivid pink, pompon-shaped flowers that are only slightly scented. The gray-green foliage is slightly crinkled, with good disease resistance.

If you feed the tall, arching plants in midsummer, they will reward you with a bounty of blossoms that are even more intensely colored in the cool days of autumn. Hardy, disease-resistant, and generous in its flowering, 'Elmshorn' was a landscape rose long before the term became commonly used. Grow it anywhere you want a fountain of bright, nonstop color.

Class: Shrub
Hardiness: Zones 4–10
Size: 5' × 4'
Uses: Mixed borders, small climbers, cut flowers, specimens
Shade: Tolerant

Flowering: Continuous
Bloom Color: Bright pink
Fragrance: Slightly fragrant
Black Spot: Slightly susceptible
Mildew: Not susceptible
Pruning: Deadhead, remove deadwood, winter maintenance

'Father Hugo's Rose'
(also called *R. xanthina* f. *hugonis*, 'Golden Rose of China')

(Species) ▪ China, c. 1899

Class: Species
Hardiness: Zones 3–10
Size: 8' × 5'
Uses: Mixed borders, hedges, wildlife plantings, specimens
Shade: Not tolerant
Flowering: Once per year

Bloom Color: Primrose yellow
Fragrance: Slightly fragrant
Black Spot: Not susceptible
Mildew: Not susceptible
Pruning: Remove deadwood, prune after flowering

'Father Hugo's Rose' is a wonderful, tough shrub for early color. It opens its silky, single, primrose yellow blossoms well before most roses—early May in most parts of the country. Sometimes the petals look slightly crumpled, like the newly emerged wings of a butterfly. Its scarlet hips ripen by late summer.

This rose is tall and arching and has brownish bronze new growth and very fine-textured, ferny, gray-green leaves. Densely armed with prickles, 'Father Hugo's Rose' is very tolerant of poor soils and so is excellent for brightening a neglected spot. On the other hand, don't banish it to the outermost reaches of your landscape—the tender yellow flowers are spectacular with spring-blooming perennials such as rock cress (*Aubrieta* × *cultorum*).

'Fritz Nobis'

('Joanna Hill' × 'Magnifica') ▪ William Kordes Söhne, Germany, 1940

One of the most beautiful and disease-resistant shrub roses you can grow, 'Fritz Nobis' has been around for more than half a century, yet it remains unknown to most gardeners. In June, this rugged rose erupts into dense, profuse clusters of double flowers in delicate apricot pink, shaded with yellow, cream, and pure pink. The flowers contain so many hues that this rose blends beautifully with just about every other plant.

Flowering lasts for several weeks and is followed by an abundant crop of bright scarlet hips that persists into winter.

The foliage of 'Fritz Nobis' is a handsome gray green that serves as a perfect foil to its flowers. You won't need to prune this shrub, other than to remove deadwood. But if you feel you must shape or thin it, do so either right after flowering or in late winter.

Class: Shrub
Hardiness: Zones 4–10
Size: 6' × 5'
Uses: Mixed borders, cut flowers, hedges, wildlife plantings
Shade: Tolerant
Flowering: Once per year

Bloom Color: Apricot pink
Fragrance: Moderately fragrant
Black Spot: Not susceptible
Mildew: Not susceptible
Pruning: Remove deadwood, prune after flowering

'Frühlingsduft'

('Joanna Hill' × *R. pimpinellifolia altaica*) ■ William Kordes Söhne, Germany, 1949

Class: Hybrid spinosissima
Hardiness: Zones 3–10
Size: 10' × 6'
Uses: Mixed borders, cut flowers, hedges
Shade: Tolerant
Flowering: Once per year

Bloom Color: Yellow with pink overtones
Fragrance: Extremely fragrant
Black Spot: Not susceptible
Mildew: Not susceptible
Pruning: Remove deadwood, prune after flowering

Like its half-brother 'Fritz Nobis' [shrub], this rose is an undiscovered treasure for organic gardeners due to its tough, wild rose heritage. Trusses of rounded, apricot-color buds open into semidouble yellow blossoms that are washed with pink, giving a soft and pleasing coral effect. When fully open, the flowers show delicate coral-red stamens that stand out nicely against the petals. This rose wafts its powerful fragrance into the air at some distance, which explains its name—German for "spring fragrance."

'Frühlingsduft' is a big, arching, vigorous shrub with dense, glossy, dark green foliage. It doesn't need pruning other than to remove deadwood. If you decide to shape it lightly or want to thin the interior of the plant, do so right after flowering or in late winter. In the landscape, 'Frühlingsduft' makes a good hedge, as well as a nice backdrop for other roses or perennials.

'Frühlingsmorgen'

(['E. G. Hill' × 'Catherine Kordes'] × *R. pimpinellifolia altaica*) ■ William Kordes Söhne, Germany, 1942

This outstanding sibling of 'Frühlingsduft' bears large, single blossoms that range from bright pink at the margins to soft primrose yellow at their centers. They are ornamented by dark red stamens that show beautifully against the pale hearts of the flowers. The pleasantly fragrant flowers are followed by an abundance of dark wine-red hips that persist into the winter.

If you are willing to sacrifice the hips, you can experiment with deadheading this rose to encourage repeat flowering throughout the summer. Other than removing deadwood occasionally, you won't need to do any other pruning of this shrub. If you feel you must to do some shaping, do it right after the initial flowering.

Class: Hybrid spinosissima
Hardiness: Zones 3–10
Size: 6' × 4'
Uses: Mixed borders, cut flowers, hedges, wildlife plantings
Shade: Tolerant

Flowering: Once per year; occasionally repeats
Bloom Color: Medium pink/yellow
Fragrance: Moderately fragrant
Black Spot: Not susceptible
Mildew: Not susceptible
Pruning: Remove deadwood

'Great Maiden's Blush'

'Geranium'

(*R. moyesii* hybrid) ▪ Royal Horticultural Society, United Kingdom, 1938

AT A GLANCE

Class: Hybrid moyesii
Hardiness: Zones 4–10
Size: 8' × 6'
Uses: Mixed borders, climbers, cutting (for hips), hedges, wildlife plantings
Shade: Tolerant

Flowering: Once per season
Bloom Color: Bright red
Fragrance: Not fragrant
Black Spot: Slightly susceptible
Mildew: Not susceptible
Pruning: Remove deadwood, prune after flowering

Compared to the species *R. moyesii*, 'Geranium' is a more graceful shrub—slightly more spreading as it matures. It bears brilliant scarlet, single flowers in profusion all along its branches, somewhat later in June than most roses. The blossoms are ornamented by pale, creamy stamens that stand out against the geranium red petals. After the annual crop of flowers comes a spectacular show of unusual hips—brilliant scarlet, slightly bristly, and urn-shaped, with a cluster of elongated sepals at their tips.

'Geranium' forms a tall, rangy shrub with small, delicate, light green leaves. To shape the plant without removing next year's flowers, prune it immediately after flowering. (This will be at the expense of the current season's hips.) Or, to enjoy the hips, prune in late winter, knowing that you'll lose some of the current season's flower buds. (*Note:* 'Geranium' also can be trained on a wall as a climber.)

'Great Maiden's Blush'
(also called 'La Séduisante' ['The Seductress'], 'Incarnata', 'La Virginale', and 'Cuisse de Nymphe' ['Nymph's Thigh'])

(Parentage unknown) ▪ Europe, pre-1550

One of my top 10 roses, 'Great Maiden's Blush' has absolutely delicious color—a translucent blushed shell pink, which gives rise to its many alternate names. Whatever its name, 'Great Maiden's Blush' is an exquisite rose that averages about 40 petals per blossom. The petals are arranged in seductive disarray when fully open, and the fragrance is refined yet intense, with the ethereal, lemony notes characteristic of the alba roses.

The shrub's graceful arching branches and extremely blue-gray foliage make it beautiful even when it isn't in bloom. And as if its beauty is not reward enough, 'Great Maiden's Blush' is among the toughest, most disease-resistant roses you can grow, flowering even in partial shade and in poor, gravelly soil. In the garden, 'Great Maiden's Blush' and English lavender (*Lavandula angustifolia*) are a match made in heaven.

Class: Alba
Hardiness: Zones 3–10
Size: 6' × 5'
Uses: Mixed borders, cut flowers, hedges, specimens, culinary, potpourri
Shade: Tolerant

Flowering: Flowers once per year
Bloom Color: Blush pink
Fragrance: Extremely fragrant
Black Spot: Not susceptible
Mildew: Not susceptible
Pruning: Remove deadwood, prune after flowering

AT A GLANCE

'Gros Choux d'Hollande'

(Parentage unknown) ▪ Date unknown

The name of this old rose means "big Dutch cabbages"—which explains why it still goes by its pleasant-sounding French name! 'Gros Choux d'Hollande' has large, cupped, extremely double flowers with silky, warm pink petals that resemble a many-layered petticoat. The blooms are richly fragrant and make spectacular cut flowers.

'Gros Choux d'Hollande' is a vigorous, upright rose that can be used either as a large shrub or a modest-size climber. For quicker rebloom, deadhead it promptly, then fertilize it after the first flush of bloom. It has a tendency to become leggy.

Class: Bourbon
Hardiness: Zones 5–10
Size: 7' × 5'
Uses: Mixed borders, climbers, cut flowers, hedges
Shade: Not tolerant
Flowering: Repeats

Bloom Color: Rose pink
Fragrance: Very fragrant
Black Spot: Slightly susceptible
Mildew: Not susceptible
Pruning: Deadhead, remove deadwood, winter maintenance

'Herbstfeuer' (also called 'Autumn Fire')

(*R. eglanteria* hybrid) ▪ William Kordes Söhne, Germany, 1961

Nearly a half a century after its introduction, 'Herbstfeuer' is finally receiving some of the acclaim it deserves. Better late than never to recognize the merits of a healthy, hardy red rose that repeat blooms *and* bears showy hips. The blossoms of 'Herbstfeuer' are fully double, nicely fragrant, and a true crimson. Yet unlike so many roses of this color, this rose rarely shows black spot on its foliage.

With its large size, this rose is a showstopper for color from early summer through fall. 'Herbstfeuer' is especially spectacular in autumn—hence the English translation of its name. It flames with clusters of pear-shaped golden hips that are burnished red, while the foliage kindles to gold and orange. Deadheading increases rebloom on this rose at the expense of the beautiful autumn hips. I vote for the hips.

Class: Hybrid eglanteria
Hardiness: Zones 4–10
Size: 6' × 4'
Uses: Mixed borders, cut flowers, hedges, wildlife plantings
Shade: Tolerant
Flowering: Repeats

Bloom Color: Crimson
Fragrance: Very fragrant
Black Spot: Slightly susceptible
Mildew: Not susceptible
Pruning: Deadhead (optional), remove deadwood, winter maintenance

'Herbstfeuer'

'Königin von Dänemark'
('Queen of Denmark')

(Parentage unknown) ▪ Booth, Denmark, 1826

Class: Alba
Hardiness: Zones 3–10
Size: 5' × 4'
Uses: Mixed borders, cut flowers, hedges, specimens, culinary, potpourris
Shade: Tolerant
Flowering: Once per year

Bloom Color: Warm pink
Fragrance: Extremely fragrant
Black Spot: Not susceptible
Mildew: Not susceptible
Pruning: Remove deadwood, prune after flowering

'Königin von Dänemark' has superbly scented, warm pink flowers that weigh down the branches in their profusion. The stubby buds are borne in clusters that open into elegant, cupped, fully double blossoms with petals that are quartered and swirled. Because of the tight packing of the petals, the buds tend to ball (or fail to open) in wet weather. Touching the tip of the bud with your fingertips usually enables the flower to spring open.

'Königin von Dänemark' is unusually thorny for an alba, and its gray-green leaves are a bit larger than those of the rest of the tribe. In fact, some sources believe this rose is a hybrid between an alba and a damask, which would explain its coarse foliage. Still, it's an elegant rose and just as easy to grow as other albas.

'Lichtkönigin Lucia'

('Zitronenfalter' × 'Cläre Grammerstorf') ▪ William Kordes Söhne, Germany, 1966

Another little-known and undergrown Kordes rose, 'Lichtkönigin Lucia' deserves much wider use for its bright lemon yellow color, hardiness, and disease resistance. This rose bears clusters of intensely colored, semidouble flowers that open to reveal dainty coral-red stamens. The fragrance is pleasant, and repeat bloom is strong.

This shrub is well armed with thorns and covered with large, dark green leaves that, for a yellow rose, are remarkably resistant to black spot. Because it is so intensely colored, be sure to pair it with other vividly colored flowers, such as delphiniums, 'Sunny Border Blue' veronica (*Veronica* 'Sunny Border Blue'), 'Summer Wine' yarrow (*Achillea millefolium* 'Summer Wine'), and prairie poppy mallow (*Callirhoe involucrata*). White shasta daisies (*Leucanthemum* × *superbum*) are also nice companions for this rose.

Class: Shrub
Hardiness: Zones 4–10
Size: 5' × 4'
Uses: Mixed borders, cut flowers, hedges, specimens
Shade: Not tolerant
Flowering: Continuous

Bloom Color: Bright yellow
Fragrance: Moderately fragrant
Black Spot: Slightly susceptible
Mildew: Not susceptible
Pruning: Deadhead, remove deadwood, winter maintenance

'Königin von Dänemark'

'Linda Campbell'

('Anytime' × 'Rugosa Magnifica') ▪ Moore, United States, 1991

Class: Hybrid rugosa
Hardiness: Zones 4–10
Size: 5' × 8'
Uses: Mixed borders, hedges, specimens
Shade: Not tolerant
Flowering: Continuous

Bloom Color: Bright red
Fragrance: Not fragrant
Black Spot: Not susceptible
Mildew: Not susceptible
Pruning: Deadhead, remove deadwood, winter maintenance

This unusual cross of a rugosa with a miniature rose yielded a very healthy, hardy plant with large clusters of semidouble, crimson flowers that repeat generously. Although 'Linda Campbell' is useful in the landscape (because it's one of the few bright red roses with good disease resistance), its flowers aren't especially graceful. But don't let that stop you from growing it if you love reds.

This plant's foliage is abundant and dark green, contrasting nicely with its bright blooms. 'Linda Campbell' is tall but tends to spread wider than its height. Consider using it as an ever-blooming hedge or toward the back of a mixed border, framed by strongly colored or silver-leaved perennials.

'Martin Frobisher'

('Schneezwerg' × unknown) ▪ Svejda, Canada, 1968

The very first of the Explorer roses, 'Martin Frobisher' remains one of the best of this series. The fully double blossoms are the color of whipped cream tinted with strawberry juice and have a clean, refreshing fragrance. Unfortunately, the wilted petals tend to hang onto the stems like little mops instead of shattering cleanly, so deadheading is a must.

The shrub grows strongly upright, and the new growth has remarkably few thorns for a rugosa. The pretty, gray-green foliage is slightly susceptible to black spot, according to the Canadian Experiment Station, so take preventive measures. But if you're looking for a hardy rose, have no fear: Rugged 'Martin Frobisher' can survive in near-polar conditions.

Class: Hybrid rugosa
Hardiness: Zones 2–10
Size: 5' × 4'
Uses: Mixed borders, hedges, specimens
Shade: Not tolerant
Flowering: Continuous

Bloom Color: Creamy pink
Fragrance: Very fragrant
Black Spot: Slightly susceptible
Mildew: Not susceptible
Pruning: Deadhead, remove deadwood

'Nevada'

(*R. moyesii* hybrid) ▪ Dot, Spain, 1927

AT A GLANCE

Class: Hybrid moyesii
Hardiness: Zones 4–10
Size: 8' × 6'
Uses: Mixed borders, hedges, specimens
Shade: Not tolerant
Flowering: Repeats

Bloom Color: Pure white
Fragrance: Moderately fragrant
Black Spot: Slightly susceptible
Mildew: Not susceptible
Pruning: Deadhead, remove deadwood

Rose experts always wax enthusiastic over this rose with single flowers, and with good reason: It is an excellent shrub, with pointed, apricot-pink buds that open into large, sometimes rumpled snow white blossoms. In bloom, the plant appears to be covered with big white butterflies. Prompt deadheading encourages repeat bloom.

Fine-textured, medium green foliage covers the vigorous, wide-spreading shrub. In wet climates, black spot may show up, but in drier climes, this rose is disease-free. In a shrub border, it looks especially nice when combined with glossy abelia (*Abelia* × *grandiflora*) and Virginia sweetspire (*Itea virginica*).

'Robusta'

(Unnamed seedling × *R. rugosa*) ▪ William Kordes Söhne, Germany, 1979

'Robusta' is probably the most intensely scarlet rose listed in this book. The large, single blossoms are very fragrant and absolutely blaze when sunlight shines through the translucent petals. But, oddly for a single rose, 'Robusta' bears no hips.

One of the best roses for hedging, 'Robusta' has strong, vigorously upright growth and viciously

thorny canes. Its foliage is deep green, large, lustrous, and fairly resistant to black spot for a red rose. In the mixed border, combine the dazzling color of this rose with similarly vivid tones, such as in sapphire blue 'Blue Nile' delphinium, flame red 'Lucifer' crocosmia (*Crocosmia* 'Lucifer') and golden false sunflower (*Heliopsis helianthoides*). (*Note:* 'Pink Robusta' has semidouble pink flowers on a tall shrub that grows up to 6 feet tall.)

Class: Shrub
Hardiness: Zones 3–10
Size: 5' × 4'
Uses: Mixed borders, hedges, specimens
Shade: Tolerant
Flowering: Continuous

Bloom Color: Intense scarlet
Fragrance: Very fragrant
Black Spot: Slightly susceptible
Mildew: Not susceptible
Pruning: Deadhead, remove deadwood, winter maintenance

AT A GLANCE

Rosa canina

(Ancient species of Europe) ▪ Date unknown

AT A GLANCE

Class: Species
Hardiness: Zones 3–10
Size: 10' × 6'
Uses: Naturalizing, wildlife
plantings, culinary
Shade: Tolerant
Flowering: Flowers once per year,
in June

Bloom Color: Pale pink
Fragrance: Moderately fragrant
Black Spot: Not susceptible
Mildew: Not susceptible
Pruning: Remove deadwood

Although big and unruly, the dog rose has a certain rustic charm. Growing wild on roadsides and in hedgerows, it is native to Britain and Europe and naturalized throughout much of North America. Its small, single flowers appear in June and are pale to blush pink and sometimes white. But its best feature comes *after* the flowers: a profusion of bright scarlet, oval hips that persist into the winter. If you like rose hip tea, jam, wine, and other such concoctions, this is the very best rose to grow—both for the abundance of hips and for their good flavor. (And if you don't eat them, the birds certainly will!)

A vigorous, arching shrub that is quite tolerant of shade, the dog rose needs absolutely no care at all. It makes a fine addition to a wild hedge and is unmatched for attracting birds.

Rosa eglanteria
(also called *R. rubiginosa*, *R. suavifolia*, and *R. walpoleana*)

(Ancient species of Europe) ▪ Date unknown

Along with the dog rose (*R. canina*), *R. eglanteria* is Europe's other widespread wild rose. Its common name, sweetbriar, comes from the delicious, fresh, green apple scent of its foliage and flowers. Its small to medium, pink, single blossoms are a shade darker than those of *R. canina*, and the two combine nicely when grown together among trees in a naturalized area.

To enjoy lots of fragrant new growth without completely sacrificing the plant's colorful hips in fall and winter, cut back sweetbriar every year, after it flowers. Sweetbriar is one of the only roses that thrives in alkaline soil.

Class: Species
Hardiness: Zones 4–10
Size: 12' × 8'
Uses: Hedges, naturalizing, wildlife
plantings
Shade: Tolerant
Flowering: Once per year

Bloom Color: Light pink
Fragrance: Very fragrant
Black Spot: Not susceptible
Mildew: Not susceptible
Pruning: Remove deadwood,
prune after flowering

AT A GLANCE

Rosa glauca

(Species) ▪ Europe, pre-1820

Class: Species
Hardiness: Zones 4–10
Size: 8' × 6'
Uses: Mixed borders, cut flowers, hedges, wildlife plantings
Shade: Tolerant
Flowering: Once per season

Bloom Color: Lilac pink
Fragrance: Not fragrant
Black Spot: Not susceptible
Mildew: Not susceptible
Pruning: Remove deadwood, winter maintenance or after flowering

Pretty *R. glauca* is known more for its foliage and hips than for its flowers. Its graceful, pointed leaves are extremely blue-gray-green with dark maroon edges and stems. New growth is purplish red, as are the nearly thornless stems. In June, the plant bears small, single, lavender-pink blooms that fade to white at their centers. These blooms are followed by shiny red hips that ripen to deep, burnished, purplish red.

In the garden, *R. glauca*'s highly ornamental foliage makes a superlative companion for other plants. I especially love this rose in front of five-stamen tamarix (*Tamarix ramossissima*), whose pale gray foliage and pink flowers are spectacularly echoed by the rose's leaves, while the rose's hips soften the tamarix's unappealing winter coarseness. *R. glauca*'s foliage and hips are also lovely in cut arrangements; in fact, the more you clip away at this rose, the more brightly colored its new growth will be.

Rosa virginiana

(Species) ▪ North America, pre-1807

This graceful, wild American rose is a good garden plant by any measure. Blooming later than most roses—toward the third week in June—it produces single, light pink blossoms with sunny yellow stamens and an apple scent. The sprays of blossoms are followed by showy, tomato red hips that persist into winter.

R. virginiana is a well-proportioned plant for a species rose, without the unruliness of some. It has few thorns, and with its mildly suckering habit, it makes an outstanding hedge. The foliage is elongated and pointed, light green and glossy, and turns warm gold and orange in autumn. Together with the clusters of red hips, this makes for a stunning fall display.

Class: Species
Hardiness: Zones 3–10
Size: 5' × 4'
Uses: Mixed borders, hedges, naturalizing, wildlife plantings
Shade: Tolerant

Flowering: Once per year
Bloom Color: Light pink
Fragrance: Slightly fragrant
Black Spot: Not susceptible
Mildew: Not susceptible
Pruning: Remove deadwood

'Roseraie de l'Haÿ'

(Sport of unknown parentage) ▪ Cochet-Cochet, France, 1901

AT A GLANCE

Class: Hybrid rugosa
Hardiness: Zones 3–10
Size: 6' × 8'
Uses: Mixed borders, hedges, specimens, culinary, potpourris
Shade: Not tolerant

Flowering: Continuous
Bloom Color: Deep cerise purple
Fragrance: Extremely fragrant
Black Spot: Not susceptible
Mildew: Not susceptible
Pruning: Winter maintenance

'Roseraie de l'Haÿ', named after one of the most famous rose gardens in the world, is an organic gardener's dream come true. This exemplary rugosa bears clusters of furled and pointed buds that unfold into large, semidouble flowers of velvety cerise. With age, the blossoms gain subtle purple overtones and show a boss of golden stamens. Their wafting fragrance is heady, rich, and spicy. Although 'Roseraie de l'Haÿ' develops few hips, it flowers almost nonstop throughout the season.

'Roseraie de l'Haÿ' is supremely hardy, vigorous, and densely covered with deep green, crinkled foliage that is immune to disease. In autumn, the leaves turn a clear gold. Its broadly rounded form makes an excellent specimen, and it requires no pruning other than to remove deadwood. Just be sure to give this lusty rose the room it needs to reach its full potential.

'Rugelda'

(Parentage unknown) ▪ William Kordes Söhne, Germany, 1989

Like many of the excellent Kordes introductions, 'Rugelda' is not well known in the United States, but it is actually a better yellow rugosa than the more widely grown 'Topaz Jewel' [hybrid rugosa], being hardier, healthier, and more graceful. Its large, semidouble flowers are soft lemon yellow tinged with coral red, and the wavy petals give the flowers a slightly ruffled look.

As with most yellow rugosa hybrids, the foliage is more glossy and leathery than it is crinkled, making it slightly more susceptible to black spot, so use preventive measures to keep the disease at bay. Vigorous 'Rugelda' grows into a strongly upright shrub that makes a handsome specimen. It's also well suited to use as a hedge or in a mixed border.

Class: Hybrid rugosa
Hardiness: Zones 4–10
Size: 5' × 4'
Uses: Mixed borders, hedges, specimens
Shade: Not tolerant
Flowering: Continuous

Bloom Color: Soft yellow tinged with coral red
Fragrance: Moderately fragrant
Black Spot: Slightly susceptible
Mildew: Not susceptible
Pruning: Deadhead, deadwood removal, winter maintenance

AT A GLANCE

'Roseraie de l'Haÿ'

'Sarah Van Fleet'

(*R. rugosa* × 'My Maryland') ■ Van Fleet, United States, 1926

Class: Hybrid rugosa
Hardiness: Zones 4–10
Size: 5' × 4'
Uses: Mixed borders, hedges, specimens
Shade: Tolerant
Flowering: Continuous

Bloom Color: Clear pink
Fragrance: Moderately fragrant
Black Spot: Not susceptible
Mildew: Slightly susceptible
Pruning: Deadhead, remove deadwood, winter maintenance

'Sarah Van Fleet', one of the more elegant rugosa hybrids, has satiny, luminous pink petals that form gracefully cupped semidouble blossoms. The flowers are borne in slightly nodding sprays, and rebloom is very strong—probably because the plant does not set hips.

'Sarah Van Fleet' has matte, gray-green foliage that is moderately prone to rust, so avoid planting it if the disease is prevalent in your region. The shrub is viciously thorny and quite upright in growth, making it an excellent hedge. In mixed borders, you can count on 'Sarah VanFleet' for almost-constant color throughout the growing season.

'Scabrosa'

(*R. rugosa* seedling) ■ Harkness, United Kingdom, 1950

One of the most outstanding rugosas, 'Scabrosa' exemplifies the best qualities of the rugosa species. Its blossoms are a beautiful, showy, bright mauve purple that stands out against the apple green foliage. Borne in dense clusters, the flowers are single, with bunches of contrasting golden yellow stamens. Enormous, tomato red hips reliably follow the flowers.

With its vigorous, bushy, upright growth habit, 'Scabrosa' needs no pruning except to remove deadwood occasionally. Its spiny canes are densely cloaked in rugged, semigloss, crinkly leaves that turn gold and orange in autumn. 'Scabrosa' makes a most stunning hedge—colorful, fragrant, and, thanks to the hops, filled with birds.

Class: Hybrid rugosa
Hardiness: Zones 3–10
Size: 6' × 4'
Uses: Mixed borders, hedges, specimens
Shade: Tolerant
Flowering: Continuous

Bloom Color: Bright mauve purple
Fragrance: Very fragrant
Black Spot: Not susceptible
Mildew: Not susceptible
Pruning: Remove deadwood

'Souvenir de Philémon Cochet'

(Sport of 'Blanc Double de Coubert') ▪ Cochet-Cochet, France, 1899

AT A GLANCE

Class: Hybrid rugosa
Hardiness: Zones 3–10
Size: 5' × 4'
Uses: Mixed borders, hedges, specimens
Shade: Tolerant
Flowering: Continuous

Bloom Color: Blush pink
Fragrance: Very fragrant
Black Spot: Not susceptible
Mildew: Not susceptible
Pruning: Deadhead, remove deadwood

This rose is similar to its parent, 'Blanc Double de Coubert' [hybrid rugosa], except that its blossoms are much more double—in fact, they are so tightly packed with petals that the fully open flowers are almost round. And instead of having snow white flowers (as on 'Blanc Double de Coubert'), the blooms of this rose are pale blush pink, with slightly deeper color at the center. The trade-off for its incredible flowers, however, is that it bears no hips.

The foliage is typically rugosa—crinkled, semigloss, and deep green. 'Souvenir de Philémon Cochet' is wonderful as part of a hedge of other big rugosas, where its subtle color can act as a bridge between more forthright tones.

'Stanwell Perpetual'

(*R. damascena* var. *bifera* × *R. spinosissima*) ▪ Lee, United Kingdom, 1838

Like most species crosses, 'Stanwell Perpetual' is a superior rose. Its very double, pure blush pink blossoms are as richly fragrant as those of its damask parent. The swirled and quartered petals are attractively disheveled, and they reflex at the center to form a button eye. It is one of the first roses to begin blooming in spring, often showing a few open blossoms during the first week of May.

'Stanwell Perpetual' is a full, gracefully arching shrub with the fine-textured, gray foliage and spiny canes of its spinosissima parent. The leaves sometimes spot with a dark maroon purple—but don't mistake this idiosyncrasy for black spot because it's quite resistant to the disease. To stimulate flowering, deadhead it promptly and cut out a few of the oldest canes each year.

Class: Hybrid spinosissima
Hardiness: Zones 4–10
Size: 5' × 5'
Uses: Mixed borders, cut flowers, hedges, specimens
Shade: Tolerant
Flowering: Repeats

Bloom Color: Blush pink
Fragrance: Extremely fragrant
Black Spot: Not susceptible
Mildew: Not susceptible
Pruning: Deadhead, remove deadwood, winter maintenance

AT A GLANCE

'Thérèse Bugnet'

'Thérèse Bugnet'

([*R. acicularis* × *R. rugosa* var. *kamtchatica*] × [*R. amblyotis* × *R. rugosa* var. *plena*] × 'Betty Bland')
■ Bugnet, Canada, 1950

Although this rose is always grouped with rugosa hybrids, 'Thérèse Bugnet' is the result of some very innovative breeding that involved several hardy species roses. Unlike typical rugosas, it has matte, pointed, gray-green foliage and few thorns. The bright pink, double blossoms open into graceful saucer shapes with wavy, ruffled petals.

'Thérèse Bugnet' is usually considered a continual bloomer, but I've found it to be a shy repeater, at best. Deadhead it promptly to keep it flowering. A vigorous grower, its elegant appearance belies its good health. Enjoy 'Thérèse Bugnet' as a specimen, in mixed borders, or in hedges.

AT A GLANCE

Class: Hybrid rugosa
Hardiness: Zones 3–10
Size: 6' × 5'
Uses: Mixed borders, cut flowers, hedges, specimens
Shade: Tolerant
Flowering: Repeats

Bloom Color: Bright pink
Fragrance: Very fragrant
Black Spot: Not susceptible
Mildew: Not susceptible
Pruning: Deadhead, remove deadwood, winter maintenance

'Wasagaming'

([*R. rugosa* × *R. acicularis*] × 'Gruss an Teplitz') ■ Skinner, Canada, 1939

This interesting cross between two very hardy species and a Bourbon rose resulted in a lovely shrub that is, unfortunately, still not widely grown. The large, double, warm pink blooms have a more elegant form than those of many rugosas and are strongly recurrent. Their fragrance is sweet.

'Wasagaming' makes a mounded shrub that is well covered with foliage. The medium green leaves have inherited a touch of black spot susceptibility from the Bourbon parent, so take the usual precautionary measures against the disease. 'Wasagaming' sometimes suckers and is easy to propagate from softwood cuttings. This very quality allows it to be offered by many growers as an own-root plant.

AT A GLANCE

Class: Hybrid rugosa
Hardiness: Zones 3–10
Size: 6' × 5'
Uses: Mixed borders, hedges, specimens
Shade: Not tolerant
Flowering: Repeats

Bloom Color: Medium pink
Fragrance: Moderately fragrant
Black Spot: Slightly susceptible
Mildew: Not susceptible
Pruning: Deadhead, remove deadwood, winter maintenance

Recommended Climbers

Just what constitutes a climbing rose is a matter of some subjectivity. I've defined a climber as a rose that can grow at least 6 feet tall in Zone 5 and one that has long, thick, strongly vertical canes. Most of these roses put out the majority of their new growth as branches from a scaffolding of mature canes. They often bloom on new as well as old wood, and many are repeat-blooming. These roses are suitable for training up the wall of a house or on a pillar, trellis, or pergola. They need to be affixed to their means of support, unlike vines (which climb on their own by means of twining, tendrils, or holdfasts). Remember that many large rose shrubs can be trained as climbers, as well.

'Alexander MacKenzie'

('Queen Elizabeth' × ['Red Dawn' × 'Suzanne']) ▪ Svejda, Canada, 1985

'Alexander MacKenzie' has big, deep cherry pink, extremely double flowers that contain as many as 50 petals each. In keeping with its tea heritage, the petals reflex backward as the buds open. Bloom occurs on several big flushes (the first and the last are the most profuse) and the fragrance is pleasantly fruity. Because of its high petal-count, 'Alexander MacKenzie' has a slight tendency to "ball" in wet weather. If this happens, just tease open the petals at the top to help the blossom pop.

'Alexander MacKenzie' is an entirely hardy and very healthy rose, especially for a red. Its lustrous, deep green foliage serves as a nice foil to its brilliantly colored blossoms. Train the canes as horizontally as possible to encourage more flowers. (*Note:* This rose can also be grown as a shrub by allowing the long canes to arch.)

Class: Shrub
Hardiness: Zones 3–10
Size: 8' × 5'
Uses: Mixed borders, short climbers, cut flowers, hedges, pillars
Shade: Not tolerant

Flowering: Repeats
Bloom Color: Deep crimson pink
Fragrance: Moderately fragrant
Black Spot: Not susceptible
Mildew: Not susceptible
Pruning: Deadhead, remove deadwood, winter maintenance

AT A GLANCE

'Awakening'

(Sport of 'New Dawn') ▪ Blatina Nurseries, Czechoslovakia, 1935

Class: Large-flowered climber
Hardiness: Zones 5–10
Size: 10' × 8'
Uses: Cut flowers, pillars, tree ramblers
Shade: Tolerant
Flowering: Continuous

Bloom Color: Blush pink
Fragrance: Very fragrant
Black Spot: Slightly susceptible
Mildew: Not susceptible
Pruning: Deadhead, remove deadwood, winter maintenance

We have English rosarian and nurseryman Peter Beales to thank for the 1992 reintroduction of this wonderful rose. A sport of the widely known 'New Dawn', this rose has extremely double flowers of classic old-rose form. The petals are cupped, swirled, and quartered, while the outermost petals reflex. The blooms are borne in generous clusters, and their sweet pink stands out to great advantage against the deep green, glossy foliage.

'Awakening' is slightly susceptible to black spot, but it can be kept reasonably disease-free by using careful sanitation and preventive practices. In late winter, prune out all extremely spindly canes to help the plant concentrate its energy on flower-bearing wood.

'Charlemagne' (also called 'President Dutailly')

(Parentage unknown) ▪ Dubreuil, France, 1888

Although this tall, rangy gallica tends to bloom a week or two later than most roses, its flowers are worth the wait. The large, extremely double blossoms are intensely perfumed and richly colored—a velvety cerise crimson tinged with purple, fading to lilac.

'Charlemagne' is only slightly thorny and has slender canes. To treat it as a climber, select about five of the thickest canes for scaffolding and suppress any others that come up from the base. Bend the scaffolding canes into horizontal arches. 'Charlemagne' will respond by covering itself with cascades of blossoms. Keep it well and evenly watered to prevent mildew.

Class: Hybrid gallica
Hardiness: Zones 4–10
Size: 6' × 4'
Uses: Mixed borders, cut flowers, hedges, pillars, culinary, potpourris
Shade: Not tolerant
Flowering: Once per year

Bloom Color: Deep crimson purple
Fragrance: Extremely fragrant
Black Spot: Not susceptible
Mildew: Slightly susceptible
Pruning: Remove deadwood, prune after flowering

'Dortmund'

'Dortmund'

(Seedling × *R. kordesii*) ▪ William Kordes Söhne, Germany, 1955

Class: Hybrid kordesii
Hardiness: Zones 3–10
Size: 8' × 6'
Uses: Pillars
Shade: Tolerant
Flowering: Repeats

Bloom Color: Crimson with white
Fragrance: Slightly fragrant
Black Spot: Slightly susceptible
Mildew: Not susceptible
Pruning: Deadhead, remove deadwood,
   winter maintenance

One of the most rugged red climbers you can grow, 'Dortmund' has dazzling, single crimson blossoms with white eyes at the center highlighting yellow stamens. The flowers are only slightly fragrant and are borne in large sprays that densely cover the plant. 'Dortmund' is a stunning sight in full bloom.

   This rose has long, vigorous, thorny canes that climb rapidly to cover a pillar or arch. Deep green, leathery, and glossy, its foliage resists disease formidably for a red rose. Deadhead 'Dortmund' promptly to encourage quick and generous rebloom. If you want a vigorous climber that shows up at a distance, 'Dortmund' is your rose.

'Henry Kelsey'

(*R. kordesii* hybrid × unknown seedling) ▪ Svejda, Canada, 1984

'Henry Kelsey' bears large clusters of semidouble, bright crimson blossoms that fade to deep magenta pink. Compared to its half-sibling 'Dortmund' [hybrid kordesii], this rose is a slightly better repeat bloomer and even more cold-hardy (to Zone 2!). Its red hue is slightly softer than that of 'Dortmund'.

   The long, vigorous canes of 'Henry Kelsey' will quickly cover a pergola or trellis, but because the canes are supple, you'll need to tie them at frequent intervals for support. Also remember to bend or wind them to grow horizontally to encourage more flowering. For a red rose, 'Henry Kelsey' is extremely healthy.

Class: Hybrid kordesii
Hardiness: Zones 2–10
Size: 8' × 6'
Uses: Pillars, tree ramblers
Shade: Tolerant
Flowering: Repeats

Bloom Color: Crimson
Fragrance: Moderately fragrant
Black Spot: Slightly susceptible
Mildew: Not susceptible
Pruning: Deadhead, remove
   deadwood, winter maintenance

'Ilse Krohn Superior'

('Golden Glow' × *R. kordesii*) ▪ William Kordes Söhne, Germany, 1957

'Ilse Krohn Superior' is a wonderfully hardy and healthy rose with the shapely, tapered buds and flowers of a tea rose. Borne in clusters of three to five, the pretty scrolled buds are slightly flushed with apricot, and they open to a warm ivory. The petals have excellent substance and the finish of heavy, matte silk. Although the fragrance is light, it is definitely perceptible.

This climber's glossy, deep green foliage is exquisitely healthy, and the plants rarely suffer from winter dieback. For heavier bloom, prune the strongly vertical growth after dormancy in early winter, and train the canes to grow horizontally. Repeat this process after the first flush of growth in mid-summer. Deadhead regularly.

Class: Hybrid kordesii
Hardiness: Zones 4–10
Size: 10' × 5'
Uses: Pillars
Shade: Tolerant
Flowering: Remontant

Bloom Color: Ivory
Fragrance: Light
Black Spot: Mildly susceptible
Mildew: Not susceptible
Pruning: Deadhead, remove deadwood, winter maintenance

'John Davis'

([*R. kordesii* × unnamed seedling] × unknown) ▪ Svejda, Canada, 1986

Of all the roses in my nursery, 'John Davis' was the best-seller in terms of sheer numbers. Customers would take one look at it blooming in the display gardens and decide that they had to have it for themselves. 'John Davis' is smothered with fully double, loose, pink blossoms that have a lightly spicy scent. The flowers are so large and borne in such huge clusters that the plant becomes a veritable fountain of bloom.

To train 'John Davis' as a climber, select about five scaffolding canes to grow up a support, and suppress any other shoots at ground level. (Without support, 'John Davis' becomes a huge, cascading shrub.)

Although this rose was prone to mildew in my nursery after its first flush of bloom, the problem never spoiled the flowers and disappeared on its own within 2 or 3 weeks. To reduce the chance of mildew, keep the plants well watered, especially during the first prodigious flush of flowers.

Class: Hybrid kordesii
Hardiness: Zones 3–10
Size: 8' × 6'
Uses: Mixed borders, cut flowers, hedges, pillars
Shade: Not tolerant
Flowering: Continuous

Bloom Color: Medium pink
Fragrance: Moderately fragrant
Black Spot: Not susceptible
Mildew: Somewhat susceptible
Pruning: Deadhead, remove deadwood, winter maintenance

'John Davis'

'Kathleen Harrop'

(Sport of 'Zephirine Drouhin') ▪ Dickson, United Kingdom, 1919

AT A GLANCE

Class: Bourbon
Hardiness: Zones 5–10
Size: 10' × 6'
Uses: Cut flowers, pillars
Shade: Tolerant
Flowering: Continuous

Bloom Color: Clear pink
Fragrance: Very fragrant
Black Spot: Slightly susceptible
Mildew: Slightly susceptible
Pruning: Deadhead, remove
    deadwood, winter maintenance

This lovely rose, one of the last Bourbon roses to be introduced, has elegant, pointed buds that open to semidouble, clear pink blossoms with sunny yellow stamens. The loose, wavy petals have pretty, reflexed edges, with deeper coloring and transparent veining on the reverse side. What's more, the flowers are wonderfully fragrant, with hints of raspberry.

Like its parent, 'Kathleen Harrop' is absolutely free of thorns, making it perfect for use in tight spots where passersby might brush against it. To prevent mildew on the gray-green foliage, keep the plant evenly watered. This rose is more tolerant of shade than most. In Zone 5, it flourishes best in a sheltered spot.

'Leverkusen'

(*R. kordesii* × 'Golden Glow') ▪ William Kordes Söhne, Germany, 1954

'Leverkusen' has been around for nearly half a century, yet few rose growers are familiar with this healthy yellow climber. Beginning in June and continuing until frost, 'Leverkusen' bears ruffled, translucent, light yellow blossoms that hold their color as they age. When the delicately fragrant blossoms are fully open, golden stamens can be seen nestled deep within their centers. Although the petals appear incredibly delicate, they stand up well to inclement weather.

Possibly the most remarkable thing about this rose, however, is that it is impervious to disease—which is not much short of miraculous for a yellow rose. Deadhead it to keep it in flower. Undoubtedly, it inherited its immaculate health from that paragon of disease resistance, *R. kordesii*.

Class: Hybrid kordesii
Hardiness: Zones 4–10
Size: 10' × 8'
Uses: Pillars
Shade: Tolerant
Flowering: Continuous

Bloom Color: Light yellow
Fragrance: Moderately fragrant
Black Spot: Not susceptible
Mildew: Not susceptible
Pruning: Deadhead, remove
    deadwood, winter maintenance

AT A GLANCE

'Mme. Plantier'

(Possibly *R. alba* × *R. moschata*) ▪ Plantier, France, 1835

Class: Hybrid alba
Hardiness: Zones 4 to 10
Size: 20' × 8'
Uses: Cut flowers, tree roses, specimens
Shade: Tolerant
Flowering: Once per year

Bloom Color: Creamy white
Fragrance: Extremely fragrant
Black Spot: Not susceptible
Mildew: Not susceptible
Pruning: Remove deadwood, prune after flowering

'Mme. Plantier' is enormous—in warm climates, it can climb to 20 feet! The fragrant, double flowers are creamy white when they first open, fading to pure white with a green button eye. The petals are elegantly arranged and reflex back, forming a flat blossom when fully open. Its foliage is gray green, and the canes are nearly thornless.

Because of its large size and vigor, this rose can be trained as a standard or tree rose even in cold climates. To do this, select the strongest cane and attach it to a post. Suppress all branches up to the point where you want to establish the "crown" of the tree, as well as all shoots growing from the base. When the branch point is reached, pinch the plant often to create a bushy top. For a rounded canopy, prune the plant after it has flowered, or allow the branches to weep naturally.

'Mme. Sancy de Parabère'
(also called 'Mme. de Sancy de Parabère')

(Parentage unknown) ▪ Bonnet, France, 1874

This little-known climber is vigorous, disease resistant, and completely thornless! What's more, it has lovely flowers: The extremely double blossoms are deep rose pink at the center, fading to lighter pink at the edges. The petals fold almost in half lengthwise, giving the flowers a pretty, tufted look. Sweetly fragrant, the flowers are almost flat when open and are borne in generous clusters. In fall, the foliage becomes ornamental as well, turning a warm gold color.

'Mme. Sancy de Parabère' does well even in poor soils and is one of the best roses for shade. No need to deadhead it because it blooms only once per year.

Class: Boursault
Hardiness: Zones 5–10
Size: 15' × 10'
Uses: Cut flowers, pillars
Shade: Tolerant
Flowering: Once per year
Bloom Color: Medium pink

Fragrance: Moderately fragrant
Black Spot: Slightly susceptible
Mildew: Not susceptible
Pruning: Remove deadwood, prune after flowering

'New Dawn'

(Sport of 'Dr. Van Fleet') ▪ Somerset Rose Company, United States, 1930

AT A GLANCE

Class: Large-flowered climber
Hardiness: Zones 4–10
Size: 20' × 8'
Uses: Pillars, tree ramblers
Shade: Tolerant
Flowering: Continuous

Bloom Color: Shell pink
Fragrance: Very fragrant
Black Spot: Slightly susceptible
Mildew: Not susceptible
Pruning: Deadhead, remove deadwood, winter maintenance

Perhaps the most-loved climbing rose of all time, 'New Dawn' was the first rose variety ever patented. The large, delicate, shell pink blossoms are borne both singly and in clusters, and they are sweetly fragrant. The thick petals resist wet weather and reflex at their edges to create pretty points, much like those of a tea rose but with a more informal charm.

This rose's hardiness, generous flowering, and disease resistance make it one of the most adaptable climbers. Although 'New Dawn' may experience some winter dieback in Zone 4, it can climb to 20 feet in warmer zones. Its supple canes are well suited to winding around a tree trunk or pillar, from which it can produce cascades of romantic-looking blossoms.

'Rosarium Uetersen'

('Karlsruhe' × seedling) ▪ William Kordes Söhne, Germany, 1977

If only this German rose had a better name and some savvy marketing, it surely would be sold in every garden center. It's vigorous, healthy, and absolutely spectacular in bloom. 'Rosarium Uetersen' has the most double flowers of any rose listed in this book, often packing as many as 100 petals into a single large blossom! Yet the petals have such substance that the flowers aren't bothered by wet weather. In full bloom,

'Rosarium Uetersen' is unforgettable: The plant becomes covered with cascades of warm pink blossoms that age to silvery pink. Its attractive foliage is plentiful and glossy dark green in color.

Grow 'Rosarium Uetersen' in your landscape either as a large climber or as an enormous cascading shrub. Prompt deadheading will encourage several encores of repeat bloom.

Class: Large-flowered climber
Hardiness: Zones 4–10
Size: 10' × 6'
Uses: Cut flowers, pillars, specimens
Shade: Tolerant
Flowering: Repeats

Bloom Color: Medium pink
Fragrance: Slightly fragrant
Black Spot: Slightly susceptible
Mildew: Not susceptible
Pruning: Deadhead, remove deadwood, winter maintenance

AT A GLANCE

'New Dawn'

'Zéphirine Drouhin'

'William Baffin'

(*R. kordesii* seedling) ▪ Svejda, Canada, 1983

Class: Hybrid kordesii
Hardiness: Zones 2–10
Size: 10' × 6'
Uses: Climbers
Shade: Tolerant
Flowering: Repeat

Bloom Color: Bright pink
Fragrance: None
Black Spot: Not susceptible
Mildew: Not susceptible
Pruning: Deadhead, remove deadwood, winter maintenance

'William Baffin' is the gold standard of hardy, healthy climbing roses. In fact, if you need a rose to climb up the wall of your igloo, this is the rose for you. The semidouble flowers are bright raspberry pink with dishevelled petals and golden stamens. Although the flowers are totally lacking in fragrance, this is an advantage if Japanese beetles are a problem in your area. 'William Baffin' can be a shy rebloomer, so be sure to deadhead regularly.

For heaviest bloom, train the long, vigorous branches horizontally. Be sure to wear gloves when you do this and when removing deadwood—this rose's canes are viciously thorny! 'William Baffin' can also be grown as a large, cascading shrub.

'Zéphirine Drouhin'

(Parentage unknown) ▪ Bizot, France, 1868

'Zéphirine Drouhin' is more prone to disease than many of the other roses listed in this book, but it isn't as weak as some authorities insist. This rose has strongly fragrant, semidouble blossoms of soft, rich, raspberry pink. The plant repeats more strongly than most Bourbon roses, and the flowers are borne in loose, graceful clusters.

'Zéphirine Drouhin' is one of the few completely thornless roses, making it great for prickle haters. It's also one of the 10 most shade-tolerant roses you can grow. Put this rose on a black spot prevention regimen and keep it evenly watered to minimize mildew. Coating the leaves of 'Zéphirine Drouhin' with an antitranspirant will give it a boost against disease. If you're like most gardeners, you'll love this rose despite its flaws.

Class: Bourbon
Hardiness: Zones 5–10
Size: 10' × 6'
Uses: Cut flowers, pillars
Shade: Tolerant
Flowering: Continuous

Bloom Color: Rich raspberry pink
Fragrance: Very fragrant
Black Spot: Moderately susceptible
Mildew: Moderately susceptible
Pruning: Deadhead, remove deadwood, winter maintenance

Recommended Ramblers

Exactly where to draw the line between rambling and climbing roses is never clear. The difference in definition lies somewhat in function, but also in their genetics and growth habits. Ramblers are great for climbing into trees or covering an eyesore. They can also tumble over a bank as a groundcover, and they look wonderful cascading over a wall. However, this doesn't prevent them from being trained up a wall much as you would a traditional climbing rose. Ramblers usually are descendents of *Rosa multiflora* or *R. wichuriana* crosses. They have long, thin, supple canes that make them ideally suited to winding around a pillar or creating a rose garland (see pages 80 and 81). Ramblers put out most of their new growth as new canes emerging at ground level. They bloom primarily on old wood and are usually once-blooming. The biggest roses in this book are in the rambler category, with some climbing to heights of 20 feet or more in warm climates. Ramblers are almost never hardy in Zone 3 and may suffer massive dieback in Zone 4.

'Albéric Barbier'

(*R. wichuriana* × 'Shirley Hubbard') ▪ Barbier, France, 1900

'Albéric Barbier', one of the finest old rambling roses, was introduced by the highly regarded Barbier Nursery in Orleans, France. This rose's big, graceful sprays of scrolled, pointed buds open into very double, creamy white, quartered blooms with a glow of yellow at their hearts. Like many of the once-flowering ramblers, this rose becomes absolutely covered with flowers. 'Albéric Barbier' is the most shade-tolerant rose in this book, flowering even with only 1 hour of full sun per day.

Its foliage is extremely dark green, leathery, and glossy, making a superb foil to the flowers. The canes are long and supple. Pruning usually isn't necessary—this rose grows so vigorously that you'll be lucky to drag out a dead cane or two every so often. If you do need to prune, do it right after the plant has finished flowering.

AT A GLANCE

Class: Hybrid wichuriana
Hardiness: Zones 4–10
Size: 15' × 10'
Uses: Climbers, bank covers, cut flowers
Shade: Tolerant
Flowering: Blooms once per year

Bloom Color: Creamy white
Fragrance: Slightly fragrant
Black Spot: Not susceptible
Mildew: Not susceptible
Pruning: Remove deadwood, prune after flowering

'Albéric Barbier'

'François Juranville'

(*R. wichuriana* × 'Mme. Laurette Messimy') ▪ Barbier, France, 1906

AT A GLANCE

Class: Hybrid wichuriana
Hardiness: Zones 5–10
Size: 16' × 10'
Uses: Climbers, bank covers, cut flowers
Shade: Tolerant
Flowering: Blooms once per year, in June or July

Bloom Color: Apricot pink
Fragrance: Very fragrant
Black Spot: Not susceptible
Mildew: Not susceptible
Pruning: Remove deadwood, prune after flowering

One of the prettiest ramblers, this rose bears bountiful garlands of medium-size, luscious apricot-pink blossoms with a heavy, fruity fragrance. The quilled, quartered petals are yellow at their bases. When fully open, the flat-shaped blossoms are positively loaded with old-rose charm. Flowering begins a bit later than for many roses, around the third week in June, but it continues over a long period. It's one of the most beautiful roses to let scramble through an old tree.

'François Juranville' has very shiny, dark green, fine-textured leaves that emerge bronzy and remain tinged with red. The canes have few prickles and are long, supple, and vigorous. Like other once-blooming ramblers, prune this one right after it flowers—or don't bother to prune it at all, other than to remove some deadwood from time to time.

'Ghislaine de Féligonde'

('Goldfinch' × unknown) ▪ Turbat, France, 1916

'Ghislaine de Feligonde' is a wonderfully hardy old rose that probably would be grown much more often if it only had a snappier name like, say, 'Carefree Garland'. This rose swathes itself in graceful garlands of small, double blossoms of warm apricot pink highlighted with gold, fading to pure pink. The blossoms

reveal their stamens when fully open and emit a fruity fragrance. Most amazing for a rambler, this rose repeat blooms, especially in autumn.

The supple canes are covered with medium green, semigloss leaves. Surprisingly (especially given its multiflora heritage), the canes are nearly thornless, making this rose much less difficult to train. Climbing among the branches of an old apple tree, 'Ghislaine de Féligonde' is breathtaking.

Class: Hybrid multiflora
Hardiness: Zones 5–10
Size: 10' × 6'
Uses: Cut flowers, pillars, specimens
Shade: Tolerant
Flowering: Repeats

Bloom Color: Apricot pink highlighted with gold
Fragrance: Moderately fragrant
Black Spot: Not susceptible
Mildew: Not susceptible
Pruning: Deadhead, remove deadwood

AT A GLANCE

'Kiftsgate'

(Sport or selection of *R. filipes*) ■ Murrell, United Kingdom, 1954

Class: Species
Hardiness: Zone 6–10
Size: 30' × 20'
Uses: Bank covers, wildlife plantings
Shade: Very tolerant

Flowering: Blooms once per year
Bloom Color: White
Fragrance: Moderately fragrant
Black Spot: Not susceptible
Mildew: Not susceptible
Pruning: Impossible!

If you live in the southern half of the country and you want a rose to smother a tree in blossoms or cover an unsightly shed, this is the rose for you. 'Kiftsgate' will billow to enormous heights (its plants are the largest of any in this book), festooned with huge heads of small, single white flowers with golden stamens. Bloom is so heavy that the plant seems smothered in drifts of snow. And because flowering occurs in late June to July, it provides a spectacular follow-up to earlier bloomers.

Clusters of ornamental scarlet hips—enough to feed entire flocks of birds—follow the blooms, adding beauty to the landscape through winter. The leaves are relatively large and tinged bronze when emerging. As a bonus, the foliage turns rich orange and gold in autumn, making a glorious show with the garlands of hips. Don't even think about trying to prune this rose—just let it go!

'Nastarana'

(Possible hybrid of *R. moschata* and *R. chinensis*) ■ Asia Minor, 1879

This exquisite rambler flowers very late—usually in July—and continues into autumn, bearing clusters of dainty, pointed, pink buds that open to small, semidouble flowers with a fruity, musk rose fragrance. 'Nastarana' is wonderful for filling the gap when other roses are napping through the hottest part of summer.

The foliage of this rambler is small, dark green, and pointed, providing a beautiful backdrop to its pale flowers. Pruning isn't necessary, but you might want to thin the spindly canes. (If you do, be careful—they're quite thorny!) Otherwise, just pull out the deadwood when it occurs. To help 'Nastarana' harden off in the northern parts of its range, withhold fertilizer after the end of July. (*Note:* Gardeners in Zone 5 can grow 'Nastarana' as a cascading shrub.)

Class: Noisette
Hardiness: Zones 6–10
Size: 15' × 10'
Uses: Climbers, bank covers, cut flowers
Shade: Tolerant

Flowering: Blooms once per year
Bloom Color: Creamy white
Fragrance: Very fragrant
Black Spot: Slightly susceptible
Mildew: Not susceptible
Pruning: Remove deadwood

'Veilchenblau'

'Seven Sisters'
(also called *R. multiflora platyphylla* and *R. cathayensis platyphylla*)

(Parentage unknown) ■ China, 1816

AT A GLANCE

Class: Hybrid multiflora
Hardiness: Zones 4–10
Size: 12' × 10'
Uses: Climbers, bank covers
Shade: Tolerant
Flowering: Blooms once per year

Bloom Color: Dark pink through pale pink
Fragrance: Very fragrant
Black Spot: Not susceptible
Mildew: Not susceptible
Pruning: Remove deadwood, prune after flowering

'Seven Sisters' is a curiosity that people often remember from their grandmothers' gardens. It owes its name to the fact that the blossoms can occur, theoretically, in seven different colors on a single truss. The truth is that the blossoms open as deep pink to fuschia, then gradually fade as they age to medium pink, lilac, and finally pale pink. The flowers are very double and have the fermented fruity scent of multifloras.

The foliage of 'Seven Sisters' is dark green and dense, and its canes are thorny. For best use in the landscape, allow this vigorous, hardy rose to cascade over a bank or climb into a tree. You won't need to do much pruning, but when you feel you must, do it right after the plant has finished flowering.

'Veilchenblau'

('Crimson Rambler' × 'Errinerung an Brod') ■ Schmidt, Germany, 1909

Although some rose catalogs make the dubious claim of having truly "blue" roses, 'Veilchenblau' comes pretty close—at least its blooms are truly purple! The violet-purple petals are white at the base, fading to blue lilac and gray. The abundant, semidouble, cupped flowers are borne in dense clusters and have an ethereal, lily-of-the-valley scent.

Although the glossy, medium green, pointy leaves are somewhat prone to black spot, the plant is so vigorous and tough that it will survive even without treatment. For a stunning effect in the landscape, combine 'Veilchenblau' with soft yellow shrub roses and the silvery foliage of artemisias (*Artemisia* spp.). The color of 'Veilchenblau' is much more dramatic when it's grown in only partial sun, making it ideal for shadier landscapes.

Class: Hybrid multiflora
Hardiness: Zones 5–10
Size: 15' × 12'
Uses: Climbers, groundcovers
Shade: Tolerant
Flowering: Blooms once per year

Bloom Color: Purple and white
Fragrance: Moderately fragrant
Black Spot: Moderately susceptible
Mildew: Not susceptible
Pruning: Remove deadwood, prune after flowering

AT A GLANCE

PART IV

design details

Most of us wouldn't consider planting a garden filled with just lilacs or hydrangeas, yet gardens consisting strictly of roses don't strike us as odd. In fact, roses have traditionally been segregated from the rest of the garden.

I feel, however, that roses should be liberated from the rose garden. Not only do I find gardens filled with nothing but roses boring, but I also know that such an arrangement makes it easier for diseases and pests to whip through your roses like wildfire.

Treat the roses in this book as the tough, serviceable plants they are. They're capable of enhancing a mixed border, providing a screening hedge, supplying food and shelter for wildlife, as well as bringing together the more formally landscaped areas of your yard.

Roses are ideal companions to other shrubs, grasses, and perennials in the mixed border, adding color, texture, and form from early summer through fall.

chapter 11

roses in the mixed border

Roses are naturals for the

mixed border. With their wide range of bloom colors and fragrances, leaf textures, and plant forms, they are perfect for weaving into the front, middle, or rear of mixed planting beds. For the organic gardener, planting roses in a mixed border has practical advantages, too. Combined with other plants, your roses will be less likely to suffer disease and insect problems than they will in a monoculture, and when pests do show up, they'll be less likely to spread. In a traditional, roses-only planting, diseases and pests can spread rapidly from one plant to the next, ruining your garden.

Just what is a *mixed border*? Compared to a perennial border, a mixed border has more structure, texture, and more winter interest because it includes shrubs and perhaps even some small trees. In addition, a mixed border can include grasses, herbs, wildflowers, vines, and even annuals—in short, any plant that adds harmony, contrast, or visual excitement. At its best, a mixed border looks attractive year-round; it offers a wealth of plant material for cutting; and it provides food and shelter for birds, butterflies, and beneficial insects. Planning a mixed border is your opportunity to use plants to create a very special garden that is both beautiful and practical.

Start with a Plan

Selecting roses—or any other plants—for your mixed border requires you to juggle several balls at once. You must consider bloom color and time, plant height and spread, texture, form, seasonal attributes, and more—all in relation to surrounding plants. That's why it's best to create your mixed border on paper first, especially if you've never planted one before. Mistakes are much easier (and less costly) to correct on paper than after you've already put the plants in the ground.

If you've never drawn a garden plan before, you might feel a bit intimidated, but there's no need to. After you've completed the tedious part (measuring the area and transferring the measurements to paper), the fun begins: selecting and grouping the plants. As you mix and match colors, textures, bloom times, and plant forms, be sure to keep your eraser handy because you're sure to make revisions as you go.

Plenty of good books explain garden mapping and planning in detail, but here's a quick overview to get you started.

When planning a mixed border, you'll need measuring tapes, sand or limestone, paper, and a pencil. Having a partner is a good idea, too—he or she will make the job go faster and more smoothly.

Outlining the Border

The first step in planning a mixed border is to outline the area on the ground, then take measurements so that you can transfer your outline accurately onto paper. To do this, you'll need some simple supplies, patience, and a little time. Here's what to do:

■ **Gather your supplies.** You'll need a hose (or rope) long enough to outline the edges of the border, a bag of sand or limestone, two measuring tapes (50 to 250 feet long, depending on the size of the area), paper for taking notes while you work, and a pencil with a good eraser. If possible, find a partner to help you with the work and to provide opinions and ideas.

■ **Choose the site.** Keep in mind that roses are sun lovers and that your palette of plants for the border will be much broader if you choose to plant your border in a sunny spot.

■ **Lay out the bed.** Use the hose or rope to experiment with the edges of the bed, moving it

around until you're sure that you're pleased with the outline. Remember that a mixed border should be at least 6 feet wide—the wider the bed, the more interesting the plant combinations you can create. When you've decided on the outline, follow along the outline with the sand or limestone to define the edges of the border. Then draw a rough sketch of the area on paper.

■ **Measure the area.** Run one long measuring tape down the length of the bed. (If your bed has a straight edge, run the tape along this edge; otherwise, place the tape down the middle of the area.) Stretch it tight and anchor it at both ends. Use the other tape to measure perpendicularly from the tape to the edges of the bed at regular intervals; 5- or 10-foot intervals usually work best. Use the fixed tape as the X axis and the other tape as the Y axis to locate points along the entire perimeter of your bed. On the rough sketch, record the measurements [X, Y] at 5- or 10-foot intervals. For example, at the 10-foot mark the edge of the bed measures 12 feet from the tape, so that point would be [10,12].

Note: If you ran the tape down the middle of the bed, you'll need to take two measurements at every increment: a positive and a negative one. For instance, at the 10-foot mark, the front edge of the bed might be [10,7] while the back edge of the bed might be [10, -4].

Creating the Map

Now turn your rough sketch into an accurate drawing on graph paper. (Regular, notebook-size graph paper will suffice, but larger, 24 × 36-inch paper—available from art supply stores—is nice because it allows you to assign a large enough scale to your drawing to denote smaller plants, such as perennials.) After you've filled in the drawing with your plant selections, you'll have a map, or blueprint, for your future border. Here's what to do:

■ **Choose a scale for your drawing.** For mixed borders, I like to work in 1 inch = 5 feet scale, but you can assign any scale you like, as long as it doesn't make your drawing too large to fit on the paper or so small that you can't define a perennial with a 1½ foot spread.

■ **Draw a light pencil line to represent the fixed measuring tape (X axis).** If the bed is 120 feet long and your scale is 1 inch = 5 feet, your pencil line would be 24 inches long. Mark off and label the measuring intervals you used along this line, beginning with zero. For example, if you used 5-foot intervals, you'd note 0 feet, 5 feet, 10 feet, 15 feet, and so on.

■ **Plot the measurements on the graph paper.** Use the pencil line together with the measurements on the rough sketch to locate the points that define the perimeter of your new bed. Also locate existing trees and other objects.

■ **Fill in your border.** Now comes the fun part—filling your border with your favorite plants! Use circles or other shapes to denote the plants. Be sure the plant symbols indicate the diameter of the

plants *at maturity*. Allow ample spacing for each plant. In very wide beds, you may want to leave room for an access path through the middle so that you can maintain your plants more easily. Also, don't forget to label each type of plant on your design. (If you don't have enough space to spell out the names of the plants, use different symbols for each type of plant or create a numbered key.)

Once you've finished your "paperwork," prepared your bed, and purchased your plants, you can begin making your plan a reality. One final word of advice as you head out the door to install your plants: Arrange the plants in the bed according to your plan while they're still in pots. Move the pots around—even if it means tweaking your design a bit—until everything looks just right. When your arrangement seems as close to perfect as it's going to get, start planting. (For an example of what a finished plan might look like, see page 202.)

In this design, roses blend harmoniously with other shrubs, perennials, grasses, and herbs to create a garden that is in flower all season long.

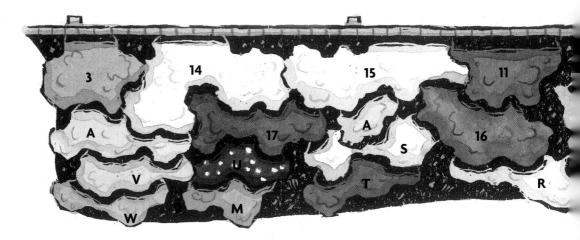

Roses in the Mixed Border—Plant List

Shrubs

1. 'Alba Maxima' [alba rose] (1)
2. 'Fritz Nobis' [shrub rose] (1)
3. 'Roseraie de l'Haÿ' [hybrid rugosa rose] (1)
4. 'Cornelia' [hybrid musk rose] (1)
5. 'Snow Queen' oakleaf hydrangea (*Hydrangea quercifolia* 'Snow Queen') (5)
6. 'Saturnalia' Virginia sweetspire (*Itea virginica* 'Saturnalia') (6)
7. 'Nordic' inkberry holly (*Ilex glabra* 'Nordic') (4)
8. 'Limelight' panicle hydrangea (*Hydrangea paniculata* 'Limelight') (3)
9. Chaste tree (*Vitex agnus-castus*) (4)
10. 'Alfred de Dalmas' [moss rose] (5)
11. 'Lochinch' butterfly bush (*Buddleia* 'Lochinch') (3)
12. 'Coral Cluster' [polyantha rose] (5)
13. 'Hidcote' St. John's wort (*Hypericum* 'Hidcote') (4)

14. 'September Beauty' summersweet (*Clethra alnifolia* 'September Beauty') (3)
15. 'Blanc Double de Coubert' [hybrid rugosa rose] (2)
16. 'Moje Hammarberg' [hybrid rugosa rose] (3)
17. 'Edward Goucher' abelia (*Abelia* 'Edward Goucher') (3)

Perennials

A. 'Hameln' fountain grass (*Pennisetum alopecuroides* 'Hameln') (7)
B. 'Siskiyou Pink' gaura (*Gaura lindheimeri* 'Siskiyou Pink') (7)
C. Catmint (*Nepeta subsessilis*) (6)
D. 'Aureola' hakone grass (*Hakonechloa macra* 'Aureola') (5)

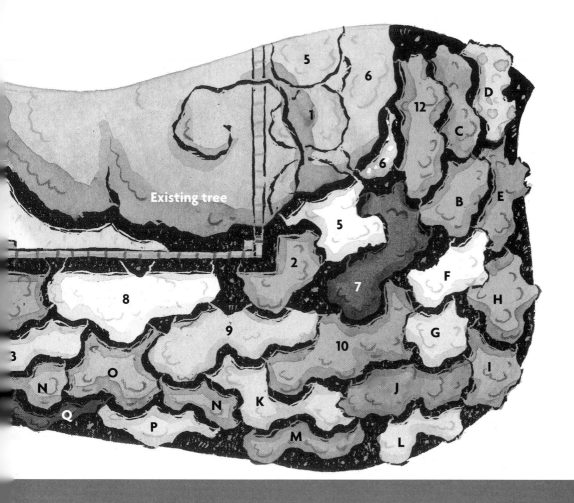

Existing tree

Tips for Mixing

Almost any rose is a candidate for a mixed border. The only exceptions are climbers and ramblers, but even these can be trained as pillars and used at the back of the border (see page 80). Otherwise, feel free to let your tastes be your guide.

Try to include at least a few roses that bear a good crop of hips. Bright scarlet rose hips provide a welcome contrast to flowers in the border and have the advantage of persisting into autumn and winter. For me, a big shrub rose laden with graceful clusters of hips epitomizes the spirit of autumn.

Avoid planting roses with an arching form right next to perennials, as the roses will overhang and shade out the perennials. Also, remember to position large roses against the back of the border (or in the center, if it is an island bed) so they don't overwhelm neighboring plants.

By the same token, keep your roses away from aggressively spreading perennials. For instance, although catmints look lovely with roses, some varieties of these vigorous plants (especially *Nepeta* × *faassenii*) can easily engulf the lower branches of a rose, while their roots form a greedy mat that sucks away available moisture and nutrients before the rose can get its share—leading to the rose's demise.

For visual interest and to prevent disease, try to position your roses next to shorter or taller plants. Or leave a little extra space around roses so that neighboring plants don't block the flow of air or shade the foliage of your roses.

In addition to plant heights and bloom colors, the most aesthetically pleasing mixed borders also take into account plant forms and leaf textures. To soften the lines of a stiff, upright shrub rose, for example, you could plant mounded, arching perennials or feathery grasses as neighbors. On the other hand, arching shrubs need adequate room to display their natural form; don't distract from their grace by crowding them with other plants. Plants with contrasting foliage textures can make good partners. For instance, roses with ferny leaves look handsome next to plants with bold foliage, such as oakleaf hydrangea (*Hydrangea quercifolia*).

Hip-bearing roses, such as *Rosa rugosa*, add a sense of grace and bounty to the mixed border, especially in autumn.

Good Company

Although a mixed border can include almost any type of ornamental plant, some plants complement roses better than others do. Plant form and size, bloom color and time, foliage texture, and fragrance all figure into the mix. Much of the fun of creating a mixed border is coming up with your own inspired combinations. Remember: It's *your* garden, so if the combination makes you happy, go for it! You can always change it later.

Here are some of my favorite plant companions for roses in the mixed border.

Small Trees

In a large border (50 feet or more in length), one to three small trees can serve as visual anchors for the planting and add winter interest. Just don't overdo the use of trees—even small trees have extensive root systems that compete with nearby plants, making the selection of suitable companions even trickier.

Top Trees for Mixed Borders

Choose trees that won't overgrow their bounds, cast too much shade, or have aggressive roots. Trees with small leaves are preferable because they cast less shade. Good candidates include the following:

- Paperbark maple (*Acer griseum*)

- Red buckeye (*Aesculus pavia*)

- Flowering dogwood (*Cornus florida*)

- 'Leonard Messel' kobus magnolia (*Magnolia* × *loebneri* 'Leonard Messel')

- Higan cherry (*Prunus* × *subhirtella*)

- 'Donald Wyman', 'Pink Spires', and 'Schmidtcutleaf' flowering crabapple (*Malus* 'Donald Wyman', 'Pink Spires', and *M. transitoria* 'Schmidtcutleaf')

- Korean Group stewartia (*Stewartia pseudocamellia* var. *koreana*)

- Japanese snowbell (*Styrax japonicus*)

Truly a four-season tree, flowering dogwood is treasured in the mixed border for its contained habit, horizontal branching, graceful spring flowers, and rich autumn color.

Select your trees carefully. They should look interesting even when not in leaf. Pay special attention to their branch structure. Flowering dogwoods, for example, are treasured for their delicately layered yet strongly horizontal branches, which add beauty to the landscape year-round.

Korean stewartia (*Stewartia pseudocamellia* var. *koreana*)—with its elegant zigzagging twigs and stunning bark patterned in a mosaic of gray, cream, and cinnabar—is another prime candidate for the mixed border. Its camellia-like, waxy white, late-summer blossoms and burnished red fall color are the icing on the cake.

Other excellent small trees for the mixed border include 'Pink Chimes' Japanese snowbell (*Styrax japonicus* 'Pink Chimes'), our native pawpaw (*Asimina tribola*), 'Pendula Rosea' Higan cherry (*Prunus* × *subhirtella* 'Pendula Rosea'), and Chinese quince (*Pseudocydonia sinensis*).

Some trees really aren't suitable for mixed borders, however. Avoid those that eventually will grow so large that they would shade the entire border, such as river birch, as well as those that are too distinctive to blend well, such as Japanese maple. Likewise, steer clear of trees that form clumps, such as clump-forming magnolias (*Magnolia stellata*); their low branches don't allow room for neighboring plants.

Companionable Shrubs

Shrubs are a must for the mixed border. They add mass and, if well chosen, will ornament the garden through the fall and winter with colorful fruits. (See "Fruit-Bearing Shrubs," below.) In fact, the more flowering shrubs you include in your mixed border, the less maintenance it will need because shrubs don't require trimming and dividing that many perennials do.

Choose shrubs that will add qualities that your border would otherwise lack. Remember to consider leaf color and texture, colorful fruits, flowering time, and plant form. Most shrubs look best when massed in groups. And don't be afraid to mass an even number of plants, if you must, rather than an odd number. Grouping an odd number of plants is usually considered "correct," but creating a graceful, well-integrated border depends more on where you place the plants than on whether you use them in even or odd numbers.

Littleleaf lilac (*Syringa pubescens* subsp. *microphylla*) blooms in both spring and fall, and its form is more graceful than that of common lilacs. As a bonus, it's among the most disease-resistant members of its tribe.

Fruit-Bearing Shrubs

Here's a partial list of shrubs that will produce pretty fruit during the colder months.

- Purple beautyberry (*Callicarpa dichotoma*)

- Fringe tree (*Chionanthus virginicus*—must be accompanied by a male for fruiting)

- Seven-son flower (*Heptacodium miconioides*)

- Sea buckthorn (*Hippophae rhamnoides*)

- 'Warren Red' possumhaw (*Ilex decidua* 'Warren Red'—must be accompanied by a male for fruiting)

- 'Winter Red', 'Cacapon', and 'Red Sprite' winterberry holly (*Ilex verticillata* 'Winter Red', 'Cacapon', and 'Red Sprite'—all of these must be accompanied by a male for fruiting)

- Spicebush (*Lindera benzoin*)

- Jet bead (*Rhodotypos scandens*)

- 'Magic Berry' and 'Hancock' snowberry, also sold as coralberry (*Symphoricarpos* × *doorenbosii* 'Magic Berry' and *S.* × *chenaultii* 'Hancock')

- 'Winterthur' smooth viburnum (*Viburnum nudum* 'Winterthur'—*Note:* This cultivar doesn't self-pollinate, so a species *V. nudum* should be planted nearby to ensure fruit)

- American cranberry bush, linden viburnum, and Sargent viburnum (*Viburnum trilobum; V. dilatatum, and V. sargentii*)

Shrubs That Stretch the Bloom Season

Here are just a few of the many noteworthy shrubs that extend the bloom season for mixed borders. They either flower when roses aren't in bloom, or they flower over a particularly long period.

Shrub	Bloom Time
Glossy abelia (*Abelia × grandiflora*)	All summer until frost
'Longwood Blue' blue mist shrub (*Caryopteris × clandonensis* 'Longwood Blue')	Late summer through fall
'September Beauty' summersweet (*Clethra alnifolia* 'September Beauty')	Fall
Winterhazel (*Corylopsis glabrescens* and *C. pauciflora*)	Late winter; early spring
'Pallida' witchhazel (*Hamamelis × intermedia* 'Pallida')	Winter
Seven-son flower (*Heptacodium miconioides*)	Late summer through late fall
'Bluebird' rose of Sharon (*Hibiscus syriacus* 'Bluebird')	Late summer
'All Summer Beauty' bigleaf hydrangea (*Hydrangea macrophylla* 'All Summer Beauty')	Summer through fall
'Unique' panicle hydrangea (*Hydrangea paniculata* 'Unique')	Late summer
Littleleaf lilac (*Syringa pubescens* subsp. *microphylla*)	Spring and fall

Shrubs with Lively Leaves

Never underestimate the importance of foliage in a mixed border. The colorful foliage of the following shrubs will complement roses in any mixed border.

Shrub	Foliage
Gold Tide ('Courtasol') forsythia (*Forsythia × intermedia* 'Courtasol')	Chartreuse foliage; wonderful with lavender-pink roses
'Picta' Japanese kerria (*Kerria japonica* 'Picta')	Soft green leaves with creamy edges; lovely with yellow roses
'Variegatus' mock orange (*Philadelphus coronarius* 'Variegatus')	Elegant, creamy white leaf margins; smashing with white and pale pink roses
'Diabolo' ninebark (*Physocarpus opulifolius* 'Diabolo')	Rich purple leaves; wonderful with pink, fuchsia, white, and yellow roses
'Sutherland Gold' European red elder (*Sambucus racemosa* 'Sutherland Gold')	Huge, ferny, chartreuse leaves (cut back often for best color); combine with pink, lavender-pink, or fuchsia roses

Perennial Partners

With the countless perennials that are available, only your climate and imagination limit their possible combinations with roses. When choosing perennial neighbors for a particular rose, consider not only bloom colors, but also the shapes of the blossoms. The large, rounded blossoms of roses look best with perennials that have a contrasting flower shape, such as spikes or small, airy blossoms. Large blossoms also make good partners for roses—for example, trumpet and Oriental lilies add to the luxuriant look of established roses.

And, again, don't forget the power of foliage. Many perennials offer invaluable silver or purple leaves that blend with even the most difficult rose blossom colors or that can act as a bridge between the rose and a nearby plant of a discordant color. Silver foliage works well with every color rose, while purple leaves contrast best with white, pale pink, and yellow roses. For a can't-miss color combination, team yellow roses with perennials that have purple flowers and silver foliage.

When it comes to color, you can take several different approaches when choosing perennial companions for roses. One approach is to complement a rose's color with a color from the other side of the spectrum, such as a powder blue bellflower for a light pink rose or mauve liatris for a pale yellow rose. Taking this approach to its extreme, you can successfully pair hues that are intensely opposite, such as the bright lemon yellow of a yarrow and the deeply saturated fuchsia purple of a gallica rose.

Another approach is to work with variations of the same color by pairing the rose with a perennial flower that is a few shades lighter or darker. For example, you might combine the warm pink of the rugosa rose 'Jens Munk' with the pale pink of 'Loddon Anna' milky bellflower (*Campanula lactiflora* 'Loddon Anna'). In this case, the rose appears to concentrate the color of the bellflowers. Even closely related colors that seem to clash, such as scarlet and fuchsia, can be successfully paired to produce an exciting visual vibration between the two tones.

(continued on page 212)

If you keep bloom and foliage color as well as blossom shape in mind when pairing roses and perennials, you'll find the possibilities for creating a beautiful display, such as this one, almost endless.

Winning Combinations

Perennials make outstanding companions for roses in the mixed border. Here's a quick guide to just a few of the many excellent choices for roses of any given color.

Perennial	Description
To accompany a scarlet or fuchsia rose, choose from:	
'Valerie Finnis' artemisia (*Artemisia ludoviciana* 'Valerie Finnis')	Silver foliage; 2'; shear off flowers
'Superba' clustered bellflower (*Campanula glomerata* 'Superba')	Rich violet flower spikes; 20"
Colewort (*Crambe cordifolia*)	Huge sprays of lacy, white flowers; 4' to 5'
'Bellamosum' delphinium (*Delphinium* 'Bellamosum')	Royal blue flower spikes; 3'
'Aqua' border pink (*Dianthus* 'Aqua')	Fragrant white flowers cover mats of blue-green foliage; 15"; shear after flowering
Gas plant (*Dictamnus albus*)	Spikes of fragrant white flowers; 2'
Amethyst sea holly (*Eryngium amethystinum*)	Metallic blue flowers; 2'
'Johnson's Blue' cranesbill (*Geranium* 'Johnson's Blue')	Large, deep violet-blue flowers; 18"; deadhead after flowering
Japanese aster (*Kalimeris mongolica*)	Sprays of small, double, white daisies; to 2½'
'Sunny Border Blue' veronica (*Veronica* 'Sunny Border Blue')	Royal blue flower spikes; to 2'
To accompany a pink rose, choose from:	
'Anthea' yarrow (*Achillea* 'Anthea')	Pale yellow flowers; silver foliage; 20"
Lady's mantle (*Alchemilla mollis*)	Sprays of chartreuse-yellow flowers; scalloped gray-green leaves; 18"
'Sea Foam' artemisia (*Artemisia versicolor* 'Sea Foam')	Unique filigreed silver foliage; 18"
'Mönch' aster (*Aster* × *frikartii*) 'Mönch'	Masses of large, sky-blue daisies; 2'
'Birch Hybrid' bellflower (*Campanula* 'Birch Hybrid')	Violet-blue bells on low mat; 6"
'Compacta Plena' baby's breath (*Gypsophila paniculata* 'Compacta Plena')	Clouds of tiny white flowers; 12" to 18"
'Souvenir d'André Chaudron' Siberian catmint (*Nepeta siberica* 'Souvenir d'André Chaudron')	Spikes of bright blue flowers; 2' to 3'

(continued)

Perennial	Description
'Lemon Silver' evening primrose (*Oenothera fremontii* 'Lemon Silver')	Large, pale lemon yellow flowers; silver foliage; 1'
Russian sage (*Perovskia atriplicifolia*)	Clouds of amethyst flowers; silver foliage; 3'
Yellow scabious (*Scabiosa ochroleuca*)	Pale yellow flowers on airy, branched stems; 2' to 3'

To accompany a **yellow** rose, choose from:

Perennial	Description
Hummingbird's mint (*Agastache cana*)	Spikes of fragrant, rosy pink flowers; 30"
Yellow columbine (*Aquilegia chrysantha*)	Delicate, lemon yellow flowers; 30"
'Powis Castle' artemisia (*Artemisia* 'Powis Castle')	Mounded, silvery-gray foliage; 30"
'Purple Dome' New England aster (*Aster novae-angliae* 'Purple Dome')	Purple daisies; 18"
Lesser calamint (*Calamintha nepeta*)	Clouds of blue-white flowers; aromatic; 18"
'Plum Pudding' coral bells (*Heuchera* 'Plum Pudding')	Wavy purple foliage; white flowers; 12" (flowers taller)
'Switzerland' Shasta daisy (*Leucanthemum* × *superbum* 'Switzerland')	White daisies with yellow centers; 2'
Blazing star (*Liatris squarrosa*)	Large mauve, buttonlike flowers; 2'
Catmint (*Nepeta subsessilis*)	Bright blue spikes; 2'
'Purple Rain' meadow sage (*Salvia verticillata* 'Purple Rain')	Chunky, smoky purple spikes; 18"

To accompany a **white** rose, choose from:

Perennial	Description
Threadleaf blue star (*Amsonia hubrectii*)	Pale blue flowers; threadlike foliage turns gold in fall; 3'
'Whirlwind' windflower (*Anemone* × *hybrida* 'Whirlwind')	Graceful, white, semidouble flowers; 2' to 3'
'Dove' columbine (*Aquilegia* 'Dove')	White flowers; 2'
'My Antonia' aster (*Aster fendleri* 'My Antonia')	White flowers with yellow centers; 1'
Milky bellflower (*Campanula lactiflora*)	Starry, pale blue flowers; 4'

Perennial	Description
'Albus' valerian (*Centranthus ruber* 'Albus')	Clusters of small, white flowers; gray foliage; 2'
Gaura (*Gaura lindheimeri*)	Airy wands of small, butterflylike white flowers; 2' to 3'
'Biokovo' alpine cranesbill (*Geranium* × *cantabrigiense* 'Biokovo')	Small, pink-tinged white flowers massed over aromatic mat of foliage; 1'
'Snowflake' catmint (*Nepeta* × *faassenii* 'Snowflake')	Spikes of tiny white flowers; gray foliage; 1'
White beardtongue (*Penstemon albidus*)	Spikes of white, tubular flowers; 15"

To accompany a **coral** rose, choose from:

Perennial	Description
'Apricot Beauty' yarrow (*Achillea millefolium* 'Apricot Beauty')	Apricot-pink flowers; 2'
'Arendsii' autumn monkshood (*Aconitum carmichaelii* 'Arendsii')	Intense blue-violet flower spikes; 3'
'Blue Fortune' anise hyssop (*Agastache* 'Blue Fortune')	Spikes of lavender-blue flowers; 2'
'Raydon's Favorite' aromatic aster (*Aster oblongifolius* 'Raydon's Favorite')	Lavender-blue flowers with yellow centers; 30"
'Telham Beauty' peach-leaved bellflower (*Campanula persicifolia* 'Telham Beauty')	Spikes of china blue bells; 30"
'Sentimental Blue' balloonflower (*Platycodon grandiflorus* 'Sentimental Blue')	Violet-blue starry flowers; 1'
'Blauhügel' perennial salvia (*Salvia* × *sylvestris* 'Blauhügel')	Rich lavender-blue flower spikes; 15"
'Butterfly Blue' small scabious (*Scabiosa columbaria* 'Butterfly Blue')	Lavender-blue flowers; 15"
Oriental skullcap (*Scutellaria orientalis*)	Pale, lemon yellow flowers; 6"
'Klaus Jelitto' Stokes' aster (*Stokesia laevis* 'Klaus Jelitto')	Large, disk-shaped, violet-blue flowers; 15"

When you pair a rose with a perennial of the same or similar hue, you create a pleasant color "echo." Color echos can also be separated from each other in the border to create a rhythmic repeat. White roses look particularly wonderful when echoed by white perennials, either nearby or repeated along the length of the border.

There's one hard-and-fast rule to keep in mind regardless of the approach you take with color: Always combine plants that have colors of similar intensity. A bright fuchsia rose, for instance, should be paired with another plant that has intensely colored blooms, such as blue-violet balloonflower or bellflower—pale blue flowers would look washed out next to this rose.

Graceful Grasses

Although it may seem an unorthodox pairing, ornamental grasses actually combine handsomely with most roses. Their fine texture, strappy foliage, and arching form are especially dynamic with shrubby, upright roses such as the rugosas, as well as with prostrate groundcover types. Taller grasses can be used as a backdrop for small- to medium-size shrub roses.

The fine texture and narrow foliage of ornamental grasses combine dynamically with shrub and groundcover roses.

Again, the combinations are almost infinite, but here are a few to consider. White variegated grasses, such as 'Morning Light' eulalia grass (*Miscanthus sinensis* 'Morning Light'), complement pink roses, while distinctly blue-green grasses, such as 'Heavy Metal' switch grass (*Panicum virgatum* 'Heavy Metal'), pair nicely with bright scarlet roses. And yellow grasses, such as yellow-variegated zebra or porcupine grass (*Miscanthus sinensis* 'Zebrinus' and 'Strictus'), are striking with yellow roses. Almost any grass will look great with white roses, but white-variegated grasses are especially attractive.

Fragrant Herbs

Herbs add beauty, fragrance, and texture to the mixed border. Some herbs are better suited than others to this role, however. The thyme genus, for instance, includes many wonderful border plants. With their low-growing, spreading form and range of flower and foliage colors, thymes are among the finest underplantings for shrub roses. 'Bressingham' pink thyme (*Thymus doerfleri*) makes a diminutive mat that blooms in Valentine pink. Gardeners in Zones 7 and southward can use rosemary as a clipped hedge around roses. And the annual herb *Perilla fiutescens* has frilly, deep purple leaves that complement all colors of roses.

For a summary of other choice herbs and their attributes, see "Herbal Companions for Roses," below.

Also, don't hesitate to include roses in the herb garden. After all, roses were used historically as herbs, and the flowers and fruits of organically grown roses are edible. Damask and gallica roses, especially the apothecary rose (*R. gallica officinalis*), are particularly appropriate for herb gardens.

Many herbs make great companions to roses in the mixed border. Here, 'Leverkusen' rose is complemented by artemisia, bronze fennel, and culinary sage.

Herbal Companions for Roses

Here's a selection of the choicest herbs to include in your mixed border.

Herb	Description
Garlic chives (*Allium tuberosum*)	Umbels of white flowers; 18" vigorous self-sower; perennial
Showy calamint (*Calamintha grandiflora*)	Mounded plant with fragrant foliage; tubular bright pink flowers for 2 months; 18" to tips of flower stalks; perennial
Bronze fennel (*Foeniculum vulgare* var. *dulce*)	Purple-bronze, anise-scented foliage; yellow flowers; 3'; annual (perennial in warm climates)
German chamomile (*Matricaria recutita*)	Sweetly fragrant; airy white flowers; 2½'; annual
Oregano (*Origanum laevigatum*)	Fragrant foliage; purple flowers in late summer attract butterflies; 12" to 18"; perennial
Rosemary (*Rosmarinus officinalis*)	Piney scent; tiny, sky blue flowers; 2' or more; perennial, but overwinter indoors in Zone 6 and colder
'Purpurascens' purple sage (*Salvia officinalis* 'Purpurascens')	Silver leaves overlaid with purple; 18" to 30"; perennial
'Argenteus' lemon-scented thyme (*Thymus* × *citriodorus* 'Argenteus')	Silver-edged aromatic foliage; 6" to 12"; perennial

The abundant blossoms and exuberant forms of many roses lend themselves perfectly to the wild garden.

roses in the wild garden

Historically, roses have been grown in "rose gardens"—rigidly formal beds featuring solid blocks of hybrid teas lined up like soldiers. But there's no rule that says roses *must* be grown this way. In fact, roses grown *en masse* are much more susceptible to pest and disease problems, resulting in more time-consuming work for you, the gardener.

So why not do exactly the opposite and allow roses to run wild, just as they would along the edge of a woodland or in some forgotten "secret" garden? With their luxuriant blossoms and exuberant forms, many roses are perfect for evoking the romantic, carefree look of a wild garden.

Although a "wild garden" might seem like a contradiction in terms, the concept really is quite simple. A wild garden is inspired by the natural world, yet shaped by the imagination and hands of the gardener. How you choose to shape *your* wild garden is up to you. Perhaps you're a native plant enthusiast who wants to grow only native American roses. Or maybe you want an informal, low-maintenance garden. Or perhaps you're striving to create an old-fashioned cottage garden, where masses of flowers and foliage mingle casually in apparent untended abundance. Whatever your goal, within this chapter you'll find an array of carefree, vigorous roses to bring alive your vision of a wild garden.

In Search of the Wild Rose

The best roses for a wild garden are, of course, wild roses—or at least roses that look wild. Most have single or semidouble blossoms that show their stamens, as the blossoms of species roses do. A few roses with fully double blossoms also exist in nature, and some of these are very well suited to cottage gardens. Blossom colors should be soft and natural, such as white, pink, soft apricot, and clear (nonorange) yellow. An occasional pure scarlet is okay, too. Avoid coral, orange, and other strident colors, which look out of place among the subtle nuances of the wild garden.

Choose roses that have a loose, natural plant form—whether tall and arching, dense and bushy, or low and spreading. Climbers and especially rambling roses, with their habit of clambering, sprawling, and intermingling, are ideal for creating a look of abandoned abundance. Among shorter roses, stick to those that have a suckering or procumbent form rather than neat, tidy, dwarf shrubs.

Finally, look for roses that bear an abundant crop of hips in a variety of colors, forms, and textures. Include species with fruits that are deep burgundy or bright golden orange, round or urn-shaped, and smooth and shiny or exotically bristled. All will be right at home in your wild garden.

Regardless of what aesthetic qualities your potential rose selections have, one thing is certain: Roses for the wild garden need to be tough! Pass on those that need lots of deadheading, spraying, or pruning. In general, native roses, as well as roses that have naturalized in your area (in other words, those that have spread on their own through local hedgerows, meadows, and woodland edges) are best adapted to your conditions and, therefore, are prime candidates for the wild garden.

Allowing a rambling rose to clamber up an ancient apple tree is a classic way to evoke the romantic look of an abandoned, wild garden.

Roses that bear decorative hips, such as the mountain rose (*Rosa woodsii fendleri*), are prime candidates for the wild garden.

Rose Alert!

Although most naturalized roses are ideal for the wild garden, *R. multiflora* is a notable exception. Introduced for use as a hedgerow plant in the early part of the last century, this Japanese species has become an invasive pest in many areas of the United States, and it also harbors rosette virus. Be sure to exclude it from your wild garden.

At the same time, try to realize that a wild garden, like nature, includes plants that would be considered "imperfect" and out of place if they were included in a more formal setting. As the gardener, you may need to adjust your attitude to reach a new understanding of what looks "beautiful." A mature species rose, for instance, may assume a craggy, asymmetrical form that would stand out disconcertingly in a formal landscape. But in the wild garden, such a rose would look absolutely stunning.

The same is true for certain "weeds" such as common fleabane (*Erigeron annus*) and woolly mullein (*Verbasum* spp.). As long as you don't let them get the upper hand, many naturalized and native plants can enhance the beauty of your wild garden by lending it a truly natural spontaneity. So before you give in to your reflex to pull every weed, ask yourself if it might not be better to let it be.

Native American Roses

One type of wild garden that you might choose to create consists primarily of native plants. To purists, a native plant is one that's indigenous only to the immediate area. But I have trouble with that view because one could argue that a plant indigenous to swampy areas is no longer "native" when grown in an average garden setting in that same geographic locale. If you limited yourself to a purist's definition of native, you'd end up with very few (if any) native roses in your garden. Because there are many interesting roses that are native to North America, I prefer to take a more inclusive approach. Just be sure to choose a species that will survive winters in your area. (See "Go Native" on page 218 for a quick reference to native North American rose species to include in your wild garden.)

Although many specialty rose nurseries sell native roses, you may have trouble finding a commercial supplier for some of the more obscure species. If you're lucky enough to find a stand growing in the wild, *do not dig up the plants.* Doing so can jeopardize the native plant population. Instead, propagate the plant by collecting and germinating seeds or rooting softwood cuttings. Either method usually works easily for species roses.

American native Virginia rose (*Rosa virginiana)* puts on a spectacular autumn display of colorful foliage and hips.

These rugged, native American roses are ideal for the wild garden. Some have been used to breed hardy modern shrubs. Although most bloom just once each year, they add interest to the garden because many bloom considerably later than most garden roses.

Name	Hardiness Range	Plant Size (Height × Width)	Features
Arkansas rose (R. arkansana)	Zones 4–10	2' × 5'	Clusters of 1" pink flowers in early summer; small red fruits; suckering stems with thin prickles; can be used as a groundcover
Hudson Bay rose, Labrador rose (R. blanda)	Zones 4–10	5' × 5'	Clusters of 2" to 2½" pink blossoms in late spring; round to oval red hips; almost no thorns
California wild rose (R. californica)	Zones 3–10	10' × 8'	Clusters of small, medium pink flowers for several weeks in early summer; rounded oval red hips; thin thorns
Carolina rose, pasture rose (R. carolina)	Zones 4–10	4' × 5'	Profuse, medium-size, warm pink flowers, produced singly in midsummer; globose red hips; suckering growth; few thorns on older stems; thick, glossy, dark green foliage
Leafy rose (R. foliolosa)	Zones 4–10	4' × 5'	Solitary, bright candy pink, 2" flowers from midsummer through fall; small, round red hips from earliest flowers only; fine-textured foliage has good autumn color; thornless; likes sandy soils; one of two repeat-blooming native roses

Name	Hardiness Range	Plant Size (Height × Width)	Features
Rosa × kochiana	Zones 4–10	3' × 3'	1½" lilac-pink flowers in midsummer; pear-shaped red hips; few large thorns; glossy, apple-green foliage turns orange and red in autumn
Nutka rose (*R. nutkana*)	Zones 4–10	5' × 5'	2½" mauve-pink flowers in midsummer; showy, rounded oval, red hips
Prairie rose (*R. setigera*)	Zones 4–10	5' × 5'	Clusters of 2½" deep pink blossoms that pale with age; inconspicuous hips; bright green foliage and hooked thorns; longest-blooming native rose (2 months)
Sacramento rose, gooseberry rose (*R. stellata mirifica*)	Zones 6–10	3' × 3'	Small, solitary, lilac-pink flowers with orangey stamens; round to urn-shaped, bristly red hips; gray-green foliage
Virginia rose (*R. virginiana*)	Zones 3–10	5' × 5'	Clusters of 2½", medium pink, slightly fragrant blossoms in midsummer; shiny, scarlet hips; bright green foliage turns yellow and orange in autumn
Mountain rose (*R. woodsii fendleri*)	Zones 3–10	6' × 5'	Small, mauve-pink blossoms borne singly or in small clusters; spectacular, cherrylike red hips; dark gray-green foliage; mildly prickly

Root Your Own Roses

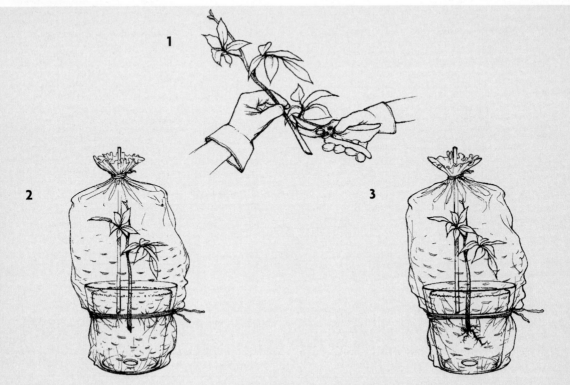

Rooting roses from softwood cuttings works well for most species roses, as well as for many hybrids. Although rooting roses takes a little time, it's a lot of fun. Plus, your homegrown plants will be more vigorous than grafted roses.

1. Take the cutting. In late spring or early summer (as soon as the first flower buds have formed), take 4- to 8-inch cuttings of healthy, vigorously growing stems. (Morning is the best time to take cuttings because the flower stems are full of water.) Snip off the buds and all but two or three leaves, removing half of their leaflets, if necessary, to reduce wilting.

2. Provide the proper conditions for rooting. Fill a sterilized, 4- to 6-inch plastic pot (with a drainage hole) with a moistened, sterile mixture consisting of 4 parts perlite to 1 part peat moss. Use a pencil to make a 2- to 3-inch-deep hole in the mix, then insert the fresh cutting. Water lightly. Enclose the entire pot and cutting in a plastic bag. Close the bag at the top and place the pot in indirect light in a warm location—a coldframe located on the north side of your house would be ideal.

3. Nurture the young plant. Monitor the pot for moisture, keeping it moist but not wet. Roots should begin to appear in 2 to 4 weeks. Remove the bag when roots are 2 inches long. (Gently remove the cutting from the pot to check for root development.) Beginning about 2 weeks after the roots start to form, fertilize the cutting with half-strength kelp emulsion every third watering. After roots have become moderately established (when the roots show at the surface of the mix when you gently tip the contents of the pot out), pot the cutting into a regular mix and harden it off outdoors. In late summer or early fall, you can plant it in the garden.

The Wide World of Wild Roses

If you're not a native plant purist, you have the option of roving the entire planet (figuratively, of course) in search of wonderful species roses for your wild garden. Both Europe and Asia are rich in roses that make marvelous additions to woodland edges, cottage gardens, or informal gardens. Like native American roses, most of these roses bloom once per year, bearing graceful single blossoms that give way to decorative hips. But European and Asian species tend to be more fragrant than North American native roses. This group also includes roses of ethereal beauty, such as the musk rose (*R. moschata*).

The plant form and structure of European and Asian roses vary widely. Some are tall and angular, while others are arching, and many are vigorous climbers. For the most pleasing effect in the wild garden, let these majestic roses assume their natural shapes without imposing any human sense of symmetry on them. (For a guide to some of the best non-native species roses to include in your wild garden, see "Exotic Species Roses for the Wild Garden" on page 222.)

The Chinese species *Rosa laevigata* is a vigorous climber that has become so naturalized in the southern United States that it is known as the Cherokee rose.

3 Oriental Beauties for the Wild Garden

Three yellow species roses hailing from China and Japan make outstanding additions to the wild garden. All are hardy to Zone 4, bloom once per year (in early spring), and have attractive, ferny foliage. 'Father Hugo's Rose' has refined, single, light yellow flowers; the plants grow 6 to 7 feet tall. *R. primula,* also known as the incense rose, has fantastically fragrant foliage and pale yellow-white flowers. And the Manchu rose (*R. xanthina*) bears single to semi-double bright yellow spring flowers.

Manchu rose (*R. xanthina*)

Exotic Species Roses for the Wild Garden

Draw on the rich variety of rose species worldwide for a palette of colors and forms to enhance your wild garden. Some of the best species follow; breeders have used many of them to develop both old and modern hybrids. (You'll find more details about some of them in "A Gallery of Roses," beginning on page 106.)

Name	Origin	Hardiness Range	Plant Size (Height × Width)	Features
The field rose (*R. arvensis*)	Europe	Zones 4–10	10' × 12'	Small, creamy white single flowers with large cluster of golden stamens; slightly fragrant; blooms in early summer; red, oval hips; deep green leaves; thorny; can be used as a rambler
'Yellow Lady Banks' rose (*R. banksiae lutea*)	China	Zones 7–10	30' × 15'	Double, bright yellow, fragrant flowers in late spring; thornless; excellent rambler and tree rose for the South and temperate coastal regions
Dog rose (*R. canina*)	Europe	Zones 3–10	12' × 6'	Small, fragrant, blush pink single flowers in early summer; profuse, bright red, oval hips; thorny
Sweetbriar rose, eglantine (*R. eglanteria*)	Europe	Zones 4–10	10' × 6'	Small, fragrant, single, light pink flowers; bristly, oval, scarlet hips; bright green, apple-scented foliage; very thorny
Rosa gigantea	China	Zones 7–10	20' × 10'	Large, single, fragrant white flowers in early summer; bottle-shaped, orange-red hips; thorny; naturalized in southern United States

Name	Origin	Hardiness Range	Plant Size (Height × Width)	Features
Redleaf rose (R. glauca)	Europe	Zones 4–10	8' × 5'	Small, clear pink flowers with tapered petals in early summer; highly ornamental scarlet hips; beautiful blue-gray foliage overlaid with red; mostly thornless
Cherokee rose (R. laevigata)	China	Zones 7–10	15' × 6'	Large, single, white, fragrant flowers in late spring; bristly, oval, orange hips; evergreen; large thorns
Musk rose (R. moschata)	Mediterranean Europe	Zones 5–10	10' × 5'	Loose clusters of small, creamy white flowers with wafting fragrance in late summer, repeating into autumn; gray-green foliage; few thorns
Rosa moyesii	China	Zones 4–10	10' × 5'	Single, dark cherry red flowers in early summer; urn-shaped, scarlet hips; small, gray-green leaves; angular growth; very thorny
Apple rose (R. pomifera)	Europe and Asia	Zones 4–10	6' × 4'	Fragrant, clear pink, single flowers; large, red, bristly, apple-shaped hips; gray-green foliage; some prickles
Rugosa rose (R. rugosa)	China and Japan	Zones 3–10	8' × 5'	Single, fragrant, bright pink to magenta flowers, repeating into autumn; large orange-red hips; apple green, crinkled leaves turn warm colors in autumn

Ancient and Modern Shrub Roses for Wild Gardens

All of the ancient roses—the albas, centifolias, damasks, and gallicas—are right at home in the wild garden. The carefree nature and generous flowering of these old roses is perfect for creating the "secret garden" look—one of abandoned abundance. Their heady perfumes and heavy double blossoms add to the sense of a forgotten paradise.

For the wildest look, choose large old shrub roses with cascading branches, such as the albas. Damasks impart a sense of timeless beauty, while gallicas are great for mingling with nearby perennials and wildflowers. If a casual-looking cottage garden is your goal, centifolias—with their heavy, old-fashioned blossoms—are an ideal choice.

But don't limit your choices to ancient roses. Any modern shrub with rugged disease resistance, subtle color, and large size can work. Examples include 'Fritz Nobis', 'Frühlingsduft', and 'Frühlingsmorgen', as well as many of the hybrid musks and noisettes. Using repeat-blooming modern shrubs such as these is an excellent way to extend the bloom season in the wild garden. Just be careful to choose cultivars that have an informal look, in keeping with the exuberance of the wild garden.

Billows of Blossom

Perhaps no other group of roses better evokes the wild garden than the ramblers. Even the name "rambling rose" conjures up a scene of gnarled old trees festooned with garlands of fragrant roses.

For the wild garden, you can't go wrong with the multiflora ramblers (not to be confused with the species *R. multiflora*) and wichurana ramblers. Allow them to clamber into trees and scramble over less desirable indigenous vegetation, covering everything in their paths with billows of blossom.

Ramblers such as 'Adélaide d'Orléans' *(above)* are well suited to the wild garden. Although most ramblers flower only in midsummer, they bear an abundance of blossoms. Most also bear a heavy crop of ornamental red hips that provide a second season of color.

Ravishing Ramblers

In addition to the rambling roses listed in "A Gallery of Roses" (see page 106), the following ramblers are fantastic for the wild garden. Some can grow to as long as 30 feet, especially in warmer climates. Most flower once per season.

All of the following roses are hardy at least to Zone 6. North of Zone 6, some will experience winter dieback. In general, the farther south you live, the bigger these roses will grow.

- 'Adélaide d'Orléans'. Pink buds open to fragrant, blushed white semidouble blossoms with golden stamens

- 'Albertine'. Fragrant, semidouble, bright pink flowers fade to blush pink with pale yellow hearts

- 'Dr. W. Van Fleet'. Fragrant, light pink, fully double blossoms age to blush white

- 'Félicité et Perpétue'. Pale pink pompom flowers; evergreen foliage; thornless

- 'Kew Rambler'. Very fragrant, single pink flowers fade to white at the center

- 'Léontine Gervais'. Semidouble blossoms of soft yellow to pale peach pink

- 'Paul's Himalayan Musk Rambler'. Pendant clusters of mauve-pink double flowers; not a musk rose (despite the name)

- 'Rambling Rector'. Dense clusters of very fragrant white flowers showing stamens; extremely vigorous

Untechniques for the Wild Garden

Cultivating a wild garden consists mostly of allowing nature to take its course. That isn't to say that a wild garden requires *no* work; you should prepare the soil just as you would for any other garden and keep the planting area free of undesirable weeds and invasive plants. But the key word here is "undesirable." Think twice before pulling what some gardeners would consider a weed, including woolly mulleins (*Verbasum* spp.), violets (*Viola* spp.), evening primrose (*Oenothera biennis*), and vervain (*Vervain* spp.). Many of these plants have a wild beauty and pleasing tendency to pop up randomly here and there, making the garden look, well, more *wild*. In Europe, even lowly weeds such as fleabane (*Erigeron annus*) are now purposefully cultivated to create the "wild" look that is at the vanguard of Dutch and German garden style.

Half the fun of wild gardening is learning to appreciate the beauty of naturalized plants, such as ox-eye daisies (*Chrysanthemum leucanthemum*).

To have a truly wild, low-maintenance garden, you must first learn to see the beauty in the flowers, seedheads, and dried forms of common, everyday wild or naturalized plants. If that seems a difficult thing to do, remember that one person's weed is another person's wildflower. For example, the corn poppies (*Papaver rhoeas*) and bachelor buttons (*Centaurea cyanus*) that we love to grow in our gardens are considered invasive weeds in European and North African cultivated fields!

I'm not suggesting you let your wild garden be overrun with dandelions, and I'm certainly not recommending you allow Canada thistles to run rampant. But do consider allowing some ornamental wild plants—whether native or exotic—to exist here and there, as you learn to appreciate their natural beauty. You'll find that as your wild garden matures under your watchful eye and caring hand, it will attain a natural balance.

Choosing Plants in the Wild Vernacular

When selecting companion plants for roses in the wild garden, let nature be your guide. Look for plants that will spread here and there in a pleasingly random—but noninvasive—manner. For the backbone of your wild garden, choose native and plain species shrubs, rather than gussied-up cultivars, to join your roses. Use the same guidelines when choosing your herbaceous perennials: Stick to species or very simple, old-fashioned cultivars, rather than double flower forms or varieties with unnatural colors. Single flowers not only look more wild, but many of them also self-sow, adding a delightfully random note to the garden composition without any help from you. Just be sure to avoid perennials that are clearly invasive, such as gooseneck loosestrife

Who says you have to grow roses in a formal garden? Allowing roses to run wild adds a carefree, exotic look to your landscape. Plus, roses in the wild garden require little in terms of pruning—and they need no deadheading—which means you'll have plenty of time to relax and enjoy their natural beauty.

(*Lysimachia clethroides*) or purple loosestrife (*Lythrum salicaria*). Within a short time, these aggressive plants will overcome their neighbors—as well as overcome the rest of your landscape.

At all costs, avoid dwarf cultivars and strains of perennials and annuals that normally are tall. These plants look very unnatural, and their tight, stunted appearance is entirely out of place in the wild garden. At the front edges of your planting, where you need short plants, use naturally diminutive plants. This is quite easy to do if your soil is dry and gravelly, as you can choose from a huge array of semi-alpine plants. In addition, many plants native to the Great Plains are naturally prostrate or diminutive, such as the lovely cups of wine (*Callirhoe involucrata*) and rose verbena (*Verbena canadensis*).

Masses and Drifts

Garden experts often harangue their readers and audiences about using plants in masses and drifts, and that advice especially applies to the use of perennials in the wild garden. A drift is nothing more than an irregular shape—one that usually is relatively smooth in outline and tapered at the ends to allow interlocking and overlap with other groups of plants. One of my favorite techniques is to plant a fairly long drift of one type of plant, then "fade out" the drift with a pair of plants of that type, and finish with a single plant that is interspersed into the neighboring group. This approximates the look of the plant populations in nature and creates soft edges between plant groups. (See the garden plan on page 228 for examples of roses and other plants suitable for the wild garden and how to arrange them in natural ways.)

Cohabitation in the Wild Garden

Don't be afraid to mingle plants in the wild garden. Nature usually populates any given square yard with several different species. Although this suggestion might seem to contradict the advice to plant in drifts, it really doesn't.

The idea is to plant a grid of two or even three different plants within a given drift. The plants you choose to combine can either bloom simultaneously (in which case their colors should blend or complement) or they could bloom in sequence so that as one type fades, another begins to bloom.

The one requirement is that the growth needs and habits—both above and below ground—of members of a given drift are relatively compatible. For example, tap-rooted columbines and fibrous-rooted penstemons or bellflowers are good companions. Likewise, butterflyweed coexists happily with pulsatilla anemones, and the two plants bloom at entirely different times of the year.

Applying this idea to roses, you might team up shrub roses with ramblers. The shrub roses would engulf the area with bloom in June, while the ramblers would clamber into a tree overhead to provide blooms later in the season. Perennial and annual companions would complement the bloom color and time of each of the roses.

Rose Care in the Wild Garden

One of the best things about a wild garden is that it requires so little maintenance. After all, you will have selected only the most rugged varieties, so disease control is practically a nonissue. And insects should be less of a problem than in any other part of your garden because the wide spectrum of plants will attract many beneficial insects and animals.

The only pruning you'll need to do will be to remove deadwood. Deadheading certainly won't be needed (and, in fact, should be avoided!) as it would discourage the formation of the beautiful hips borne by most of these roses after flowering.

Limit your fertilizing to applications of compost, which will meet all of the nutrient needs of the mostly once-flowering roses in the wild garden. And while newly planted roses need just as much water in the wild garden as they do anywhere else, the mature wild garden should need no irrigation. That's because you will have selected rugged plants that can thrive under normal rainfall conditions in your area.

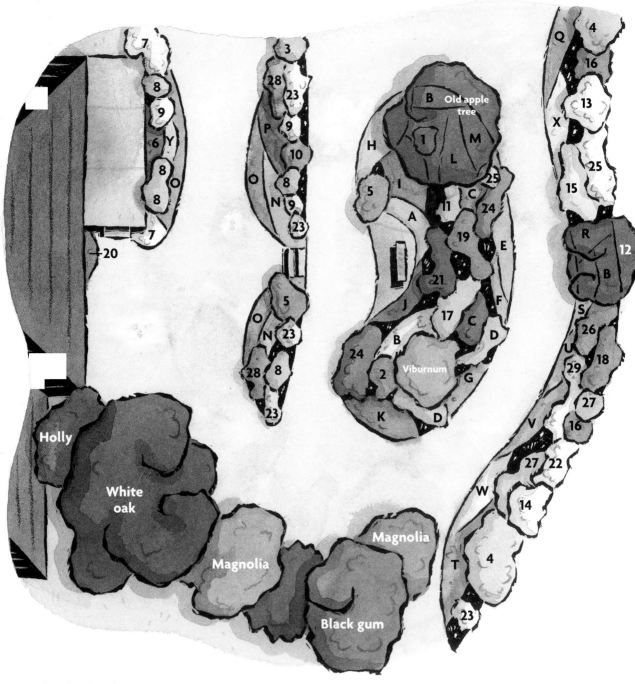

In this plan for a backyard wild garden, the look of the planting beds shifts from more formal and traditional near the house to meadowy, wild, and woodsy as you approach the natural woodland edge at the rear of the property. The complexity of the plantings also increases as you move away from the house. Thus the porch is smothered in rambling roses, but not much else is planted next to the house. The focus is on luxuriant wild color behind the retaining wall and beyond. The island bed breaks up what would otherwise be a sea of lawn, without breaking a vista to a white flowering dogwood centered in the woodland edge. A picturesque and rustic bench provides another visual focus from the house and makes for a sublime perch among the flowers.

Trees, Roses, and Other Shrubs

1. 'Adélaide d'Orléans' hybrid sempervirens rose (1)
2. 'Fritz Nobis' [shrub rose] (1)
3. 'Ghislaine de Féligonde' [hybrid multiflora rose] (1)
4. Shrub rose R. *eglanteria* ('Sweetbriar') (3)
5. 'Raubritter' [shrub rose] (2)
6. 'Veilchenblau' [hybrid multiflora rose] (1)
7. 'Albéric Barbier' [hybird wichurana rose] (2)
8. 'Danaë' [hybrid musk rose] (6)
9. 'Penelope' [hybrid musk rose] (3)
10. 'Cornelia' [hybrid musk rose] (1)
11. 'Frühlingsduft' [hybrid spinosissima rose] (1)
12. Flowering dogwood (*Cornus florida*) (1)
13. 'Alba Semi-plena' [alba rose] (1)
14. Species rose field rose R. *arvensis* (1)
15. Species rose R. *spinosissima altaica* (3)
16. Species rose apple rose R. *pomifera* (2)
17. Species rose Father Hugo's rose (2)
18. Species rose R. *woodsii fendleri* (3)
19. 'Petite Lisette' [centifolia rose] (4)
20. 'New Dawn' [large-flowered climber rose] (1)
21. Bush clover (*Lespedeza thunbergii*) (4)
22. Smooth hydrangea (*Hydrangea arborescens*) (4)
23. Bearberry (*Arctostaphylos uva-ursi*) (7)
24. 'Early Amethyst' purple beautyberry (*Callicarpa dichotoma* 'Early Amethyst') (8)
25. 'Ruby Spice' summersweet clethra (*Clethra alnifolia* 'Ruby Spice') (8)
26. Roseshell azalea (*Rhododendron prinophyllum*) (5)
27. 'Summer Stars' bush honeysuckle (*Diervilla rivularis* 'Summer Stars') (7)
28. 'Blue Billow' hydrangea (*Hydrangea serrata* 'Blue Billow') (10)
29. 'Blue Mist' dwarf fothergilla (*Fothergilla gardenii* 'Blue Mist') (5)

Perennials and Grasses

A. Golden marguerite (*Anthemis tinctoria*), rose verbena (*Verbena canadensis*), and northern sea oats (*Chasmanthium latifolium*)
B. Bugbane (*Cimicifuga simplex*) and quamash (*Camassia quamash*)
C. 'Purple Bush' Joe Pye weed (*Eupatorium purpureum* 'Purple Bush') (5)
D. Tickseed (*Coreopsis tripteris*) (9)
E. Butterfly weed (*Asclepias tuberosa*), 'Corbett' columbine (*Aquilegia canadensis* 'Corbett'), and 'October Skies' aromatic aster (*Aster oblongifolius* 'October Skies')
F. Rose campion (*Lychnis coronaria*), 'Corbett' columbine (*Aquilegia canadensis* 'Corbett'), and 'Coombe Fishacre' aster (*Aster* 'Coombe Fishacre')
G. 'Snow Sport' yarrow (*Achillea millefolium* 'Snow Sport'), quamash (*Camassia quamash*), and harebell (*Campanula rotundifolia*)
H. Northern sea oats (*Chasmanthium latifolium*) and yellow scabious (*Scabiosa ochroleuca*)
I. Tall larkspur (*Delphinium exaltatum*), gaura (*Gaura lindheimeri*), and 'Kanaria' sneezeweed (*Helenium* 'Kanaria')
J. 'Snow Sport' yarrow (*Achillea millefolium* 'Snow Sport'), rose campion (*Lychnis coronaria*), and 'Lewsii' perennial flax (*Linum perenne* 'Lewsii')

K. Quamash (*Camassia quamash*), 'Snow Sport' yarrow (*Achillea millefolium* 'Snow Sport'), and 'Purple Dome' aster (*Aster novae-angliae* 'Purple Dome')
L. Scented cranesbill (*Geranium macrorrhizum*) and 'Anja's Choice' aster (*Aster* 'Anja's Choice')
M. Northern sea oats (*Chasmanthium latifolium*), meadow rue (*Thalictrum aquilegifolium*), and blue-stemmed goldenrod (*Solidago caesia*)
N. Yellow scabious (*Scabiosa ochroleuca*)
O. Calamint (*Calamintha nepeta* spp. *nepeta*)
P. 'Omega Skyrocket' Stokes' aster (*Stokesia laevis* 'Omega Skyrocket')
Q. Mist flower (*Eupatorium coelestinum*)
R. Bowman's root (*Gillenia trifoliata*)
S. 'Clouds of Perfume' woodland phlox (*Phlox divaricata* 'Clouds of Perfume') and blue wood aster (*Aster cordifolius*)
T. Threadleaf blue star (*Amsonia hubrectii*)
U. Wood spurge (*Euphorbia amygdaloides* var. *robbiae*)
V. Prairie phlox (*Phlox pilosa*) and 'Bluebird' smooth aster (*Aster laevis* 'Bluebird')
W. 'Autumn Bride' coral bells (*Heuchera villosa* 'Autumn Bride')
X. Harebell (*Campanula rotundifolia*), 'Corbett' columbine (*Aquilegia canadensis* 'Corbett'), and blue-stemmed goldenrod (*Solidago caesia*)
Y. 'Valerie Finnis' artemisia (*Artemisia ludoviciana* 'Valerie Finnis')

A hedge of rugosa roses provides not only a colorful screen but also a bounty of fragrant petals for cooking and making potpourri.

roses for hedging

Hedges are nearly as old

as gardening is. People have always planted shrubs close together to mark property boundaries or to define areas within their property, but contemporary gardeners plant these versatile living fences for many other reasons, too. Hedges can:

- create privacy,
- set limits,
- direct foot traffic,
- emphasize an entrance,
- provide the "walls" for a garden room,
- form a barrier against unwanted animals,
- provide a background for another planting, such as a perennial border,
- create a protected microclimate, and
- serve an aesthetic role, such as to emphasize a contour or provide a gradation of height between, say, a stone path and taller plantings.

Although most people picture a "hedge" as a formal, boxy band of clipped boxwood, privet, or yew, a hedge can be quite informal and colorful. Informal hedges are not clipped (although they may be pruned). Instead, the plants merge their natural shapes to provide a "ribbon" of vegetation that may be short, tall, or in-between. Roses are among the best shrubs for this sort of informal hedge, although some are much better suited to this application than others.

Choosing Roses for Hedges

When selecting roses for hedges, avoid types and varieties that are sparsely foliated, as well as those that grow wider than they do tall or that have an excessively arching, angular, or lanky form (such as hybrid teas). None of these roses will provide the dense growth needed to make an effective hedge. Instead, look for roses that have a relatively upright form and that are thickly cloaked with healthy foliage. Other key considerations for hedging roses include height, hardiness, and—of course—health.

Height, Hardiness, and Health

For a hedge, you'll want to choose rose varieties that will have a mature size that is the same as (or close to) the desired height of your hedge. After all, why spend any more time than necessary hacking away at

Most rugosa roses, with their dense, bushy growth, are excellent candidates for a flowering hedge. 'Jens Munk' *(above)* is especially suitable because of its extremely upright habit.

the tops of the plants to keep your hedge at its intended height? (A rose variety that matures to a height that's 6 to 12 inches taller than the target height of your hedge isn't a big problem, though. Just lightly shear the tops of the plants every other year or so to control the height and stimulate dense new growth.)

Keep in mind that the ultimate height of any given rose cultivar can vary widely through its useful range, depending on the degree of winter dieback it suffers. For hedging, the rule of thumb is to select a variety that is solidly hardy in your zone, rather than one that is at its limit of cold-hardiness in your area. That way your hedge will be dense and solid and will achieve the height you expect.

Another reason to choose clearly hardy roses for your hedge is that your selection will reduce the amount of deadwood you'll need to prune away each year. Because roses are planted much more densely in a hedge than in other garden settings, cutting out lots of deadwood each year would quickly become too much work!

In addition to considering the height and winter-hardiness of your potential hedge roses, be sure to choose healthy varieties. Because roses in a hedge are planted in such close proximity to one another, disease problems can spread rapidly from one plant to the next. That's why rugosa roses—which are practically immune to black spot—are really the ultimate hedging roses. Whatever roses you choose, practice good pest prevention. Reduce overwintering disease spores by raking up all leaf debris in late fall, along with the topmost layer of mulch, and then replacing it with fresh mulch.

Recommended Roses for Hedges

Two large classes of roses provide the best candidates for hedging: the rugosas and the hybrid musks. But many roses from other classes can be used for hedging with great success, even if the other members of their classes aren't suitable. Part of the decision depends on the "look" you want to achieve with your hedge and how formal or informal the setting is. For instance, a hedge of the American species *Rosa virginiana* can look splendid as a boundary marker for your backyard if your property line runs through a somewhat wild woodland edge. And, of course, many other wild species roses, such as *R. eglanteria, R. canina,* and *R. arvensis,* are spontaneous and natural—but mostly large-growing—hedgerow plants. However, if you want a rose as a hedge along the walkway approaching the front entrance of your home, a better choice would be a more petite, refined variety, such as the dwarf polyantha 'White Pet' or the repeat-blooming small moss rose 'Alfred de Dalmas'.

If the rose you are considering for your hedge doesn't repeat bloom, be sure it has some other ornamental trait to give it value throughout the season, such as colorful hips through fall and winter or highly attractive foliage (preferably with good autumn color). If your hedge is to function as a true barrier, especially against animals, choose a densely thorny variety, such as a rugosa. For a sampling of the best roses for hedging, see "Best Bets for a Hedge of Roses" on page 234. (Also refer to "A Gallery of Roses" on page 106. Roses suitable for hedging are noted in the "Uses" category.)

Planting and Caring for a Rose Hedge

To thrive, roses in hedges need the same things that other roses do—good soil, adequate water, excellent drainage, and routine maintenance. But due to their close spacing, roses in hedges demand a bit more from the soil than roses in other situations do.

Preparing the Soil and Planting

Because the plants in your rose hedge will be tightly spaced, you'll need to prepare the soil with super diligence. Before planting, add 25 percent more organic matter than you would normally to ensure that your hedge fills in rapidly and stays full and healthy.

Plant the shrubs at about half the distance apart that you would plant them normally. You want the

(continued on page 236)

Rugged rugosa roses make a great informal hedge for a backyard or other informal area *(left)*. Some polyantha roses, such as 'China Doll' *(right),* also work well when used as a hedge.

Best Bets for a Hedge of Roses

The following roses make excellent hedges. For additional suggestions, see "A Gallery of Roses" on page 106.

Cultivar	Hardiness Range	Bloom Color	Bloom Period	Comments
Small Hedges (2–3 feet)				
'Charles Albanel' [hybrid rugosa]	Zones 3–10	Crimson pink	Repeats	Rugosa; big, orange-red hips; good fall color; may sucker
'Coral Cluster' [polyantha]	Zones 5–10	Coral pink	Continuous	No fragrance; good for formal areas
'Corylus' [shrub]	Zones 3–10	Medium pink	Continuous	Shrub rose; beautiful hips and fall color; may sucker
'Dart's Dash' [hybrid rugosa]	Zones 3–10	Magenta pink	Continuous	Rugosa; tomato red hips; good fall color; may sucker
'De Montarville' [shrub]	Zones 3–10	Medium pink	Continuous	Hardiness of rugosa with looks of modern landscape roses
'Dornröschenschloss Sababurg' [shrub]	Zones 5–10	Clear pink	Continuous	Fully double; striking for formal areas
'Rose de Rescht' [damask (Portland)]	Zones 4–10	Fuchsia red	Repeats	Extremely fragrant; excellent form for hedge
'Rose du Roi' [damask (Portland)]	Zones 4–10	Fuschsia red	Repeats	Extremely fragrant; excellent form for hedge
'Schneezwerg' [hybrid rugosa]	Zones 3–10	White	Continuous	Beautiful hips; tight form makes it suitable for both formal and informal areas
'White Pet' [polyantha]	Zones 5–10	White	Continuous	No fragrance; pomponlike blossoms; good for formal areas
Medium Hedges (3–5 feet)				
'Alfred de Dalmas' [moss]	Zones 4–10	Blush pink	Continuous	Repeat-blooming moss; very refined; excellent near the house
'Autumn Damask' [damask]	Zones 4–10	Warm pink	Repeats	Excellent for old-fashioned look

Cultivar	Hardiness Range	Bloom Color	Bloom Period	Comments
'Ballerina' [hybrid musk]	Zones 4–10	Medium pink to white	Continuous	Enormous flower power; takes well to shearing after first bloom; good in the South
'Felicia' [hybrid musk]	Zones 5–10	Salmon pink	Continuous	Takes well to shearing after first bloom flush; excellent in the South
'Félicité Parmentier' [alba]	Zones 3–10	Creamy pink	Once	Beautiful gray-green foliage; narrowly upright habit; super fragrance
'Fimbriata' [hybrid rugosa]	Zones 3–10	White blushed pink	Repeats	Beautiful hips and excellent fall color; thickly thorny and foliated
'Frau Dagmar Hartopp' [hybrid rugosa]	Zones 3–10	Pale pink	Continuous	Naturally compact, rounded form; fantastic hips and fall color
'Henry Hudson' [hybrid rugosa]	Zones 3–10	White	Continuous	Distinctive rounded form makes it unsuitable for mixing with other rugosas; needs deadheading
'Hunter' [hybrid rugosa]	Zones 4–10	Crimson	Continuous	Best true red hedge
'Jens Munk' [hybrid rugosa]	Zones 3–10	Lavender pink	Continuous	Upright form makes it a natural for hedge; tomato red hips
Tall Hedges (over 5 feet)				
'Alba Maxima' [alba]	Zones 3–10	Pure white	Once	Spectacular bloom; dense gray-green foliage makes great backdrop
'Belle Poitevine' [hybrid rugosa]	Zones 3–10	Clear pink	Repeats	Few hips, so you may choose to deadhead to increase bloom

(continued)

Cultivar	Hardiness Range	Bloom Color	Bloom Period	Comments
Tall Hedges (over 5 feet)				
'Cornelia' [hybrid musk]	Zones 4–10	Apricot pink	Continuous	Strong bloomer; takes to shearing well after first flowering; good for the South
'Frühlingsmorgen' [hybrid spinosissima]	Zones 3–10	Pink to yellow	Slight repeat	Excellent show of hips
'Herbstfeuer' [hybrid eglanteria]	Zones 4–10	Scarlet	Repeats	Brilliant scarlet; good disease resistance; fine hips
'Lichtkönigin Lucia' [shrub]	Zones 4–10	Bright yellow	Continuous	Good disease resistance for a yellow rose
'Robusta' [shrub]	Zones 3–10	Fiery scarlet	Continuous	Rugosa hybrid; best barrier; viciously thorny; upright
Rosa glauca [species]	Zones 4–10	Pink	Once	Fantastic blue-gray foliage overlaid with deep red; splendid red hips
'Roseraie de l'Haÿ' [hybrid rugosa]	Zones 3–10	Deep fuschia	Continuous	Extremely fragrant; elegant
'Scabrosa' [hybrid rugosa]	Zones 3–10	Bright fuchsia pink	Continuous	Rugosa; strongly upright; spectacular hips

plants to merge together as quickly as possible to form a solid band of vegetation, rather than to show off their individual forms. For faster results, you can space the plants even more closely. In France (a nation of particularly hedge-crazed gardeners), it's not unusual for even large hedging roses to be planted only 1 foot apart. Just remember to leave enough space—at least 18 inches—in front of and behind the hedge to allow you to feed, mulch, and prune the mature plants.

After you plant your rose hedge, water it very thoroughly, and mulch the ground around it immediately. An even, 3-inch-deep layer of organic mulch will help get your rose hedge off to a vigorous start by keeping the soil moist and blocking the growth of weeds.

Watering and Feeding

Roses planted as a hedge require more water than roses planted in a bed or by themselves. This is due to the closeness of their roots. The best way to ensure a steady, adequate supply of water for your rose hedge right from the start is to install drip irrigation when you plant.

You may be tempted to install a line with one emitter for each rose (an emitter every 2 feet if your roses are planted 2 feet apart, for example), but your roses will fare better in the long run if the emitters are spaced only 1 foot apart. That way, the dense roots of your rose hedge will receive plenty of water even when fully mature, and they will therefore be able to support the hedge's dense topgrowth.

Rose Alert!

To install a drip system for a rose hedge, lay the line about 4 inches away from the crowns of the shrubs. If your budget allows, install a drip line on *both* sides of the hedge. After you've placed and connected the line, cover it with a layer of mulch.

If you don't install drip irrigation, plan to handwater your rose hedge a lot, especially during the first 2 to 3 months after planting. Overhead irrigation—never recommended for roses anyway—is especially ineffective for roses planted in a hedge. Because of the density of the shrubs, water applied from above tends to run off the leaves and penetrate only the dripline.

The roses in your hedge will grow more quickly and densely if you fertilize them a bit more often than your other roses—ideally, about 20 percent more often. For instance, if you ordinarily feed your roses with a diluted solution of kelp emulsion every 21 days, you would fertilize your rose hedge with dilute kelp emulsion every 16 or 17 days. Don't worry too much about being precise with the math, however; the important thing to remember is that you should feed your hedge roses a bit more often than your other roses.

Pruning Your Rose Hedge

Most rose varieties recommended in this book for hedging require little or no pruning, except to remove deadwood. In addition, roses used for hedging can sometimes benefit from "heading" cuts—pruning just above an outward-facing leaf or bud—to help make the hedge more dense and leafy. You can do this type of pruning in late winter, but I believe it's better to do it right after the first flush of bloom, so the shrubs don't lose any of their first flowers.

Ideally, you will have selected your hedge roses with their mature size in mind. If your hedge is outgrowing its boundaries, however, you can control its size by cutting it back more severely right after the first flush of flowers. Rugosas respond best to this treatment.

Whatever you do, *don't* uniformly shear your roses with hedge clippers, as if they were yews or boxwoods. Shearing roses will remove most of their flowering wood and leave the plants looking as though they had been through an amputation. (Exception: In Zones 7 through 10, you *can* lightly shear some of the densely twiggy hybrid musks recommended for hedging. Do this right after their first flush of bloom to control their height or to stimulate denser growth and more flowers.)

Special Effects

If you're an adventurous gardener who thrives on novelty, you might want to try your hand at one of the more complex hedging arrangements. For a tapestry hedge, you'll need to do a bit more planning than for a single-variety rose hedge. For a two-tier hedge, you'll need more lateral space.

Tapestry Hedges

Instead of using just one rose variety for a hedge, you can combine several varieties to create a colorful tapestry hedge that blooms over an extended period.

Creating a tapestry hedge of roses requires some careful planning because the roses need to have not only compatible bloom colors but also similar plant forms and heights. If the roses are of dissimilar forms and heights, they will look like a ragged row, not an integrated hedge. For an effective tapestry hedge, stick to roses of the same class, such as rugosas or hybrid musks, and use either single- or double-flowered roses, but not both.

The varieties can be of two or three different bloom colors, but I find two-color hedges more difficult to work with. To successfully carry off a two-color rose hedge, you'll need two closely allied colors, such as soft peach and soft yellow, or white and blush pink. You'll also need to devise an informal pattern for varying the colors within the hedge, which is a bit more difficult with two colors than with three. (Alternating the plants one by one is *not* a good idea—it looks much too rigid! For one possible arrangement, see the top illustration at right.)

A tapestry of three different but closely allied colors is easier to execute. Rugosas are the best class of roses to choose from for this because they offer not only the largest number of cultivars suitable for hedging, but also many different shades of pink that blend well together. I like to use a rich fuchsia, a blush pink, and a white, but plenty of other combinations are possible, too. With three different roses, you can more easily devise a graceful, irregular pattern, such as one that repeats in frames (XYYYZZ-XYYYZZ, and so on). Or you could simply mix them randomly (XYYXXZZZYXXZ YYYZZ). Personally, I prefer the latter. (See the bottom plan at right for an example of a three-hedge tapestry.)

You can also plant a wild tapestry rose hedge, using species roses. Because of the generally more unruly growth habits of the species, this sort of hedge looks best in a more untended part of your property, such as a back boundary. Choose roses of roughly similar size from the lists of species roses on pages 222 and 223. Your wild tapestry rose hedge will quickly become home to myriad bird species.

Two-Tier Hedges

You can achieve a very sophisticated, formal effect by planting an ordinary hedge of a single rose variety and then planting another, shorter hedge of a sheared evergreen shrub, such as a boxwood, in front of the rose hedge. This arrangement, obviously, re-

Plant List—Two-Color Hedge

1. 'Danaë' [hybrid musk]
2. 'Cornelia' [hybrid musk]

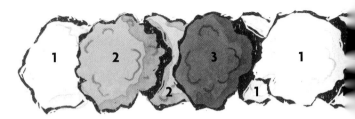

Plant List— Three-Color Hedge

1. 'Blanc Double de Coubert' [hybrid rugosa]
2. 'Souvenir de Philémon Cochet' [hybrid rugosa]
3. 'Roseraie de l'Haÿ' [hybrid rugosa]

quires quite a bit more lateral space than a simple hedge of just roses does. But the effect can be spectacular, especially if you choose the rose variety so that it contrasts well with the formal outlines of the evergreen. Some of the more upright rugosas, such as 'Robusta' and 'Jens Munk', lend themselves very well to this treatment. You also could use some of the hybrid musks. Just be careful not to let the musks overhang the evergreens. If they cast too much shade, the evergreens may lose their leaves or needles.

Here's a simple plan for a two-color rose tapestry hedge that will grow 4 to 5 feet tall in most climates. The two roses I've chosen—'Danaë' and 'Cornelia'—are both hybrid musks of similar height, habit, and flower form. 'Danaë' is soft yellow, fading to almost white, and 'Cornelia' is peachy pink, also fading to almost white. These two colors work well together and are united by their tendency to pale before wilting. The two roses are repeated in a random pattern. They are planted on 18-inch centers for quick effect; spacing could be increased to 2 feet.

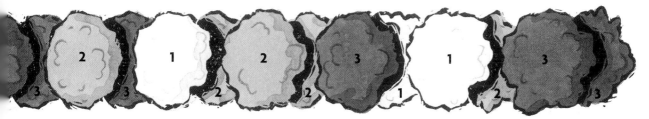

I've chosen three large rugosa roses for a tapestry hedge that will reach at least 6 feet tall. 'Blanc Double de Coubert' is sparkling white; 'Souvenir de Philémon Cochet' is pale blush pink; and 'Roseraie de l'Haÿ' is a rich, deep, purple magenta. All three of these roses have nearly identical heights and habits: thick, bushy, and upright. The blush pink serves as the bridge between the white and the deep fuchsia and in fact gives the impression of being the blending of those two color extremes. These roses, arranged in a random repeat, are planted on 2-foot centers for quick effect; spacing could be increased to 3 feet.

A romantic and very classic variation of the two-tier hedge is to front the roses with lavender (*Lavandula angustifolia*). For this use, the best lavender cultivar by far is the compact 'Nana', but the taller 'Hidcote' will work, too. If you live in Zone 7 or south, where lavender is more vigorous, you can even use the sprawling cultivar 'Munstead', if you shear it back heavily in late winter.

And if you're lucky enough to grow your roses in a mild coastal region (Zone 8 and warmer), you can use rosemary for the fragrant front row of a two-tier hedge. In Mediterranean-type climates, such as that of southern coastal California, you can even shear rosemary much as you would a boxwood hedge.

A two-tier hedge can lend a very sophisticated look to your landscape. Here, roses are paired with boxwood for an elegant effect.

Many shrub roses offer a second season of interest by providing a feast of nutritive rose hips to songbirds through fall and winter.

chapter 14

roses for wildlife gardens

The liquid notes of birds

singing from tree to tree…the desultory floating flight of a butterfly on a warm June day…the zipping whir of a hummingbird…these are just a few of the magical moments that wildlife can add to your garden. If you're interested in attracting wildlife to your landscape, roses make a great addition. They provide food and shelter for many birds, butterflies, and—for better or worse—a few mammals, such as squirrels, rabbits, and deer. Paradoxically, a thick hedge of very tall roses also makes one of the best barriers to deer that are marauding your landscape. At maturity, such a hedge is too wide for deer to leap and so dense that deer are less tempted to move in, as they can't see the other side.

If you're like most gardeners, you'll want to bring in as many of those birds, butterflies, and other benign (or beneficial) creatures as possible. Within the pages of this chapter, you'll find out how to extend the welcome mat—by planting roses that produce hips for birds and perennials that provide nectar for butterflies—as well as other ways to turn your garden into a haven for wildlife.

For the Birds

Many rose varieties produce masses of bright crimson or orange fruits (rose hips) that are rich in vitamin C and contain have seeds that are a good source of protein for foraging birds. And because rose hips are relatively dry, they remain on the plant for months.

By growing hip-bearing shrub roses, you'll be able to provide both migrating and resident birds with a bountiful feast from fall into early spring, when other food sources are scarce and birds' nutritional requirements are high. (For a quick reference to roses that bear hips, see "Hips, Hips, Hooray!" below.)

If you're considering buying a new rose to attract birds but you aren't sure whether it bears hips, remember that fully double roses usually are sterile (don't bear hips). The roses that are most likely to bear hips are those that show their stamens—including all of the species and most of the single-flowering roses.

Hips, Hips, Hooray!

Any rose that bears hips will attract birds to feast on its fruits, but the following hip-bearing roses are among the best varieties for organic gardens. (For details on these varieties, see "A Gallery of Roses" beginning on page 106.)

Small Shrubs and Groundcovers
- 'Charles Albanel' [hybrid rugosa]
- 'Corylus' [shrub]
- 'Dart's Dash' [hybrid rugosa]
- 'Immensee' [shrub]
- 'Paulii' [shrub]
- 'Rosalina' [hybrid rugosa]
- 'Schneezwerg' [hybrid rugosa]

Medium Shrubs
- 'Delicata' [hybrid rugosa]
- 'Felicia' [hybrid musk]
- 'Frau Dagmar Hartopp' [hybrid rugosa]
- 'Jens Munk' [hybrid rugosa]
- 'Marie-Victorin' [hybrid kordesii]
- 'Moje Hammarberg' [hybrid rugosa]
- *Rosa gallica officinalis* [species]
- 'Rugosa Magnifica' [hybrid rugosa]

Large Shrubs
- 'Duplex' [miscellaneous old garden rose]
- 'Fritz Nobis' [shrub]
- 'Frühlingsmorgen' [hybrid spinosissima]
- 'Geranium' [hybrid moyesii]
- 'Herbstfeuer' [hybrid eglanteria]
- *Rosa canina* [species]
- *Rosa eglanteria* [species]
- *Rosa glauca* [species]
- *Rosa virginiana* [species]
- 'Roseraie de l'Haÿ' [hybrid rugosa]
- 'Scabrosa' [hybrid rugosa]

Rambler
- 'Kiftsgate' [species]

Because rose hips contain little water, they persist on the plant through extremely low winter temperatures, making them a major food source for overwintering and migratory birds.

Making Your Garden Part of a Wildlife Web

Selecting the right roses is only one way to attract birds and other wildlife to your garden. In addition, frogs, toads, and helpful reptiles will also visit or take up residence as you begin to transform your garden into a more natural environment.

When you eliminate pesticides and chemical fertilizers and include a richer variety of plants, you provide more food for a whole world of animals. Eliminating pesticides allows insects—an important link in the food chain—to proliferate in a balanced way. And soil that is nourished by compost and organic nutrients begins to teem with earthworms and other scavengers, which, in turn, provide additional food for birds and reptiles.

Besides supplying food, large shrub roses provide birds with nesting sites and safe cover, night and day. Birds' nests are particularly safe when lodged in a thorny bower of roses. In fact, your most viciously thorny rose will likely host the greatest number of avian residents. Birds seem to sense the safe harbor, and their feathers protect them from the thorns.

Another favorite nesting site is among the canes of a climbing or rambling rose (even one that doesn't bear hips), especially one trained against a high wall. The brambles afford protection, while the wall offers birds warmth and shelter.

Including water—no matter how small the source—can boost the bird population in your garden enormously, especially if you can keep the water from freezing in winter. A pool also provides a habitat for frogs and other beneficial amphibians, and it attracts beneficial dragonflies and butterflies, as well.

In addition to roses, plant other fruiting trees and shrubs to provide food for birds year-round.

Thorny rose canes provide one of the safest havens for nesting birds.

Including water in your landscape will attract flocks of birds, beneficial insects, and amphibians.

Beautyberry (*Callicarpa* spp.), coralberry or snowberry (*Symphoricarpos* spp.), devil's walking stick (*Aralia spinosa*), elders (*Sambucus* spp.), hawthorns (*Crataegus* spp.), hollies (*Ilex* spp.), and viburnums (*Viburnum* spp.) are just a few of the plants you can include. All of them are highly ornamental and will provide a banquet for birds.

Flowering perennials and annuals provide nourishing seeds for birds. Many birds are particularly fond of sunflower seeds, and with so many beautiful varieties of sunflowers now available, you're sure to find one suited to your landscape. Even compact varieties will provide a feast for birds if you allow the seeds to ripen on the plants. (In my garden, the goldfinches didn't wait that long—they began ripping green seeds from the heads!) For birdseed-bearing flowers, see "A Perennial Smorgasbord for the Birds" on the opposite page.

Perennials for a Bounty of Butterflies

Butterflies sip nectar from flowers that have many small parts, such as daisies, butterfly bush, and asters. But don't forget that every butterfly is preceded by a hungry caterpillar! To nourish the highly specific needs of caterpillar species, include plenty of larval food sources, such as milkweeds, members of the carrot family (such as dill and parsley), spicebush (*Lindera benzoin*), and false indigo (*Baptisia australis*).

The following perennials attract adult butterflies to their flowers:

- Anise hyssops (*Agastache* spp.)
- Lead plant (*Amorpha canescens*; deciduous shrub)
- Bastard indigo (*Amorpha fruticosa*; deciduous shrub)
- Pearly everlasting (*Anaphalis margaritacea*; also provides food for caterpillars)
- Butterfly weeds (*Asclepias* spp.)
- Asters (*Aster* spp.)
- Boltonia (*Boltonia asteroides*)
- Butterfly bush (*Buddleia davidii*; shrub in Zones 6 and southward)
- Blue mist shrub (*Caryopteris* × *clandonensis*; shrub in Zone 6 and southward)
- Chrysanthemums (*Chrysanthemum* spp.)
- Purple prairie clover (*Dalea purpureum*)
- Purple coneflowers (*Echinacea* spp.)

- Globe thistle (*Echinops ritro*)
- Joe Pye weeds (*Eupatorium* spp.)
- Blanketflowers (*Gaillardia* spp.)
- Hardy gazania (*Gazania linearis*)
- Sneezeweeds (*Helenium* spp.)
- Candytuft (*Iberis sempervirens*)
- Shasta daisy (*Leucanthemum* × *superbum*)
- Blazing stars (*Liatris* spp.)
- Catmints (*Nepeta* spp.)
- Ornamental oregano (*Origanum laevigatum*)
- Coneflowers (*Rudbeckia* spp.)
- Pincushion flowers (*Scabiosa* spp.)
- Solidaster (× *Solidaster luteus*)
- Stokes' aster (*Stokesia laevis*)
- Rose verbena (*Verbena canadensis*)

Sunflowers (*Helianthus* spp.) are just one of scores of perennials and grasses you can grow to provide food for birds.

Of course, you also could supply seed by installing one or more birdfeeders in your garden. Just remember that the hulls of sunflower seeds are toxic to many landscape plants, including grass.

If you are interested in enticing hummingbirds to your rose garden, try planting brightly colored tubular flowers—ideally ones that bloom at the same time your roses do, such as penstemons—next to your roses. That way, when the hummers arrive to sip the nectar from the tubular flowers, they may go on to feast on any aphids present on your roses. Aphids are a major source of protein in the hummer's diet.

Think about the nonfood needs of wildlife, too. Include both evergreen and deciduous trees in your landscape to provide shelter, nesting sites, and perches for birds. And if you like the idea of rabbits and other mammals frequenting your garden, try to create a green "highway" of plants to connect your landscaped areas with nearby wild areas. Wild animals, inherently shy, will be more likely to visit your landscape if there's a safe, "undercover" way for them to approach and leave.

A Perennial Smorgasbord for the Birds

These perennials provide nourishing seeds for birds. Refrain from deadheading to allow the seedheads to form. Also, delay cutting down the perennials until early spring, so that birds can profit from this natural seed stock all winter long.

- Spikenard (*Aralia racemosa*)
- Asters (*Aster* spp.)
- Blackberry lily (*Belamcanda chinensis*)
- Chocolate daisy (*Berlandiera lyrata*) (perennial only in Zones 7–10)
- Boltonia (*Boltonia asteroides*)
- Tickseeds (*Coreopsis* spp., especially *C. tripteris*)
- Cardoon (*Cynara cardunculus*) (perennial only in Zones 6–10)
- Purple coneflowers (*Echinacea* spp.)

- Sea hollies (*Eryngium* spp.)
- Joe Pye weeds (*Eupatorium* spp.)
- Sneezeweeds (*Helenium* spp.)
- Perennial sunflowers (*Helianthus* spp.)
- Plantain lilies (*Hosta* spp.; seed-forming varieties)
- Blazing stars (*Liatris* spp.)
- Gray-headed coneflower (*Ratibida pinnata*)
- Coneflowers (*Rudbeckia* spp.)
- Prairie docks (*Silphium* spp.)

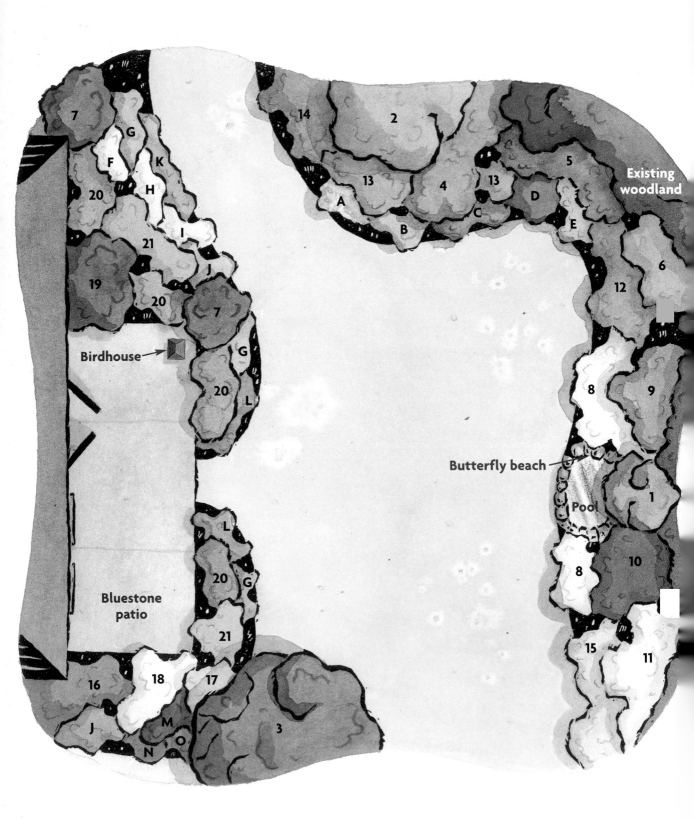

Existing woodland

7

14

2

G

F

K

H

20

13

13

5

I

A

4

D

21

B

C

E

J

19

6

20

12

7

Birdhouse

G

L

8

9

20

Butterfly beach

Pool

1

L

8

10

20

G

15

11

Bluestone
patio

21

16

18

17

3

J

M

O

N

Trees and Shrubs

1. Pagoda dogwood (*Cornus alternifolia*): SB (1)
2. White fir (*Abies concolor*): SB (1)
3. Black gum (*Nyssa sylvatica*): SB (1)
4. Red-leaved rose (*Rosa glauca*): SB (4)
5. 'Blue Muffin' arrowwood (*Viburnum dentatum* 'Blue Muffin'): SB (5)
6. Spice bush (*Lindera benzoin*): BU, SB (2)
7. Fringe tree (*Chionanthus virginicus*): SB (2)
8. 'Immensee' [shrub rose]: SB (6)
9. 'Magic Berry' coralberry (*Symphoricarpos × doorenbosii* 'Magic Berry'): SB (4)
10. 'Moje Hammarberg' [hybrid rugosa rose]: SB (4)
11. 'Brilliantissima' red chokeberry (*Aronia arbutifolia* 'Brilliantissima'): SB (5)
12. 'Corylus' [shrub rose]: SB (4)
13. 'Pink Delight' butterfly bush (*Buddleia* 'Pink Delight'): BU, HB (4)
14. 'Frau Dagmar Hartopp' [hybrid rugosa rose]: SB (5)
15. 'Blue Billow' hydrangea (*Hydrangea serrata* 'Blue Billow'): BU (8)
16. 'Scabrosa' [hybrid rugosa rose]: SB (3)
17. 'Robin Hill' serviceberry (*Amelanchier × grandiflora* 'Robin Hill'): SB (1)
18. 'Schneezwerg' [hybrid rugosa rose]: SB (5)
19. Chaste tree (*Vitex agnus-castus*): BU (4)
20. 'Felicia' [hybrid musk rose]: SB (10)
21. 'Nordic' inkberry holly (*Ilex glabra* 'Nordic'): SB (10)

Perennials

A. 'My Antonia' aster (*Aster fendleri* 'My Antonia'): BU, SB (6)
B. Yellow scabious (*Scabiosa ochroleuca*): BU (7)
C. Rocky Mountain penstemon (*Penstemon strictus*): HB (7)
D. Northern sea oats (*Chasmanthium latifolium*): SB (7)
E. 'Leuchtstern' purple coneflower (*Echinacea purpurea* 'Leuchtstern'): BU, SB (6)
F. Milky bellflower (*Campanula lactiflora*): HB (5)
G. 'Yellow Queen' yellow columbine (*Aquilegia chrysantha* 'Yellow Queen'): HB (13)
H. Pearly everlasting (*Anaphalis margaritacea*): BU (7)
I. White beardtongue (*Penstemon albidus*): HB (8)
J. Catmint (*Nepeta subsessilis*): HB (13)
K. 'Butterfly Blue' pincushion flower (*Scabiosa columbaria* 'Butterfly Blue'): BU (8)
L. 'Walker's Low' catmint (*Nepeta × faassenii* 'Walker's Low'): BU (12)
M. Wild hyssop (*Agastache cana*): BU, HB (4)
N. Butterfly weed (*Asclepias tuberosa*): BU (4)
O. Stokes' aster (*Stokesia laevis*): BU (6)

Key: BU=butterflies; HB=hummingbirds; SB=songbirds

Here's a plan for a backyard wildlife garden where every single plant attracts either butterflies, hummingbirds, songbirds, or a combination of the three. Providing a visual focus at the back of the property is a small, natural pool that invites birds and other animals to its steady source of water. At one end of the pool is a shallow area lined with river rocks or other stones just at the water's surface. This "butterfly beach" allows butterflies (who must sip from the surface of wet stones or sand and can't drink from open water) to drink from the pool.

This garden—suitable for Zones 4 through 9—is both colorful and low maintenance, using large massings of flowering shrubs, tough roses, and easy perennials. The roses have been chosen for the nourishing hips they provide to birds.

Rose Gallery at a Glance

Cultivar	Class	Hardiness Range	Size (Height x Width)	Uses	Shade Tolerance
Small Shrubs and Groundcovers (under 3 Feet)					
'Aspen'	Shrub	Zones 4–10	1½' × 3'	CO, GC	NT
'Charles Albanel'	Hybrid rugosa	Zones 2–10	1½' × 3'	GC, H, MB, WL	NT
'Coral Cluster'	Polyantha	Zones 5–10	1½' × 2½'	CO, H, MB	T
'Corylus'	Shrub	Zones 3–10	2½' × 3'	GC, MA, MB, WL	T
'Dart's Dash'	Hybrid rugosa	Zones 3–10	3' × 4'	GC, H, MB, WL	NT
'De Montarville'	Shrub	Zones 3–10	3' × 3'	H, MB	NT
'Dornröschenschloss Sababurg'	Shrub	Zones 5–10	3' × 3'	CF, H, MB	T
'Goldmarie 82'	Floribunda	Zones 5–10	2' × 2'	CF, CO, MA, MB	NT
'Grüss an Aachen'	Floribunda	Zones 5–10	1½' × 1½'	CF, CO, MB	T
'Immensee'	Shrub	Zones 4–10	1½' × 6'	CL, GC, TR, WL	NT
'Lexington'	Shrub	Zones 4–10	2½' × 3'	CO, MA, MB	NT
'Max Graf'	Hybrid rugosa	Zones 4–10	2' × 8'	GC	NT
'Mystic'	Shrub	Zones 4–10	2½' × 2½'	CO, MA, MB	NT
'Palmengarten Frankfurt'	Shrub	Zones 4–10	2' × 4'	CO, GC, MB	NT
'Paulii'	Shrub	Zones 4–10	3' × 10'	GC, WL	T
'Pink Bassino'	Shrub	Zones 4–10	2' × 4'	GC, H, MB	NT
'Raubritter'	Shrub	Zones 5–10	3' × 6'	CF, CL, GC, MB	T
'Rosalina'	Hybrid rugosa	Zones 4–10	2½' × 4'	GC, H, MB	NT
'Rose de Rescht'	Damask (Portland)	Zones 4–10	3' × 2'	CF, CO, H, MB, PP	T
'Rose du Roi'	Portland	Zones 4–10	3' × 3'	CF, CU, H, MB, PP	NT
'Schneezwerg'	Hybrid rugosa	Zones 3–10	3' × 3'	CO, H, MB, WL	T
'Snow Pavement'	Hybrid rugosa	Zones 3–10	2½' × 4'	GC, H, MB	NT
'The Fairy'	Polyantha	Zones 5–10	2' × 4'	CF, CO, GC, H, MB,	T
'Topaz Jewel'	Hybrid rugosa	Zones 5–10	3' × 3'	MB	NT
'Tumbling Waters'	Shrub	Zones 4–10	2' × 3'	CO, GC	NT
'White Pet'	Polyantha	Zones 5–10	2' × 2½'	CO, GC, H, MA, MB	T

KEY - Uses: BC = bank cover, CF = cut flower, CH = cutting hips, CL = climber, CO = containers, CU = culinary, GC = groundcover, H = hedge, MA = massing, MB = mixed border, N = naturalizing, PP = potpourri, PR = pillar rose, S = specimen, TR = tree rambler, WL = wildlife plantings
Shade Tolerance: NT = not tolerant, T = tolerant

Flowering	Bloom Color	Fragrance	Black Spot Susceptibility	Mildew Susceptibility	Pruning Requirements
C	Sunny yellow	F	MS	SS	DH, DWR, WM
R	Crimson pink	FF	NS	NS	DWR
C	Coral pink	NF	SS	SS	DH, DWR, WM
C	Silvery pink	FFF	NS	NS	DWR
C	Bright magenta	FFF	NS	NS	DWR
C	Medium pink	F	SS	NS	DH, DWR, WM
C	Clear pink	FF	NS	NS	DH, DWR, WM
C	Lemon yellow	FF	NS	NS	DH, DWR, WM
C	Creamy peach pink	F	SS	NS	DH, DWR, WM
O	White/pink	F	NS	NS	DWR
C	Soft yellow	FF	MS	SS	DWR, WM
O	Clear pink	FFF	NS	NS	DWR
C	Salmon pink	F	SS	SS	DH, DWR, WM
C	Bright pink	F	NS	NS	DH, DWR, WM
O	Pure white	FFF	NS	MS	DWR, RP
C	Light pink	F	NS	NS	DH, DWR, WM
O	Pure pink	FF	NS	MS	AF, DWR
C	Mauve pink	FF	NS	NS	DWR, WM
R	Fuchsia red	FFFF	SS	NS	DH, DWR, WM
R	Mauve fuchsia	FFFF	SS	NS	DH, DWR, WM
C	Pure white	FFF	NS	NS	DH, DWR
C	White/pale pink	FFF	NS	NS	WM
C	Medium pink	NF	SS	SS	DH, DWR, WM
C	Primrose yellow	FF	MS	NS	DH, DWR, WM
C	Crisp white	FFF	NS	NS	DWR, RP
C	White/pink	F	SS	SS	DH, DWR, WM

Flowering: C = continuous, O = once-blooming, R = repeat **Fragrance:** F = slightly fragrant, FF = moderately fragrant, FFF = very fragrant, FFFF = extremely fragrant, NF = not fragrant **Black Spot and Mildew Susceptibility:** NS = not susceptible, SS = slightly susceptible, MS = moderately susceptible **Pruning Requirements:** AF = after flowering, DH = deadheading, DWR = deadwood removal, RP = renewal pruning, WM = winter maintenance

Cultivar	Class	Hardiness Range	Size (Height x Width)	Uses	Shade Tolerance
Medium Shrubs (3 to 5 Feet)					
'AC Marie-Victorin'	Hybrid kordesii	Zones 3–10	5' × 4'	MB, WL	NT
'Alfred de Dalmas'	Moss	Zones 4–10	3' × 2'	CF, CO, H, MA, MB	T
'Autumn Damask'	Damask	Zones 4–10	4' × 3'	CF, CU, H, MB, PP	NT
'Ballerina'	Hybrid musk	Zones 4–10	4' × 3'	CO, H, MA, MB	T
'Belle de Crécy'	Hybrid gallica	Zones 3–10	4' × 3'	CF, CU, MB, PP	NT
'Belle Story'	Shrub	Zones 5–10	4' × 4'	CF, MB	NT
'Camaieux'	Hybrid gallica	Zones 4–10	3' × 3'	CF, CO, CU, H, MB, PP	NT
'Cardinal de Richelieu'	Hybrid gallica	Zones 4–10	4' × 3'	CF, CU, MB, PP	NT
'Charles de Mills'	Hybrid gallica	Zones 4–10	4' × 4'	CF, CU, MB, PP	NT
'Danaë'	Hybrid musk	Zones 5–10	4' × 4'	CF, MA, MB	T
'Delicata'	Hybrid rugosa	Zones 3–10	3' × 3'	H, MB, WL	T
'Felicia'	Hybrid musk	Zones 5–10	4' × 4'	CF, CO, H, MB, S	NT
'Félicité Parmentier'	Alba	Zones 3–10	4' × 3'	CF, CU, H, MB, PP	T
'Ferdinand Pichard'	Hybrid perpetual	Zones 5–10	5' × 4'	CF, MB, S	T
'Fimbriata'	Hybrid rugosa	Zones 3–10	4' × 4'	CF, H, MB	T
'Frau Dagmar Hartopp'	Hybrid rugosa	Zones 3–10	3' × 3'	H, MB, N, WL	NT
'Frau Karl Druschki'	Hybrid perpetual	Zones 4–10	5' × 3'	CF, MB, S	NT
'Frontenac'	Shrub	Zones 3–10	3½' × 3½'	H, MB	NT
'Henry Hudson'	Hybrid rugosa	Zones 3–10	4' × 4'	H, MB	NT
'Hunter'	Hybrid rugosa	Zones 4–10	4' × 3'	CO, H, MB	T
'J. P. Connell'	Shrub	Zones 3–10	4' × 4'	CF, MB	NT
'Jacques Cartier'	Portland	Zones 4–10	3' × 2'	CF, CU, H, MB, PP	T
'Jens Munk'	Hybrid rugosa	Zones 2–10	5' × 3'	H, MB, WL	NT
'Léda'	Damask	Zones 4–10	3' × 4'	CF, CO, CU, H, MB, PP, S	NT
'Louise Odier'	Bourbon	Zones 5–10	5' × 4'	CL, MB, S	T
'Moje Hammarberg'	Hybrid rugosa	Zones 3–10	4' × 4'	GC, H, MB, WL	T
'Nur Mahal'	Hybrid musk	Zones 5–10	5' × 4'	CF, H, MB, S	T
'Penelope'	Hybrid musk	Zones 5–10	5' × 4'	CF, H, MB, S	T

KEY - Uses: BC = bank cover, CF = cut flower, CH = cutting hips, CL = climber, CO = containers, CU = culinary, GC = groundcover, H = hedge, MA = massing, MB = mixed border, N = naturalizing, PP = potpourri, PR = pillar rose, S = specimen, TR = tree rambler, WL = wildlife plantings
Shade Tolerance: NT = not tolerant, T = tolerant

Flowering	Bloom Color	Fragrance	Black Spot Susceptibility	Mildew Susceptibility	Pruning Requirements
C	Peach pink	F	NS	NS	DH, DWR, WM
C	Blush pink	FFF	SS	NS	DH, DWR, WM
R	Clear pink	FFFF	SS	SS	AF, DH, DWR
C	Pink/white	F	NS	NS	DH, DWR, WM
O	Cerise purple	FFFF	NS	MS	AF, DWR
C	Shell pink	FFF	SS	MS	DH, DWR, WM
O	Pink/mauve	FFF	NS	NS	DWR, WM
O	Purple	FFFF	NS	SS	DWR, WM
O	Carmine purple	FFFF	NS	SS	DWR
C	Medium yellow	F	SS	NS	DH, DWR, WM
R	Clear pink	FFFF	NS	NS	DWR
C	Salmon pink	FF	SS	NS	DH, DWR, WM
O	Light pink	FFFF	NS	NS	AF, DWR
R	White-striped fuchsia	FFFF	MS	NS	DH, DWR, WM
R	White/pink blush	FFF	NS	NS	DH, DWR
C	Silvery pink	FFF	NS	NS	DWR
C	Pure white	NF	SS	NS	DH, DWR, WM
C	Medium pink	F	SS	SS	DH, DWR, WM
C	White	FFF	NS	NS	DH, DWR
C	Crimson	F	SS	NS	DH, DWR
R	Pale yellow	F	MS	NS	DH, DWR, WM
C	Clear pink	FFFF	SS	NS	DH, DWR, WM
C	Lavender pink	FFF	NS	NS	DWR
O, R	Pale pink, red picotee	FFFF	NS	NS	AF, DWR
C	Rose pink	FFFF	MS	NS	DH, DWR, WM
C	Fuchsia purple	FFF	NS	NS	DWR
C	Carmine rose	F	NS	NS	DH, DWR, WM
C	Pale pink white	FF	NS	MS	DH, DWR, WM

Flowering: C = continuous, O = once-blooming, R = repeat   **Fragrance:** F = slightly fragrant, FF = moderately fragrant, FFF = very fragrant, FFFF = extremely fragrant, NF = not fragrant   **Black Spot and Mildew Susceptibility:** NS = not susceptible, SS = slightly susceptible, MS = moderately susceptible   **Pruning Requirements:** AF = after flowering, DH = deadheading, DWR = deadwood removal, RP = renewal pruning, WM = winter maintenance

(continued)

Cultivar	Class	Hardiness Range	Size (Height x Width)	Uses	Shade Tolerance
Medium Shrubs (3 to 5 Feet)—CONTINUED					
'Petite de Hollande'	Centifolia	Zones 4–10	4' × 3'	CF, CO, MB, PP	NT
'Petite Lisette'	Centifolia	Zones 4–10	3' × 3'	CF, CO, MB, PP	T
Rosa gallica officinalis	Species	Zones 4–10	3' × 3'	H, MB, WL	T
'Rugosa Magnifica'	Hybrid rugosa	Zones 3–10	4' × 5'	H, MB, WL	T
'Soupert et Notting'	Moss	Zones 4–10	3' × 2'	CF, CO, CU, MB, PP	NT
'Tuscany Superb'	Hybrid gallica	Zones 4–10	4' × 3'	CF, CU, MB, PP	NT
Large Shrubs (over 5 Feet)					
'Abraham Darby'	Shrub	Zones 5–10	6' × 4'	CL, CF, MB	NT
'Alba Maxima'	Alba	Zones 4–10	6' × 5'	H, MB, S	T
'Alba Semi-plena'	Alba	Zones 4–10	8' × 5'	CF, H, MB, S	T
'Belle Poitevine'	Hybrid rugosa	Zones 3–10	6' × 5'	H, MB, S	T
'Blanc Double de Coubert'	Hybrid rugosa	Zones 3–10	5' × 4'	H, MB, S, WL	T
'Blush Noisette'	Noisette	Zones 5/6–10	7' × 4½'	CF, CL, MB, S	T
'Celestial'	Alba	Zones 3–10	6' × 4'	CF, CU, H, MB, PP	T
'Celsiana'	Damask	Zones 4–10	6' × 4'	CF, CU, MB, PP	NT
'Champneys' Pink Cluster'	Noisette	Zones 6–10	15' × 8'	C, CF, MB, S	NT
'Cornelia'	Hybrid musk	Zones 4–10	5' × 5'	CF, H, MB	T
'Duplex'	Misc. Old Garden Rose	Zones 4–10	5' × 4'	H, S	T
'Elmshorn'	Shrub	Zones 4–10	5' × 4'	CF, CL, MB, S	T
'Father Hugo's Rose'	Species	Zones 3–10	8' × 5'	H, MB, S, WL	NT
'Fritz Nobis'	Shrub	Zones 4–10	6' × 5'	CF, H, MB, WL	T
'Frühlingsduft'	Hybrid spinosissima	Zones 3–10	10' × 6'	CF, H, MB	T
'Frühlingsmorgen'	Hybrid spinosissima	Zones 3–10	6' × 4'	CF, H, MB, WL	T
'Geranium'	Hybrid moyesii	Zones 4–10	8' × 6'	CH, CL, H, MB, WL	T
'Great Maiden's Blush'	Alba	Zones 3–10	6' × 5'	CF, CU, H, MB, PP, S	T
'Gros Choux d'Hollande'	Centifolia	Zones 5–10	7' × 5'	CF, CL, H, MB	NT
'Herbstfeuer'	Hybrid eglanteria	Zones 4–10	6' × 4'	CF, H, MB, WL	T

KEY - Uses: BC = bank cover, CF = cut flower, CH = cutting hips, CL = climber, CO = containers, CU = culinary, GC = groundcover, H = hedge, MA = massing, MB = mixed border, N = naturalizing, PP = potpourri, PR = pillar rose, S = specimen, TR = tree rambler, WL = wildlife plantings
Shade Tolerance: NT = not tolerant, T = tolerant

Flowering	Bloom Color	Fragrance	Black Spot Susceptibility	Mildew Susceptibility	Pruning Requirements
O	Warm pink	FFFF	SS	NS	AF, DWR
O	Medium pink	FFFF	SS	NS	AF, DWR
O	Magenta	FFFF	SS	SS	DWR
C	Bright mauve	FFF	NS	NS	DWR
R	Deep pink	FFFF	SS	MS	AF, DH, DWR
O	Deep magenta red	FFFF	NS	NS	AF, DWR
C	Apricot pink	FFF	MS	NS	DH, DWR, WM
O	Pure white	FFFF	NS	NS	AF, DWR
O	White	FFFF	NS	NS	AF, DWR
R	Clear pink	FF	NS	NS	DH, DWR
R	Pure white	FFFF	NS	NS	DWR
C	Pale lavender pink	FF	SS	SS	DH, DWR, WM
O	Soft pink	FFFF	NS	NS	AF, DWR
O	Pale pink	FFFF	NS	NS	AF, DWR
C	Blush pink	FFF	NS	NS	DH, DWR, WM
C	Coral pink	FF	NS	NS	DH, DWR, WM
R	Clear pink	FF	NS	NS	DH, DWR
C	Bright pink	F	SS	NS	DH, DWR, WM
O	Primrose yellow	F	NS	NS	AF, DWR
O	Apricot pink	FF	NS	NS	AF, DWR
O	Yellow/pink	FFFF	NS	NS	AF, DWR
O, R	Pink/yellow	FF	NS	NS	DWR
O	Bright red	NF	SS	NS	AF, DWR
O	Blush pink	FFFF	NS	NS	AF, DWR
R	Rose pink	FFF	SS	NS	DH, DWR, WM
R	Crimson	FFF	SS	NS	DH, DWR, WM

Flowering: C = continuous, O = once-blooming, R = repeat **Fragrance:** F = slightly fragrant, FF = moderately fragrant, FFF = very fragrant, FFFF = extremely fragrant, NF = not fragrant **Black Spot and Mildew Susceptibility:** NS = not susceptible, SS = slightly susceptible, MS = moderately susceptible **Pruning Requirements:** AF = after flowering, DH = deadheading, DWR = deadwood removal, RP = renewal pruning, WM = winter maintenance

(continued)

Cultivar	Class	Hardiness Range	Size (Height x Width)	Uses	Shade Tolerance
Large Shrubs (over 5 Feet)—CONTINUED					
'Königin von Dänemark'	Alba	Zones 3–10	5' × 4'	CF, CU, H, MB, PP, S	T
'Lichtkönigin Lucia'	Shrub	Zones 4–10	5' × 4'	CF, H, MB, S	NT
'Linda Campbell'	Hybrid rugosa	Zones 4–10	5' × 8'	H, MB, S	NT
'Martin Frobisher'	Hybrid rugosa	Zones 2–10	5' × 4'	H, MB, S	NT
'Nevada'	Hybrid moyesii	Zones 4–10	8' × 6'	H, MB, S	NT
'Robusta'	Shrub	Zones 3–10	5' × 4'	H, MB, S	T
Rosa canina	Species	Zones 3–10	10' × 6'	CU, N, WL	T
Rosa eglanteria	Species	Zones 4–10	12' × 8'	H, N, WL	T
Rosa glauca	Species	Zones 4–10	8' × 6'	CH, H, MB, WL	T
Rosa virginiana	Species	Zones 3–10	5' × 4'	H, MB, N, WL	T
'Roseraie de l'Haÿ'	Hybrid rugosa	Zones 3–10	6' × 8'	CU, H, MB, PP, S	NT
'Rugelda'	Hybrid rugosa	Zones 4–10	5' × 4'	H, MB, S	NT
'Sarah Van Fleet'	Hybrid rugosa	Zones 4–10	5' × 4'	H, MB, S	**T**
'Scabrosa'	Hybrid rugosa	Zones 3–10	6' × 4'	H, MB, S	T
'Souvenir de Philémon Cochet'	Hybrid rugosa	Zones 3–10	5' × 4'	H, MB, S	T
'Stanwell Perpetual'	Hybrid spinosissima	Zones 4–10	5' × 5'	CF, H, MB, S	T
'Thérèse Bugnet'	Hybrid rugosa	Zones 3–10	6' × 5'	CF, H, MB, S	T
'Wasagaming'	Hybrid rugosa	Zones 3–10	6' × 5'	H, MB, S	NT
Climbers					
'Alexander MacKenzie'	Shrub	Zones 3–10	8' × 5'	CF, CL, H, MB, PR	NT
'Awakening'	Large-flowered climber	Zones 5–10	10' × 8'	CF, PR, TR	T
'Charlemagne'	Hybrid gallica	Zones 4–10	6' × 4'	CF, CL, CU, H, MB, PR	NT
'Dortmund'	Hybrid kordesii	Zones 3–10	8' × 6'	CL, PR	T
'Henry Kelsey'	Hybrid kordesii	Zones 2–10	8' × 6'	CL, PR, TR	T
'Ilse Krohn Superior'	Hybrid kordesii	Zones 4–10	10' × 5'	CL, PR	T
'John Davis'	Hybrid kordesii	Zones 3–10	8' × 6'	CF, CL, H, MB, PR	NT

KEY - Uses: BC = bank cover, CF = cut flower, CH = cutting hips, CL = climber, CO = containers, CU = culinary, GC = groundcover, H = hedge, MA = massing, MB = mixed border, N = naturalizing, PP = potpourri, PR = pillar rose, S = specimen, TR = tree rambler, WL = wildlife plantings
Shade Tolerance: NT = not tolerant, T = tolerant

Flowering	Bloom Color	Fragrance	Black Spot Susceptibility	Mildew Susceptibility	Pruning Requirements
O	Warm pink	FFFF	NS	NS	AF, DWR
C	Bright yellow	FF	SS	NS	DH, DWR, WM
C	Bright red	NF	NS	NS	DH, DWR, WM
C	Creamy pink	FFF	SS	NS	DH, DWR
R	Pure white	FF	SS	NS	DH, DWR
C	Intense scarlet	FFF	SS	NS	DH, DWR, WM
O	Pale pink	FF	NS	NS	DWR
O	Light pink	FFF	NS	NS	AF, DWR
O	Lilac pink	NF	NS	NS	AF, DWR, WM
O	Light pink	F	NS	NS	DWR
C	Cerise purple	FFFF	NS	NS	WM
C	Soft yellow	FF	SS	NS	DH, DWR, WM
C	Clear pink	FF	NS	SS	DH, DWR, WM
C	Bright mauve	FFF	NS	NS	DWR
C	Blush pink	FFF	NS	NS	DH, DWR
R	Blush pink	FFFF	NS	NS	DH, DWR, WM
R	Bright pink	FFF	NS	NS	DH, DWR, WM
R	Medium pink	FF	SS	NS	DH, DWR, WM
R	Crimson pink	FF	NS	NS	DH, DWR, WM
C	Blush pink	FFF	SS	NS	DH, DWR, WM
O	Crimson purple	FFFF	NS	SS	AF, DWR
R	Crimson/white	F	SS	NS	DH, DWR, WM
R	Crimson	FF	SS	NS	DH, DWR, WM
R	Ivory	FF	MS	NS	DH, DWR, WM
C	Medium pink	FF	NS	MS	DH, DWR, WM

Flowering: C = continuous, O = once-blooming, R = repeat **Fragrance:** F = slightly fragrant, FF = moderately fragrant, FFF = very fragrant, FFFF = extremely fragrant, NF = not fragrant **Black Spot and Mildew Susceptibility:** NS = not susceptible, SS = slightly susceptible, MS = moderately susceptible **Pruning Requirements:** AF = after flowering, DH = deadheading, DWR = deadwood removal, RP = renewal pruning, WM = winter maintenance

(continued)

Cultivar	Class	Hardiness Range	Size (Height x Width)	Uses	Shade Tolerance
Climbers—CONTINUED					
'Kathleen Harrop'	Bourbon	Zones 5–10	10' × 6'	CF, CL, PR	T
'Leverkusen'	Hybrid kordesii	Zones 4–10	10' × 8'	CL, PR	T
'Mme. Plantier'	Hybrid alba	Zones 4–10	20' × 8'	CF, CL, S	T
'Mme. Sancy de Parabère'	Boursault	Zones 5–10	15' × 10'	CF, CL, PR	T
'New Dawn'	Large-flowered climber	Zones 4–10	20' × 8'	CL, PR, TR	T
'Rosarium Uetersen'	Large-flowered climber	Zones 4–10	10' × 6'	CF, CL, PR, S	T
'William Baffin'	Hybrid kordesii	Zones 2–10	10' × 6'	CL	T
'Zéphirine Drouhin'	Bourbon	Zones 5–10	10' × 6'	CF, CL, PR	T
Ramblers					
'Albéric Barbier'	Hybrid wichuriana	Zones 4–10	15' × 10'	BC, CF, CL	T
'François Juranville'	Hybrid wichuriana	Zones 5–10	16' × 10'	BC, CF, CL	T
'Ghislaine de Féligonde'	Hybrid multiflora	Zones 5–10	10' × 6'	CF, CL, PR, S	T
'Kiftsgate'	Species	Zones 6–10	30' × 20'	BC, WL	T
'Nastarana'	Noisette	Zones 6–10	15' × 10'	BC, CF, CL	T
'Seven Sisters'	Hybrid multiflora	Zones 4–10	12' × 10'	BC, CL	T
'Veilchenblau'	Hybrid multiflora	Zones 5–10	15' × 12'	BC, CL, TR	T

KEY - Uses: BC = bank cover, CF = cut flower, CH = cutting hips, CL = climber, CO = containers, CU = culinary, GC = groundcover, H = hedge, MA = massing, MB = mixed border, N = naturalizing, PP = potpourri, PR = pillar rose, S = specimen, TR = tree rambler, WL = wildlife plantings
Shade Tolerance: NT = not tolerant, T = tolerant

Flowering	Bloom Color	Fragrance	Black Spot Susceptibility	Mildew Susceptibility	Pruning Requirements
C	Clear pink	FFF	SS	SS	DH, DWR, WM
C	Light yellow	FF	NS	NS	DH, DWR, WM
O	Creamy white	FFFF	NS	NS	AF, DWR
O	Medium pink	FF	SS	NS	AF, DWR
C	Shell pink	FFF	SS	NS	DH, DWR, WM
R	Medium pink	F	SS	NS	DH, DWR, WM
R	Bright pink	NF	NS	NS	DH, DWR, WM
C	Medium bright pink	FFF	MS	MS	DH, DWR, WM
O	Creamy white	F	NS	NS	AF, DWR
O	Apricot pink	FFF	NS	NS	AF, DWR
R	Apricot pink/gold	FF	NS	NS	DH, DWR
O	White	FF	NS	NS	Impossible!
O	Creamy white	FFF	SS	NS	DWR
O	Pink	FFF	NS	NS	AF, DWR
O	Purple/white	FF	MS	NS	AF, DWR

Flowering: C = continuous, O = once-blooming, R = repeat **Fragrance:** F = slightly fragrant, FF = moderately fragrant, FFF = very fragrant, FFFF = extremely fragrant, NF = not fragrant **Black Spot and Mildew Susceptibility:** NS = not susceptible, SS = slightly susceptible, MS = moderately susceptible **Pruning Requirements:** AF = after flowering, DH = deadheading, DWR = deadwood removal, RP = renewal pruning, WM = winter maintenance

Rose Care Calendar

Consider this calendar a *general* guide to help you remember what to do for the roses in your garden each month. Keep in mind that your area's particular climatic variations and weather patterns affect the suitability of any given task.

Month	Zones 3–4	Zones 5–6	Zones 7–8	Zones 9–10
January	■ Plan additions to the garden. ■ Order new roses. ■ Check canes under snow for rodent damage; set traps if necessary. ■ Secure or prune any long canes whipping in wind. ■ Remove snow load from roses.	■ Plan additions to the garden. ■ Order new roses. ■ Check canes under snow for rodent damage; set traps if necessary.	■ Prepare new beds. ■ Plant bareroot roses. ■ Prune and train established roses. ■ Clean up and dispose of rose debris. ■ Spray dormant oil if you had high numbers of mites and scale last season.	■ Prepare new beds. ■ Plant bareroot roses. ■ Prune and train established roses. ■ Clean up and dispose of rose debris. ■ Spray dormant oil if you had high numbers of mites and scale last season. ■ Apply compost. ■ Renew mulch.
February	■ Check canes under snow for rodent damage; set traps if necessary. ■ Remove snow load from roses.	■ Clean up and burn rose debris. ■ Renew mulch. ■ Spray dormant oil if you had high numbers of mites and scale last year. ■ Prune and train established roses. ■ Begin planting bareroot roses at end of month.	■ Prune and train established roses. ■ Prepare new beds. ■ Plant bareroot roses. ■ Apply compost. ■ Renew mulch.	■ Prepare new beds. ■ Finish planting bareroot roses. ■ Finish winter pruning. ■ Check irrigation systems. ■ Sow annual seeds to attract beneficial insects.
March	■ Check plants for ice damage; prune broken wood. ■ Prune and train established roses. ■ Plant bareroot roses. ■ Clean up and burn rose debris during thaw. ■ Apply compost. ■ Renew mulch.	■ Clean up and burn rose debris. ■ Apply compost. ■ Renew mulch. ■ Plant bareroot roses. ■ Prune and train established roses. ■ Check plants for ice damage; prune broken wood. ■ Prepare new beds if weather permits.	■ Finish planting bareroot roses early in month. ■ Finish winter pruning early in month. ■ Check irrigation systems. ■ Sow annuals to attract beneficial insects.	■ Plant containerized roses.

Month	Zones 3–4	Zones 5–6	Zones 7–8	Zones 9–10
April	■ Prepare new beds if weather permits. ■ Plant bareroot roses. ■ Finish winter pruning. ■ Sow annual seeds to attract beneficial insects.	■ Prepare new beds. ■ Plant bareroot roses. ■ Sow annual seeds to attract beneficial insects. ■ Finish winter pruning at beginning of month. ■ Plant containerized roses toward end of month. ■ Check irrigation systems.	■ Plant containerized roses.	■ Begin monitoring for diseases and insects. ■ Plant containerized roses. ■ Monitor water needs, especially of new plantings. ■ Release beneficial insects if necessary.
May	■ Prepare new beds. ■ Finish planting bareroot roses by end of month. ■ Plant containerized roses. ■ Check irrigation system.	■ Finish planting bareroot roses by beginning of month. ■ Plant containerized roses. ■ Begin monitoring water needs, especially of new plantings. ■ Release beneficial insects if necessary.	■ Release beneficial insects if necessary. ■ Plant containerized roses. ■ Gather roses for drying and culinary use. ■ Begin deadheading repeat bloomers. ■ Begin monitoring for diseases and insects. ■ Monitor water needs, especially of new plantings and plants in bloom.	■ Gather roses for drying and culinary use. ■ Begin deadheading repeat bloomers. ■ Treat for insects and diseases if necessary. ■ Release beneficial insects if necessary. ■ Eliminate new rootstock suckers. ■ Monitor water needs, especially of plants in bloom. ■ Prune once-flowering roses immediately after bloom. ■ Train new shoots on climbers horizontally.
June	■ Continue fertilizing. ■ Monitor water needs, especially of plants in bloom. ■ Gather roses for drying and culinary use. ■ Begin deadheading repeat bloomers. ■ Treat for insects and diseases if necessary. ■ Release beneficial insects if necessary.	■ Monitor water needs, especially of plants in bloom. ■ Gather roses for drying and culinary use. ■ Deadhead repeat-bloomers. ■ Treat for insects and diseases if necessary. ■ Prune once-flowering roses immediately after bloom. ■ Train new shoots on climbers horizontally at end of month.	■ Monitor water needs, especially of plants in bloom. ■ Gather roses for drying and culinary use. ■ Deadhead repeat-bloomers promptly. ■ Eliminate new rootstock suckers. ■ Prune once-flowering roses immediately after bloom. ■ Treat for insects and diseases if necessary. ■ Train new shoots on climbers horizontally.	■ Monitor water needs. ■ Check irrigation frequency. ■ Gather roses for drying and culinary use. ■ Deadhead repeat-bloomers. ■ Treat insects and diseases if necessary. ■ Finish pruning once-blooming roses.

(continued)

Rose Care Calendar—CONTINUED

Month	Zones 3–4	Zones 5–6	Zones 7–8	Zones 9–10
July	■ Monitor water needs. ■ Check irrigation frequency; increase through hot weather. ■ Stop deadheading hip-producing repeat-bloomers so they can form hips for fall. ■ Continue deadheading other repeat-bloomers. ■ Eliminate new rootstock suckers. ■ Prune once-blooming roses after bloom. ■ Treat for insects and diseases when necessary. ■ Train new shoots on climbers horizontally.	■ Monitor water needs. ■ Check irrigation frequency. ■ Continue deadheading repeat bloomers. ■ Eliminate new rootstock suckers. ■ Treat for insects and diseases if necessary.	■ Monitor water needs. ■ Check irrigation frequency. ■ Continue deadheading repeat bloomers. ■ Treat for insects and diseases if necessary.	■ Monitor water needs. ■ Check irrigation frequency. ■ Continue deadheading repeat bloomers. ■ Treat for insects and diseases if necessary.
August	■ Give roses a foliar feeding of kelp mid-month. ■ Monitor water needs. ■ Stop deadheading hip-producing repeat-bloomers so they can form hips for fall. ■ Continue deadheading other repeat bloomers. ■ Treat for insects and diseases if necessary.	■ Give roses a kelp foliar feeding at end of month. ■ Stop deadheading hip-producing repeat-bloomers so they can form hips for fall. ■ Treat for insects and diseases if necessary.	■ Monitor water needs. ■ Stop deadheading hip-producing repeat-bloomers so they can form hips for fall. ■ Continue deadheading other repeat bloomers. ■ Treat for insects and diseases if necessary.	■ Monitor water needs. ■ Continue deadheading repeat bloomers. ■ Treat for insects and diseases if necessary.
September	■ Give roses a kelp foliar feeding first week of month. ■ Monitor water needs. ■ Prepare new beds.	■ Give roses a kelp foliar feeding midmonth. ■ Monitor water needs. ■ Prepare new beds.	■ Give roses a kelp foliar feeding midmonth. ■ Monitor water needs. ■ Order new roses.	■ Give roses a kelp foliar feeding at end of month. ■ Monitor water needs. ■ Order new roses.

Month	Zones 3–4	Zones 5–6	Zones 7–8	Zones 9–10
October	■ Rake up and dispose of all rose debris. ■ Check to make sure all graft unions are well covered. ■ Renew mulch. ■ Prepare new beds.	■ Rake up and dispose of all rose debris. ■ Check to make sure all graft unions are well covered. ■ Renew mulch. ■ Prepare new beds.	■ Prepare new beds.	■ Prepare new beds.
November	■ Trim any long canes that may whip in wind. ■ Make sure all climbers are securely tied to supports.	■ Trim any long canes that may whip in wind. ■ Make sure all climbers are securely tied to supports.	■ Prepare new beds. ■ Plant new bareroot roses. ■ Trim any long canes that may whip in wind. ■ Make sure all climbers are securely tied to supports. ■ Rake up and dispose of all rose debris. ■ Check to make sure all graft unions are well covered. ■ Renew mulch.	■ Prepare new beds. ■ Plant new bareroot roses. ■ Make sure all climbers are securely tied to supports. ■ Rake up and dispose of all rose debris. ■ Check to make sure all graft unions are well covered. ■ Renew mulch
December	■ Mound mulch over tender varieties after ground freezes.	■ Mound mulch over tender varieties after ground freezes.	■ Continue planting new bareroot roses.	■ Continue planting new bareroot roses.

Glossary

Axil. The angle between the cane and the upper surface of the leaf stalk.

Bareroot. A common method of shipping roses. Dormant roses are dug out of the ground and packed for shipment without soil around their roots.

Bud. A young, undeveloped leaf, flower, or shoot.

Bud union. The swollen point where the grafted bud is joined with the rootstock.

Cane. A long, woody stem of a rose plant.

Climber. A tall rose that can be trained to grow on a trellis, an arbor, a pergola, or a wall. Climbers bloom on the lateral shoots of the scaffold.

Continuous-flowering. Roses that begin blooming in early summer and continue blooming through early fall. (Also called continuous-blooming, repeat-blooming, and repeat-flowering.)

Crown. The point on the rose where the canes join the root system.

Cultivar. Short for "cultivated variety," a cultivar is any plant that is bred for specific characteristics such as color, fragrance, and disease resistance and is propagated vegetatively.

Deadhead. Removing spent flowers. Finished rose blooms should be cut back to the third eye (leaf node) below the blossom.

Dormant. A state of rest that enables plants to survive winter. Roses drop their leaves before going dormant.

Feeder roots. Thin, fine-textured roots that absorb nutrients and water from the soil; also called hair roots.

Grafting. The process of joining a stem or bud of one cultivar onto the rooted stem of another cultivar for propagation purposes.

Harden off. Gradually exposing tender seedlings or young plants to the outdoors in a protected area for a week prior to transplanting them to the garden.

Heeling in. Temporarily planting bareroot plants in a soil-filled trench before planting in a permanent location.

Hip. The fruit or seedpod of the rose. Some roses have very showy hips that add color and beauty to fall and winter landscapes.

Inflorescence. A cluster of flowers arranged on one stem.

Lateral cane. A side branch arising from a main cane. Climbing roses bloom on lateral canes.

Leaf/leaflet. A rose leaf is compound and has three or more leaflets that make up the true leaf.

Main shoot. A strong lateral cane.

Modern rose. A rose cultivar that was bred and introduced after 1867, the year the modern hybrid tea rose was first introduced.

New wood. A cane of the current year's growth. Some roses bloom only on new wood, while others bloom on the previous year's growth and some bloom on both.

Node. The area where the leaf joins the stem on a plant.

Old roses. Roses that were bred before 1867, the year the modern hybrid tea rose was first introduced.

Old wood. A cane of the previous year's growth or older.

Once-blooming. Roses that bloom heavily in early summer and do not repeat bloom. (Also called once-flowering.)

Own-root roses. Roses grown from cuttings that develop their own roots, rather than roses grafted onto the rootstock of another plant.

Pralinage. A slurry of equal parts garden soil and aged manure that is mixed with water. Applied to bareroot roses before planting.

Rambler. Similar to climbing roses, ramblers can be trained to grow on fences and into trees. They are once-blooming roses that flower on the previous year's growth. They're often much bigger than climbing roses, and they have more supple canes than climbing roses do.

Remontant. Roses that bloom heavily in early summer and then have a second, lighter flowering in early fall.

Reversion. Suckers from the rootstock choking out or taking over from the growth of the bud union.

Rootstock. The host plant or root portion (understock) onto which a bud of another type of rose is grafted.

Scion. The technical term for the bud grafted onto a rootstock.

Standard. A rose that is grafted to a single cane which in turn is grafted to a rootstock, meaning that there are two bud unions on a standard rose. These roses can be planted in the ground in Zone 7 and southward or used in containers as accent plants.

Stem. A branch of a cane that emerges from a bud eye and bears leaves and at least one flower.

Sucker. A growing stem that arises from a rootstock below the bud union.

Thorn. The prickle, or sharp spine, found on the stems of roses.

Understock. The base of the plant (the root system) onto which the scion or bud of another rose is grafted; also called the rootstock.

Vegetative bud. A bud that will develop into a leaf or a shoot but will not develop into a flower.

Recommended Reading and Resources

Recommended Reading

Beales, Peter. *Classic Roses.* New York: Henry Holt, 1997.

Beck, Hallie. *Roses in a Desert Garden.* Phoenix, AR: Phoenix Home and Garden Magazine, 1996.

Botanica's Roses. Forward by William A. Grant. San Diego, CA: Laurel Gold Publishing, 2000.

Bünemann, Otto. *Roses: The Most Beautiful Roses for Large and Small Gardens.* Hauppauge, NY: Baron's Educational Series, 1994.

Dickerson, Brent C. *The Old Rose Adventurer: The Once-Blooming Old European Roses, and More.* Portland, OR: Timber Press, 1999.

Druitt, Liz. *The Organic Rose Garden.* Dallas, TX: Taylor Publishing, 1996.

Hawthorne, Linden. *Roses.* New York: DK Publishing, 1999.

Jones, Louisa. *The French Country Garden: Where the Past Flourishes in the Present.* Boston, MA: Little, Brown, and Co., 2000.

Lord, Tony. *Designing with Roses.* North Pomfret, VT: Trafalgar Square Pub., 1999.

McHoy, Peter. *The Essential Rose Garden.* New York: Hermes House, 1998.

McKeon, Judith C. *Gardening with Roses: Designing with Easy-Care Climbers, Ramblers, and Shrubs.* New York: Friedman/Fairfax, 1997.

————. *The Encyclopedia of Roses: An Organic Guide to Growing and Enjoying America's Favorite Flower.* Emmaus, PA: Rodale, 1995.

Olson, Jerry, and John Whitman. *Growing Roses in Cold Climates.* Lincolnwood, IL: Contemporary Book, 1998.

Osborne, Robert A. *Hardy Roses: An Organic Guide to Growing Frost- and Disease-Resistant Varieties.* Pownal, VT: Storey Communications, 1991.

Reddell, Rayford C. *The Rose Bible.* New York: Harmony Books, 1994.

Thomas, Graham Stuart. *The Graham Stuart Thomas Rose Book.* Portland, OR: Sagapress/Timber Press, 1994.

Verrier, Suzanne. *Rosa Gallica.* Deer Park, WI: Capability's Books, 1995.

————. *Rosa Rugosa.* Deer Park, WI: Capability's Books, 1991.

Welch, William C. *Antique Roses for the South.* Dallas, TX: Taylor Publishing, 1990.

Resources

Antique Rose Emporium
9300 Lueckemeyer Road
Brenham, TX 77833
Phone: (800) 441-0002
Fax: (979) 836-0928
Web site:
    www.antiqueroseemporium.com

Chamblee's Rose Nursery
10926 U.S. Highway 69 North
Tyler, TX 75706
Phone: (800) 256-7673
Fax: (903) 882-3597
Web site:
    www.chambleeroses.com

The Fertrell Company
Box 265
Bainbridge, PA 17502
Phone: (717) 367-1566
Fax: (717) 367-9319
Web site: www.fertrell.com

Great Lakes Roses
49875 Willow Rd.
PO Box 65
Belleville, MI 48112-0065
Phone: (734) 461-1230
Fax: (734) 461-0360
Web site:
    www.greatlakesroses.com

Heritage Rosarium
211 Haviland Mill Road
Brookeville, MD 20833-2311
Phone: (301) 774-6890
E-mail: heritagero@aol.com

High Country Roses
9122 E. Highway 40
PO Box 148
Jensen, UT 84035
Phone: (800) 552-2082
Fax: (435) 789-5517
Web site:
    www.highcountryroses.com

Hortico Nurseries, Inc.,
723 Robson Road, R.R. 1
Waterdown, Ontario
Canada LOR 2H1
Phone: (905) 689-9323
Fax: (905) 689-6566
Web site: www.hortico.com

William Kordes Söhne
Rosenstrasse 54
25365 Klein Offenseth
Sparrieshoop
Germany
Phone: 04121-4870-0
Fax: 04121-847-45
Web site: www.kordes-rosen.com

La Roseraie De Berty
07110 Largentière
France
Phone: 33-4-7588-3056
Fax: 33-4-7588-3693

**Les Roses Anciennes
de Andre Eve**
Lieu-dit Morailles
BP 206 Pithiviers-le-Vieil
45302 Pithiviers Cedex
France
Phone: 33-2-3830-0130
Fax: 33-2-3830-7165
Web site:
    www.roses-anciennes-eve.com

Lowe's Own-Root Roses
6 Sheffield Road
Nashua, NH 03062
Phone: (603) 888-2214

Michael's Premier Roses
9759 Elder Creek Road
Sacramento, CA 95829
Phone: (916) 369-7673
Fax: (916) 361-1141
Web site: www.michaelsrose.com

Old Rose Nursery
1020 Central Road
Hornby Island, BC
Canada VOR 1Z0
Phone: (250) 335-2603
Fax: (250) 335-2602
Web site:
    www.oldrosenursery.com

Peaceful Valley Farm Supply
PO Box 2209
Grass Valley, CA 95945
Phone: (888) 784-1722
Fax: (530) 272-4794
Web site: www.groworganic.com

Peter Beales Classic Roses
London Road
Attleborough, Norfolk
England NR17 1AY
Phone: 44-1953-454727
Fax: 44-1953-456845
Web site: www.classicroses.co.uk

Pickering Nurseries, Inc.
670 Kingston Road
Pickering, ON
Canada L1V 1A6
Phone: (905) 839-2111
Fax: (905) 839-4807
Web site:
    www.pickeringnurseries.com

The Roseraie at Bayfields
PO Box R
Waldoboro, ME 04572
Phone: (207) 832-6330
Fax: (800) 933-4508
Web site: www.roseraie.com

Royall River Roses
PO Box 370
Yarmouth, ME 04096
Phone: (800) 820-5830
Fax: (207) 846-7603

Russian Roses for the North
5680 Hughes Road
Grand Forks, BC, Canada V0H1H0
Phone: (250) 442-1266
Fax: (250) 442-1266
Web site:
    www.russianroseforthenorth.com

Russian Roses for the North
PO Box 339
Danville, WA 99121
Phone: (250) 442-1266
Fax: (250) 442-1266
Web site:
    www.russianroseforthenorth.com

**Vintage Gardens Antique
Roses**
2833 Old Gravenstein Highway,
South
Sebastopol, CA 95472
Phone: (707) 829-2035
Web site:
    www.vintagegardens.com

Photo Credits

Agriculture & Agri-Food Canada 13, 111 (bottom), 126, 138, 141 (top), 178

Heather Angel 4 (bottom right)

Art Archive 7

Rich Baer 85 (bottom), 87, 123 (top), 144 (bottom), 160 (top), 172, 182 (top)

Matthew Benson 34 (left and right), 55, 62

Derek Fell 233 (left)

Jim Block 230

Richard Day/Daybreak Images 245

Ken Druse 77

Garden Picture Library/David Askham 121, 148, 159, 164, 192 (top)

Garden Picture Library/John Beedle 243 (bottom left)

Garden Picture Library/Mark Bolton 116 (bottom)

Garden Picture Library/Philippe Bonduel 85 (top)

Garden Picture Library/Linda Burgess 193 (top)

Garden Picture Library/Brian Carter 150

Garden Picture Library/Bob Challinor 169 (bottom)

Garden Picture Library/Kensey Clyne 185 (bottom)

Garden Picture Library/Nigel Francis 94

Garden Picture Library/John Glover x, 56 (left), 158, 160 (bottom), 174 (bottom)

Garden Picture Library/Georgia Glynn-Smith 165

Garden Picture Library/Marijke Heuff 161 (bottom)

Garden Picture Library/Jacqui Hurst 18 (right)

Garden Picture Library/Lamontagne 56 (right), 86 (bottom), 128, 142, 206

Garden Picture Library/Mayer/Le Scanff 90, 192 (bottom), 214

Garden Picture Library/Clive Nichols 24, 39, 95, 243 (top)

Garden Picture Library/Howard Rice 184 (top), 221 (bottom), 239

Garden Picture Library/J. S. Sira 92, 205, 243 (bottom right)

Garden Picture Library/Janet Sorrell 49

Garden Picture Library/Micky White 123 (bottom)

John Glover 70, 83, 86 (top), 204

Bill Grant/Rogersroses.com 179 (bottom)

Jerry Harper 208, 216 (left)

Jessie M. Harris 171 (bottom)

Hazel Le Rougetel/Natural Visions 110 (bottom), 134, 137 (top), 168 (bottom), 224

Saxon Holt 4, 10, 28, 64 (bottom left), 106, 122 (bottom), 130, 132 (top), 141 (bottom), 146 (top and bottom), 152 (top), 198, 221 (top), 233 (right)

Stephen Ingram 216 (right)

Andrew Lawson 11

Susan McKessar, Justourpictures. com 129

Bill Marchel 240

Alison Miksch 11, 22, 30, 32 (left and right), 38, 40, 44, 48, 50, 58, 65 (left, middle, and right), 200, 212, 226

Ralph Paonessa 98

Jerry Pavia 99, 124 (bottom), 139, 140 (top), 147 (top), 151, 154, 180, 185 (top), 186, 189, 193 (bottom), 195

Roger Phillips/Rogersroses.com 119, 144 (top)

Poulsen Roser Pacific, Inc. 116 (top)

Regina, Justourpictures.com 117 (top)

Doug Seidel 71

Richard Shiell 12, 64 (top, right), 76, 102, 109 (bottom), 111 (top), 143, 147 (bottom), 161 (top), 170 (bottom), 176, 181 (bottom), 183

Hugh Skinner 177, 232

Howard Sooley ii, 2, 16, 42, 104, 120, 122 (top), 127, 132 (bottom), 133 (top), 135, 136 (top & bottom), 137 (bottom), 145 (bottom), 149, 153 (top), 155, 162, 163, 167, 169 (top), 170 (top), 171 (top), 173, 175 (top), 179 (top), 187, 188, 191, 194, 196

Mark Turner 61, 225

W. Kordes Sohne 84, 112 (top), 113, 115, 118, 166, 184 (bottom)

Rachel Weill viii, 14, 18 (left), 52, 91, 109 (top), 114, 117 (bottom), 124 (top), 125 (top), 131, 133 (bottom), 145 (top), 152 (bottom), 153 (bottom), 156, 157, 168 (top), 174 (top), 175 (top)

John Woodworth 217

Index

USDA Plant Hardiness Zone Map

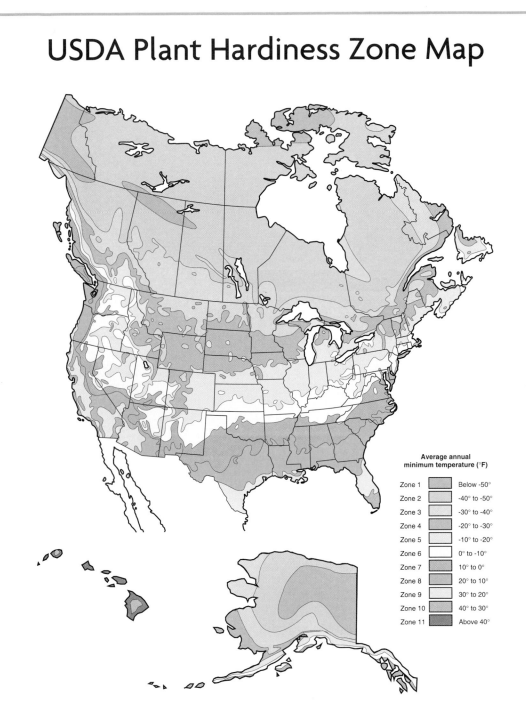

Average annual minimum temperature (°F)

Zone 1		Below -50°
Zone 2		-40° to -50°
Zone 3		-30° to -40°
Zone 4		-20° to -30°
Zone 5		-10° to -20°
Zone 6		0° to -10°
Zone 7		10° to 0°
Zone 8		20° to 10°
Zone 9		30° to 20°
Zone 10		40° to 30°
Zone 11		Above 40°

Revised in 1990, this map is recognized as the best indicator of minimum temperatures available. Look at the map to find your area, then match its color to the key at the right. When you've found your color, the key will tell you what hardiness zone you live in. Remember that the map is a general guide; your particular conditions may vary.